LOCAL GAZETTEER

THE ANDAMAN AND NICOBAR ISLANDS

GYAN

Published by

GYAN

Gyan Publishing House
5, Ansari Road
Daryaganj, New Delhi-110002
Phone: 011-47034999, 9811692060
E-mail: books@gyanbooks.com

Distribution Network
gyanbooks.com
India, USA, Canada, UK, Australia, France

ISBN : 978-81-212-3127-5 (PB)
First Published, 1908

2nd Impression 2020

Printed at: Gyan Press, Delhi.

The Andaman and Nicobar Islands

THE ANDAMAN
AND
NICOBAR ISLANDS

LOCAL GAZETTEER

The Andainan and Nicobar Islands

CALCUTTA
SUPERINTENDENT GOVERNMENT PRINTING, INDIA
1908

TABLE OF CONTENTS.

CHAPTER I.—THE ISLANDS.

CHAPTER II.—THE ANDAMANS.

CHAPTER III.—THE NICOBARS.

CHAPTER IV.—THE PENAL SETTLEMENT.

BIBLIOGRAPHY.

CHAPTER I.

THE ISLANDS.

GEOGRAPHY.

The Andamans and Nicobars.

The Andaman Islands, large and small, are said to number 204 and lie in the Bay of Bengal, 590 geographical miles from the Hooghly mouth, 120 miles from Cape Negrais in Burma, the nearest point from the mainland, and about 340 from the north extremity of Sumatra. Between the Andamans and Cape Negrais intervene two small groups, Preparis and Cocos; between the Andamans and Sumatra intervene the Nicobar Islands, all indicating a submarine range connected with the Aracan Yoma Range of Burma, stretching in a curve, to which the meridian forms a tangent, between Cape Negrais and Sumatra; and though this curved line measures 700 miles, the widest sea space is about 91 miles. The extreme length of the Andaman Group is 219 miles, with an extreme width of 32 miles. The principal outlying islands are the North Sentinel, a dangerous island of about 28 square miles, lying about 18 miles off the west coast of the South Andaman; the remarkable marine volcano, Barren Island, 1,158 feet, quiescent for the last hundred years, 71 miles to the North-East of Port Blair; and the equally curious isolated mountain, the extinct volcano known as Narcondam, rising 2,330 feet out of the sea, 71 miles east of the North Andaman. To the west of the Andamans, distant about 18 miles, are the dangerous Western Banks and Dalrymple Bank, rising to within a few fathoms of the surface of the sea and forming, with the two Sentinel Islands, the tops of a line of submarine hills parallel to the Andamans: to the east, some 40 miles distant, is the Invisible Bank with one rock just awash, and 34 miles south-east of Narcondam is a submarine hill rising to 377 fathoms below the surface of the sea. Narcondam, Barren Island, and the Invisible Bank, a great danger of these seas, are in a line almost parallel to the Andamans inclining somewhat towards them.

Certain physiological facts have long been held, in combination with phenomena exhibited by the fauna and flora of the respective terminal countries, to point to the former existence of a continuous range of mountains, thought to be sub-aerial, from Cape Negrais in Burma on the north to Achin Head in Sumatra on the south. According to the doubtful authority of Wilford, Hindu legends notice this remarkable range, ascribing it to Rama, who attempted here first to bridge the sea, an enterprise afterwards transferred to the south of India, and accomplished by the god at

A

the more practicable point known as Adam's Bridge. The tradition of the South Andaman, or Bojigngiji, group of tribes is that Maia Tomola, the ancestral chief of the nation from which they all sprung, dispersed them after a cataclysm, which caused a subsidence of parts of a great island, divided it up into the present Andaman Islands, and drowned large numbers of the old inhabitants together with many large and fierce beasts that have since disappeared. As a matter of physical geography such a subsidence need not have been more than of 20 fathoms or 120 feet to convert one single island into the present Andaman group. It has also been noted as tending to show the junction of the Andaman Islands with the mainland, that besides the South Andaman tradition, the people of the Little Andaman have names for animals which do not now exist and which they cannot describe.

The acceptable evidence on this subject that is so far available goes to show, on the assumption that except in the case of isolated volcanic peaks 200 fathoms is the extreme limit of the rising and sinking of land on the earth's surface, the possibility of there having been a time when the whole Andaman group with Preparis and the Cocos formed one continuous hill connected with Cape Negrais, and that this hill was separated by a strait of, say, 400 fathoms deep and, say, 30 miles wide, from the Nicobars considered as one island and the general Nicobar Island again from Sumatra by a strait of, say, 600 fathoms deep, and perhaps not more than 30 miles wide. The 100 fathom line connects the Preparis Group with Burma (Cape Negrais), converts all the Andamans with the Cocos Group into one island and, except for a few deeper soundings, all the Nicobars into another island. It would also convert the Invisible Bank, 40 miles East of the South Andamans, now a mere "rock awash" in mid ocean, into a considerable island and would considerably enlarge the area of Barren Island, but it would leave Narcondam Island as it is. So that in reality, as above indicated, the Andamans and Cocos are, geographically speaking, exhibitions of one summit and the Nicobars of another of the submarine range between Burma and Sumatra, whose Eastern outlying spurs are expressed by the Invisible Bank and Barren Island. Narcondam belongs to the Asiatic Continent (Burma).

The accepted conclusive argument proving the isolation of the Andaman Sea from the connected oceans is that of Carpenter, who showed that the temperature of its great depths involved the existence all round it of submarine hills, the greatest depth of which below sea level could not be more than about 750 fathoms. The contours of the depths of this sea from such data as the available charts at my disposal afford seem to fully support Carpenter's conclusion. The openings into the Andaman Sea from the connected oceans are:—from Bay of Bengal, the North and South Preparis

Channels, the Coco Channel, Duncan Passage, Ten Degrees Channel, and the Great Channel:—from the Gulf of Siam, the Straits of Malacca. This last has a bar only a few fathoms deep and clearly isolates the Andaman Sea from the Gulf. The greatest depths in the other Channels are as under: North Preparis Channel, 47 fathoms; South Preparis Channel, 150 fathoms; Coco Channel, 36 fathoms; Duncan Passage, 17 fathoms; Ten Degrees Channel, 565 fathoms; Great Channel, 798 fathoms.

On either side the line of the Andamans and Nicobars the sea rapidly deepens to 1,000 fathoms and thence on the west in the Bay of Bengal to over 2,000 fathoms within 60 miles of the Nicobars and probably within 100 miles of the Andamans; and on the east in the Andaman Sea to 2,000 fathoms within 85 miles of the Nicobars and within about 95 miles of the Andamans. The contours thus show beyond doubt the existence of a lofty range of submarine mountains between Cape Negrais and Acheen Head rising from the ocean depths up to 15,000 feet and nowhere less than 6,000 feet on the east, and up to 15,000 feet and nowhere less than 10,000 feet on the west, thus separating the Bay of Bengal from the Andaman Sea. Of this great Range 700 miles long, taking 100 fathoms as a base, the continental and island summits are shown in one central line north to south as (1) Cape Negrais (Arakan Yomas) and Preparis Islands, (2) Cocos and Andaman Islands, (3) Nicobar Islands, (4) Acheen Head (Sumatra). The Western Banks, the Sentinel Islands and Dalrymple Bank are lower summits to the west of the central line. According to the contours outlying summits of detached spurs of the central line to the east are Barren Island and the Invisible Bank. They also show that Narcondam and the submarine hill to its south-east are separated from the Central Andaman and Nicobar Range, being summits of outlying spurs of the Yomas attached to Cape Negrais. This last fact supports the old assumption that the dormant Barren Island volcano belongs to the *immediate* Sunda group of volcanoes, while the long extinct Narcondam Volcano belongs to the Pegu group, both belonging to the *general* Sunda group.

Narcondam and Barren Island are, as already noted, properly volcanoes belonging to the Sunda Group, and lie, with the Nicobars, along one of the principal lines of weakness in the earth's surface. The Andamans are just off this and escape the violent earthquakes to which the others are liable.

The general geographical phenomena are in fact the same as those of the Japan Islands off the East coast of the Asiatic Continent (China), and of other groups of islands similarly situated on various parts of the earth's surface. They indicate the existence of a submarine range of great length and height, showing above the sea surface as a string of islands, on the outer fringe of a Mediterranean Sea bordering a continental shore, having volcanoes on it or between it and the mainland.

Port Blair.

Port Blair, the head-quarters of the Administration is situated by sea routes 780 miles from Calcutta, 740 miles from Madras and 360 miles from Rangoon, with which ports there is regular communication. It is 140 miles from Car Nicobar, 225 miles from Nancowry Harbour, 265 miles from Great Nicobar, 105 miles from Narcondam and 71 miles from Barren Island, the chief outlying points for local visits.

Area and Population.

The land area of the islands under the Andaman Administration is 3,143 sq. miles: 2,508 sq. miles in the Andamans and 635 sq. miles in the Nicobars. The population of the whole area was returned at the Census of 1901 as 24,649: Andamanese, 1,882; Nicobarese, 6,511; the Penal Settlement, 16,256.

The Andamanese population is decreasing to an alarming extent. It is now taken at under 2,000, whereas up to a generation ago it must have been stationary at about 5,000, an estimate supported by the density figures given in the Census Report which work out to about two to the square mile, a reasonable figure to adopt for the old indigenous population before contact with Europeans. The children now number only a fourth of the adults. The cause of the diminution of the population is infectious and contagious disease, the result of contact with an advanced civilisation. Epidemics, all imported, of pneumonia (1868), syphilis (1876), measles (1877), and influenza (1892), together with exposure to the sun and wind in cleared spaces, the excessive use of tobacco (but not of intoxicants) and overclothing, have been the means of destroying them. It is disease, introduced by the carelessness and callousness of individuals in the first instance, and spread broadcast among the savages by their own ignorance in the next place, that has worn down the actual numbers of the tribes in contact with civilised man to a fifth of their former total in one generation, and has apparently rendered the union of the sexes infructuous in three-fourths of the cases.

It has been well known for years past that the Andamanese population was even a generation ago far more numerous than it is now and a fairly accurate estimate of the old normal population can be arrived at by following the principles below for governing the estimate: (1) the population has always been stationary, (2) the population has been limited by habits as to food production and by the area of productive occupation, (3) the relative size of the

Tribes as gauged by their present strength combined with exposure to devastating contagious or infectious diseases, (4) the capacity of each Tribe to hold its own with neighbouring Tribes. On these grounds the combined Onge-Jarawa Tribe can be assumed to have been always of its present estimated strength and the other Tribes as under, keeping to the further principle that the adults and children have always been about equal and that the sexes also have been about equal: preponderance in favour of women over men and of male over female children. The following table gives an estimate of the old normal population:—

Name of Tribe.	Adults.		Children.		Total.	Occupied area in square miles.	Density per square mile.
	Male.	Female.	Male.	Female.			
Chāriār . .	20	25	30	25	100	47	2·13
Kôrâ . . .	105	120	140	135	500	137	3·65
Tabo . . .	40	50	60	50	200	158	1·27
Yēre . . .	150	165	200	185	700	198	3·50
Kede . . .	105	120	140	135	500	371	1·35
Jūwai . . .	60	75	90	75	300	110	2·73
Köl . . .	20	25	30	25	100	161	0·62
Bojigyâb . .	60	75	90	75	300	148	2·03
Balawa . . .	60	75	90	75	300	141	2·12
Bêa . . .	105	120	140	135	500	444*	1·13
Jarawa . . .	130	140	170	160	600	220†	2·73
Onge . . .	150	165	200	185	700	373	1·88
	1,005	1,155	1,380	1,260	4,800	2,508	1·91

Males—2,385 Females—2,415 = Total 4,800.
Adults—2,160 Children—2,640 = Total 4,800.

* Including 327 square miles now occupied by the Penal Settlement.

† The Jawara density being divided up as per footnote to paragraph thus:—

·86 | Great Andaman.
4·17 | North Sentinel.
6·62 | Rutland.

The Nicobarese population is stationary. In the Census of 1901 the Shom Pen Tribe and foreign traders were included, but not in that of 1883. Excluding the extra figures, the population compares thus:—in 1883 it was 5,942; in 1901 it was 5,962. This result supports the abstract argument that savage and semi-civilised populations quickly reach the limit of increase, that limit depending on their method of gaining their livelihood in the area they occupy. As long as such people adhere to their habits of life, the population remains stationary after a short period of occupation of a new territory. When the territory occupied consists of islands, the population is especially limited by habits as to food production and by the area of productive occupation.

ETHNIC AFFINITIES.

The inhabitants of the Andaman Islands, living so near to countries that have for ages attained a considerable civilisation and have been the seat of important empires, and close to the track of a great commerce which has gone on for at least 2,000 years, have continued to our day to be savages as low in civilisation as almost any known upon earth, though close observation of them discloses the immense distance between them and the highest of the brute beasts in mental development, one most notable fact being that they eat nothing raw, cooking all their food however slightly and making pots for the purpose, and this from time immemorial.

The Andamanese are still a standing puzzle to ethnologists. The various tribes form one race of Negritos, speaking varieties of one fundamental language. The safest thing to say about them is that they are probably relics of a bygone Negrito race, now represented by themselves, the Semangs of the Malay Peninsula and the Aetas of the Philippines, which in very ancient times occupied the South-Eastern portion of the Asiatic Continent and its outlying islands, before the irruptions of the oldest of the peoples, whose existence or traces can now be found there. In this view the Andamanese are of extreme enthnological interest, as probably preserving, owing to an indefinite number of centuries of complete isolation, in their persons and customs the last pure remnant of the oldest kind of man in existence. The possibility of their representing the archaic type of the Negrito and the consequent extreme ethnological interest they arouse was long since pointed out by Sir W. Flower. It is to be noted however that Professor Owen considered them to be not connected on anatomical grounds with the people of any existing continent. A notice of the points on which Semangs and Andamanese agree and differ will be found in Appendix A.

The antiquity of the Andamanese on their present site is proved by their kitchen-middens, rising from 12 ft. to 15 ft. and more in height, and in some cases having fossilised shells at the base. These show that the Andamanese still gets his food just as he did when the now fossil shells contained living organisms. The largest and traditionally the oldest, the original, home of the race by a consensus of Andamanese opinion and worth scientific exploration (any other to be greatly deprecated), is the kitchen-midden of Wota-Emi on Baratang in Elphinstone Harbour on the east coast of the South Andaman. In reference to such remains it is worth noting that all Andamanese tradition commences with the cataclysm accompanied by a subsidence of a large portion of the surface of their old country already noticed, and the people point to certain ancient kitchen-middens, such as that at Port Mouat, on the sea level to prove it. They say that these were commenced by the survivors of the cataclysm and that the sites were previously high up on the mountain sides, where no one could build a kitchen-midden.

It has also been pointed out that an estimate of the old population can be arrived at from locating and enumerating the existing kitchen-middens of the Andamanese, on the assumptions that each midden represents the head-quarters of a Sept of 30 people and that apparently each Sept, owing to the habits of the people, would require four to five such head-quarters. A population of 5,000 would therefore require, say, 600 middens, *i.e.*, there should be a midden to every four square miles of territory. The value of the kitchen-midden argument comes out thus:—(1) The size, 50 feet diameter usually, does not permit more than 30 people to live on it; (2) change of head-quarters is frequently necessary owing to (*a*) monsoons, (*b*) exhaustion of food in the neighbourhood, (*c*) nomadic instincts, (*d*) stench from discarded food thrown around. As a matter of practice the Andamanese do not return for three months after they have left a midden, nor for about a year after a death in one, and occasionally they abandon a midden for many years, and cannot occupy one for more than a few weeks at a time from the stench about it. These considerations fix four as the smallest number of middens per 30 people.

As has been above noted the middens also beyond all doubt prove that the Andamanese are now as they were an exceedingly long time ago. There are but few "newer" middens, and the older ones show great age: newness and age being gauged by height. They contain generally the remains of the same kind of food throughout, except that certain shell-fish have been fashionable at one period and certain others at another, and at their bases are found the same refuse and the same pottery as we find shown on the surface to-day. Here then we have a people unaltered in habits from primeval time and whose numbers, if these premises be correct, we should be able to estimate from existing data, as they must have been stationary through all time. The questions on this argument really are therefore:—(1) how many middens are there? (2) where are they? To these questions it is worth while obtaining answers at the next Census or even as opportunity occurs, as the answers will either upset the theory or afford an approximate estimate of the old Andamanese population and of the strength of each tribe.

It is not at all easy to present a brief, clear and yet adequate account of the Nicobarese, and quite impossible to present an authoritative one, because of the insufficient study that has as yet been practicable of the people, the great number of more or less inaccurate notes extant about them by observers of widely different equipment for the purpose and scattered over publications difficult of access, the many unsettled controversial points regarding them, and complicated extent of their civilisation. However, despite local differences, they can be fairly treated as one people (crosses, except a few with the allied Burmese, Siamese and wild Malay races being almost unknown and due to visits of trading vessels and strayed boats from the Malay Peninsula and these are not fruitful), whose affinities may be established from the following characteristics of some or other, but not necessarily all, of the inhabitants of the various islands:—Their houses are on piles; they stain the teeth with betel; they perforate and enlarge the lobe of the ear; they artificially deform the heads of infants by flattening the occiput and forehead; they have an aversion to milk; the marriage tie is weak and brittle, and women have free choice of husbands; they practise the couvade (paternal lying-in); they sniff for kissing; they have no caste; they are independent and undisciplined by nature; they are sociable and the sexes freely mix without restraint; their religion consists of spirit-scaring; they have holy days in certain months; they have definite courting customs; their mode of hospitality is to allow any stranger to enter the house and take what he wishes without question; they have special ceremonies for the disposal of the revered dead; they are fond of sport and matches; they eat dog's flesh; only the women will carry loads on the head and men's heavy loads are carried on a yoke; their language. All these points show them to be a Far-Eastern and not an Indian people. Their own idea of themselves is that they came from the Pegu-Tenasserim coast, an idea borne out by physical structure, social habits, trend of civilisation and language. Everything so far ascertained about them points to an origin from the Indo-Chinese, as distinguished from the Tibeto-Burmese or Malay tribes or nations. There is an old charge of cannibalism against them which may be said to be quite untrue, though a rare, secret and considered disreputable form of ceremonial cannibalism has been discovered on Camorta, as in India and elsewhere. It seems to be punished by murder and subsequent mutilation when discovered, as reported by the Missionary Haensel (1779-87), and as shown by some otherwise mysterious murders much later in our own time.

The Nicobarese idea of their origin is that they came from the Pegu-Tenasserim Coast, an idea borne out by physical structure social habits, trend of civilisation and language. On the facts ascertained about them the accepted general opinion supports an origin from the Indo-Chinese, as distinguished from the Tibeto-Burmese or Malay, tribes or nations. In the view that they represent that portion of the Indo-Chinese race, which has been the longest isolated and freest from disturbing influences, they are of the highest ethnological interest.

Opinions, however, on a subject such as this are subject to continual change as research proceeds, and the last word on the ethnic affinities of the Nicobarese (Pater W. Schmidt, Die Mon-Khmer-Völker) demands a modification to some extent of the above remarks. According to the writer, with whom Dr. G. A. Grierson is in accord, it may be now considered as established that the Nicobarese speak a language and possibly belong to a race which is neither Tibeto-Burman nor Simitic (Chinese), and which he terms Austro-Asiatic, including in this group scattered tribes of the Lower Himalayas, the Khasis and Mundas of India, the Was, Palaungs and other tribes of Burma, the Mon-Khmer peoples of Indo-China, the aboriginal tribes of the Malay Peninsula and the Nicobarese. Pater Schmidt further shows that this Austro-Asiatic race is essentially related to the peoples of Oceania and thus that they form together one great united whole which he calls the Austric family covering a vast extent of the globe from the Panjab Hills to Madagascar off the coast of Africa and Easter Island off South America, from the Himalaya to New Zealand—the most widely spread family of mankind whose existence has yet been proved. In this view, too, which is strongly supported by Skeat and Blagden's *Pagan Races of the Malay Peninsula*, it is worth while scientifically to carefully study the Nicobarese.

Revenue.

It is not the policy of the Government to raise revenue from the aboriginal population of the islands, and all the revenue and expenditure accounts are confined to the Penal Settlements, in which financially the requirements of convict discipline and management are placed before revenue. On this basis the expenditure for 1901-2 was £116,443 and the revenue, chiefly the result of convict labour on productive works, was £43,898. Of this sum about one half was raised from convict labour devoted to forest produce.

Administration.

The Islands are administered by the Chief Commissioner of the Andaman and Nicobar Islands, who is also Superintendent of the

Penal Settlement. All the officials reside in the Penal Settlement, except the Government Agents at Mus in Car Nicobar, and in Nancowry Harbour (Camorta). Such slight control as is necessary over the Andamanese is exercised by the Officer in charge of the Andamanese, who is one of the executive magisterial officers of the Penal Settlement, appointed for that purpose by the Chief Commissioner. The control of the Nicobars is exercised by judicial and executive officers deputed to visit the islands at short periods by the Chief Commissioner and under his orders.

SURVEYS.

The whole of the Andamans and the outlying islands were completely surveyed topographically by the Indian Survey Department under Colonel J. R. Hobday in 1883-6 and a number of maps on the scale of two miles to the inch were produced, which give an accurate coast line everywhere and astonishingly correct contours of the inland hills, considering the difficulties presented by the denseness of the forests with which they are covered. For Port Blair and neighbourhood a series of maps on the scale of four inches to the mile were made. The exact latitude and longitude of Chatham Island in Port Blair Harbour were determined astronomically by Mr. Nicholson of the Great Trigonometrical Survey in 1861: latitude 11° 41′ 13″ N.; longitude 92° 42′ 44″ E. The marine surveys of the Andamans date back many years and one can go back to the days of Ritchie (1771) and of Blair and Moorsom (1788-96) for partial charts which are still usable. Brooker's surveys of 1867 added much knowledge about Port Blair, but the serious dangers of the western coral banks were not removed by surveys till 1888-9 under Commander A. Carpenter, when a great advance in the charts generally was made. His general chart is that now in use, corrected by subsequent surveys up to 1899. The coasts on the whole are fairly well charted, but some most necessary work still remains to be done before a voyage round these dangerous coral-bound coasts can be said to be free from anxiety. It is, however, worth noting that the long standing notice on charts that "the dangers of the North Andaman have not been surveyed" is now at last removed, and that of the Coco Channel is made safe for ships. A fresh issue of the two-miles-to-the-inch maps with many additional names was effected in 1902-3. As the Andamanese have names of their own for places known to Europeans by other names it will be useful for visitors and explorers to have access to the native place-names and they are therefore given in Appendix B.

The whole of the Nicobars and outlying islands were surveyed topographically by the Indian Survey Department under Colonel G. Strahan in 1886-7, and a number of maps on the scale of 2 miles to the inch were produced, giving an accurate coast line. The longitude of the (former) Camorta Observatory in Nancowry Harbour, has been fixed at 93° 31′ 55·05″ east. The marine surveys of these islands date back to the days of Ritchie (1771) and Kyd (1790), and are still meagre and not satisfactory. The chart in use is that of the Austrian frigate *Novara* (1858) combined with the Danish Chart of 1846, with corrections up to 1889. There is also a large scale chart of Nancowry Harbour, which is that of Kyd in 1790 with additions up to 1869. There are beacons for running in at Mus and Sawi Bay in Car Nicobar, at Bengala in Teressa, and (now doubtful) buoys in the eastern entrance to Nancowry Harbour. A voyage round these coral-bound and sparsely-sounded coasts is one to be made with caution. The Eastern Extension Company's cable from Madras to Penang lies between the Central Group and Car Nicobar, the whole line across the Andaman Sea being, of course, charted.

At page 146 of the Census Report, 1901, is a series of Nicobarese village maps, which should, however, be used with the caution there given, because of the very different habits of the populations of the various islands. In Car Nicobar, Chowra, and Bompoka the village sites are fixed and the same may be said of Teressa, but in the last case a tendency to move them is to be noticed. In the rest of the islands, where the population is thin, the village sites are moved about as convenient from time to time. It is nevertheless of value to the visitor to have a distinct indication of recognised village names and for that reason an alphabetical list is given of the existing village names on every island in Appendix C.

CHAPTER II.

THE ANDAMANS.

Physical Aspects.

The Andamans are a group of islands in the Bay of Bengal administered by the Chief Commissioner of the Andaman and Nicobar Islands. The main part of the Andaman Group is a band of five chief islands, so closely adjoining and overlapping each other, that they have long been known as one: *viz.*, the Great Andaman. The five islands are (North to South):—North Andaman, Middle Andaman, South Andaman, Baratang, Rutland Island. The axis of this band of islands forms almost a meridional line 156 statute miles long. Four straits part these islands:—*viz.* (North to South), Austen Strait, Homfray's Strait,

Middle or Andaman Strait, Macpherson's Strait. Attached to the main islands are the Landfall Islands to the North, Interview Island to the West, the Labyrinth Islands to the South-West, Ritchie's or Andaman Archipelago to the East separated by Diligent Strait. Little Andaman, roughly 26 m. by 16 m., is 31 miles to the South across Duncan Passage, in which lies the Cinque Islands, forming Manners Strait, the commercial highway between the Andamans and the Madras Coast. Besides these there are a great number, said to be altogether 204, islands lying off the shores of the main islands. The extreme length of the Andaman Group is 219 miles and the extreme breadth is 32 miles. The outlying islands are the North Sentinel, 28 sq. m., 18 miles off the West Coast, Barren Island, 1,158 ft., a marine volcano, and Narcondam, 2,330 ft., an extinct volcano, each 71 miles from the East Coast.

THE HILLS AND RIVERS.

The islands forming Great Andaman consist of a mass of hills enclosing very narrow valleys, the whole covered by an exceedingly dense tropical jungle. The hills rise, especially on the east coast, to a considerable elevation, the chief heights being, in the North Andaman. Saddle Peak, 2,400 feet; in the Middle Andaman, Mount Diavolo behind Cuthbert Bay, 1,678 feet; in the South Andaman, Koiob, 1,505 feet; and Mount Harriet, 1,193 feet; the Cholunga range, 1,063 feet; in Rutland Island, Ford's Peak, 1,422 feet. Little Andaman, with the exception of the extreme north, is practically flat. There are no rivers and few perennial streams in the islands.

THE HARBOURS.

The coasts of the Andamans are deeply indented, giving existence to a number of safe harbours and tidal creeks, which are often surrounded by mangrove swamps. The chief harbours, some of which are very capacious, are, starting northwards from Port Blair, the great harbour of South Andaman—*East Coast*, Port Meadows, Colebrooke Passage, Elphinstone Harbour (Homfray's Strait), Stewart Sound, Port Cornwallis, the last three are very large;—*West Coast*, Temple Sound, Interview Passage, Port Anson or Kwangtung Harbour (large), Port Campbell (large), Port Mouat, Macpherson's Strait. There are besides many other safe anchorages about the coasts for sea-going vessels: notably Shoal Bay and Kotara Anchorage in the South Andaman, Cadell Bay and the Turtle Islands in the North Andaman, and Outram Harbour and Kwangtung Strait in the Archipelago.

The Scenery.

The scenery of the islands is everywhere strikingly beautiful and varied, and the coral beds of the more secluded bays in its harbours are conspicuous for their exquisite assortment of colour. The scenery of the harbours has been compared to that of Killarney by Professor V. Ball, and no doubt they do recall the British Lakes. One view of Port Blair Harbour is strongly reminiscent of Derwentwater as seen from the Keswick end.

Origin of Name.

The name has always been in all historical times and for all countries some form of Andaman, which more than probably represents Handuman, the Malay form of Hanuman, designating the islands to be the abode of the Hindu mythological "monkey people," *i.e.*, of savage aboriginal antagonists of the Aryan immigrants into India. The Chinese and Japanese knew the Islands respectively as Yeng-t'o-mang and Andaban in the first millenium A.D. (*vide* Takakasu's Edition of I-tsing pp. xxx and xxviii ff), which clearly represent the Andaman of the *Arab Relations* of 851 A.D. Then comes Marco Polo with his Arabic dual form Angamanian in 1292. After which we have Nicolo Conti in 1430 with Andemania, and after him almost every eastern traveller and map-maker with some form of "Andaman." All these terms seem obviously to be based on the Malay name for the islanders, as the Malays of the Peninsula have, for many centuries, used the islands for their piratical practices and for a trade in Andamanese slaves to their own country and Siam (this up to about 1860) and have known them by the term Handuman. In the great Tanjore inscription of 1050 A.D. the Andamans are mentioned under a translated name along with the Nicobars, as Timaittivu, "Islands of Impurity" and as the abode of cannibals. In the Chinese *History of the T'ang Dynasty* (618-906 A.D.) they are called the land of the Rakshasas, and the Andamanese are to-day regarded as Rakshasas (or ogres, *i.e.*, traditional savage antagonists of the Aryans) by the Natives of India on being first seen, and were so called at once when they appeared in the streets on a visit to Calcutta in 1883. As the abode of the Rakshasas the Andamans were also known to the Southern Indians in mediæval times and this persistence in regarding the Andamanese as the Rakshasas or their descendants confirms the ancient derivation of "Andaman" as a name from Hanuman through Malay Handuman. The Andamanese have returned the compliment and know all Orientals as Chauga or ancestral ghosts, *i.e.*, demons, and have preserved an ancient knowledge of them in a term for trepang or sea-slug as the "Oriental's slug," the collection of this valuable edible and of the equally valuable birds'-nests being one object of the visits of the Malays, Burmese and Chinese in days gone by, in addition to trapping slaves, which last practice no doubt had something to do with the savage hostility of the Andamanese towards all who landed on their shores.

Geology.*

There has been no geological survey of the Andamans, but expeditions by experts have been officially undertaken to make preliminary examinations of the islands. These examinations have been carried on under practical difficulties of every kind, not the least being the dense and lofty forests with which the entire islands are covered. Geologically the Andaman Islands form a southward continuation of the Arakan Yoma Range. Two sedimentary series only have so far been distinguished, the Port Blair and Ritchie's Archipelago. With these are associated some altered igneous intrusions of great interest and some volcanic rocks. The Port Blair series, evidently the same as the Negrais rocks of Arakan, consists principally of non-calcareous grey sandstone and imbedded shales, with occasional nests of poor coal, conglomerates and pale grey-limestone. The limestone is recognised by its peculiar honey-combed weathering. The Archipelago series consist of soft limestone formed of coal and shell sand, soft calcareous sandstones and white clays with occasional conglomerates. The Port Blair series is older than the Archipelago. Volcanic fragmentary rocks, apparently younger, occur in the Port Blair series, at Entry Island in Port Meadows on the East Coast of the South Andaman, and indurated and altered intrusions of serpentine in the Cinque Islands and elsewhere. This serpentine contains chromites, is associated with gabbro and is similar to the great intrusions in the Arakan Yomas. Chromite, asbestos and valuable minerals should be looked for here. There is coral along the coasts everywhere and the Sentinel Islands are composed of the newer rocks with a superstructure of coral, but no atoll is known in the vicinity of the islands. Other valuable substances that have been found are hard volcanic breccias at Namunaghar in the Penal Settlement, yielding an excellent building stone; good red clay for bricks in pockets; abundant old coral valuable for lime and pockets of workable limestone; a pretty reddish marble in the Penal Settlement, red ochre (*koiob*) in pockets, making when mixed with gurjan oil (a local product) an excellent covering for shingle roofs; mica in workable quantities about Navy Bay Hill in Port Blair Harbour.

There has been a comparatively recent raising in parts of the Andamans, especially in the Archipelago, and sinking in others, chiefly along the East Coast. A theory of a still continuing sub-

* The information under this head is chiefly based on an official note by Mr. T. H. Holland of the Geological Survey.

sidence of the islands was first formed by Kurz on his investigation of the vegetation in 1866 and has since been confirmed by Oldham in his geological report of 1884, though with some reluctance owing to the fact that the Arakan Coast to the north and the Nicobars are showing signs of recent elevation. Signs of the continuance of the subsidence are to be found at several places:—Port Mouat, Rangu-chang on the East Coast of the South Andaman near Port Blair, Outram Harbour and Havelock Island in the Archipelago, the northern ends of the Little Andaman, the North Sentinel, and the North Andaman.

The extremely interesting islands of Narcondam and Barren Island are volcanoes of the general Sunda group, the extinct volcano of Narcondam belonging apparently to what is known as the Pegu group and the quiescent Barren Island to the Sunda group proper. Barren Island was last in eruption in 1803, but there is still a thin column of steam from a sulphur bed at the top and a variable hot spring at the point where the last outburst of lava flowed into the sea, showing lately a temperature of 107° Fahr.

BOTANY AND FORESTS.*

The vegetation of the Andamans is an almost unbroken tropical forest, of a distinctly Indo-Chinese type with a strong admixture of Malayan types. The forest consists of two clearly marked divisions, the littoral and the non-littoral, the former of which is the most valuable economically. The sandstone ledges and the fringing coral reefs around the coasts are wonderfully free from marine vegetation and the seaweeds are as a rule inconspicuous and scarce. The beaches, sand and shingle, are, however, covered with two varieties of *ipomea*, which are valuable as shore protectors, and the mangrove beach forest is very extensive and valuable. The sea fence contains, among other species, the *pandanus* and the nipa palm of economic value. But the absence here of the cocoanut and the *casuarina* is remarkable, as the former is plentiful in the Nicobars to the South and in the Cocos to the North, and the latter so near as the Little Andaman. The whole beach forest is characteristically Indo-Malayan, and provides no special indications as to connection with the Asiatic Continent or the Malay Archipelago.

The true Andaman forests are filled with evergreen trees, often with huge buttresses and usually heavily laden with climbers, though considerable patches of deciduous forest, with occasional glades of bamboo, are to be met with. Usually in the evergreen tracts the ridges are found to be covered with small or stunted trees inextricably tangled with masses of creepers, the fine forests being

* Much of the information on this subject is based on notes by Major D. Prain I.M.S., Superintendent of the Royal Botanic Gardens, Calcutta.

confined to the slopes. The bamboo groves are usually associated with patches of indurated chloritic rock or sandstone. On the whole the non-littoral Andaman flora is found to comprise a considerable number of endemic forms and to include a perceptible contingent of forms that are to be found, outside the Andamans, only in Tenasserim on the opposite shore of the Andaman Sea. The preponderance of Indo-Chinese types is thoroughly in accordance with what one would expect from the physiographical relationships of the islands.

The timber available for economic purposes is both plentiful and various. It is divided for commercial objects into three classes, known by their commercial names thus:—First class, Padouk, Koko, Chuglam, Marble-wood, Satin-wood; Second class, Pyimma, Bombway, Chai, Lakuch, Lalchini, Pongyet, Thitmin, Mowha, Khaya, Gangaw, Thingan; Third class, Didu, Ywegyi, Toungpeingyi and Gurjan. Padouk is the chief timber for export to Europe at a very high price per ton, but other first class timbers also find a market there. Third class timbers find a ready market in Calcutta, while the second class are extensively used locally.

Padouk (*pterocarpus dalbergioides*) can be used for buildings and boats, for furniture and fine joinery, and for all purposes to which teak, mahogany, hickory, oak, and ash are applied. It seasons quickly and easily, and is immune from the attacks of white ants and borers, except the marine worm (*teredo navalis*), and from rot of all kinds: colour, pale and dark red and brown. Koko (*albizzia lebbek*) is used for battens and furniture; colour, greenish grey, light brown and chocolate with dark markings. White Chuglam (*terminalia bialata*) and black Chuglam (*myristica irya*) are used for furniture, oars, shafts, and planking; colour, grey with darker markings. Marble or zebra wood (*diospyros kurzii*) makes furniture and joinery; colour, ebony with streaks of grey or light brown. Satin-wood (*murraya exotica*), which is not the satin-wood of Ceylon (*chloroxylon swietenia*), makes delicate furniture; colour, yellow. The proper names for the woods of the second class are as follow:—Pyimma, *lagerstræmia hypoleuca*: Bombway, *terminalia procera*: Chai, *alphonsea ventricosa*: Lakuch, *artocarpus lakoocha*: Lalchini, *calophyllum spectabile*: Ponyet, *calophyllum inophyllum*: Thitmin, *podocarpus neriifolia*: Mowha, *mimusops littoralis*: Khaya, *mimusops elenchi*: Gangaw, *messua ferrea*: Thingan, *hopea odorata*. These are used for a great variety of economic purposes locally connected with the building, ship and carriage making, furniture and joinery trades. Of the third class timbers, Didu (*bombax insigne*) is used for tea boxes and packing cases; Toungpeingyi (*artocarpus chaplasha*) for cases and planking; Ywegyi (*adenanthera pavonina*) for inferior cabinet furniture; Gurjan (*dipterocarpus turbinatus*) for slabs and planking and wood-paving. Lakuch and Ywegyi yield a yellow dye, Khaya the pagoda gum of Madras, Gurjan a resin and the well known oil. The great mangrove swamps supply unlimited fire-wood of the best quality, and the bark of the trees a tan, as does also that of the bombway. The best mixture for steeping wooden shingles, is 3 lbs. of gurjan oil, 1 lb. of crude petroleum, 1 lb. of red ochre or metallic paint: the first and third ingredients are produced in the Andamans. Other minor products of the forests are several species of bamboo and cane and two thatching palms, *nipa fruticans* and *licuala peltata*. The cane roots are largely used in Calcutta for walking sticks: the majority of those sold by street vendors there from 4 annas to 8 annas each are from the Andamans. The inner bark of the *sterculia villosa* is used for making elephant harness for dragging timber, and the long climbing canes for ferry ropes and boat fenders. As regards general capabilities the Andaman forests, in addition to the invaluable and largely spread padouk, there is an extremely abundant supply of gurjan, gangaw (the Assam iron-wood) suitable for sleepers, and didu for tea boxes. Labour only is required to bring them on to the suitable markets. Safe anchorages are numerous and there is no difficulty in providing convenient points at which to ship the timber when extracted, especially as the localities of the valuable timbers are situate on, or near to, navigable creeks leading direct to the sea and thus rendering the forests capable of easy and economical working. The woods chiefly used by the Andamanese for their own purposes are mangrove, padouk, *melochia velutina*, some of the sterculiaceæ, *bombax insigne*, *areca laxa*, pandanus, bamboo, *anadendron paniculatum*. They also gather and eat the fruit of a great variety of trees and use the leaves of the following for medicinal purposes:—*trigonostemon longifolius*, *alpinia* species, *Calamosagus laciniosus*.

A section of the general Forest Department of India has been established in the Andamans since 1883 and, in the neighbourhood of Port Blair, 156 square miles have been formally set apart for regular forest operations. The activity of the department is strictly limited by the amount of convict labour from time to time available, as there is no indigenous labour. In the last few years the islands have been carefully explored, and on the expiry of the term for which an exclusive contract has been given for the extraction of *padauk*, it is proposed to offer a long lease for the exploitation of these valuable forests. It is estimated that the annual yield of both *padauk* and *gurjan* will be 10,000 to 12,000 tons. The financial results at present are shown in the article on PORT BLAIR.

Among the intentionally introduced plants and trees, elaborately reported on by both Kurz and Prain, may be mentioned tea (*camellia theifera*), Liberian coffee (*coffea liberica*), Cocoa (*theobroma cacao*), Ceara rubber (*manihot glaziovii*) which has not done well, Manilla hemp (*musa textilis*), teak (*tectona grandis*), cocoa-nut (*cocos nucifera*), besides a number of shade and ornamental trees, fruit trees especially of the anti-scorbutic kinds, vegetables and garden plants. Among the shade trees, the most interesting is the flourishing rain-tree (*pithecolobium saman*) of the West Indies and American Continent, and among the vegetables the Otaheite potato (*dioscorea species*). An attempt has also been made to introduce the Bahamas aloe (*agave sisalana*), but though it has flowered and given out bulbils in quantities, success is not yet assured. Tea is grown in considerable quantities and the cultivation is under a department of the Penal Settlement. The outturn for the last seven years has been on an average 2,519 chests per annum.

The crops chiefly raised are paddy, pulse, maize, sugarcane and turmeric. In the cleared places about Port Blair the grazing appears to be abundant, but is not really so, owing to the action of two destructive weeds: the needle bearing grass (*avena fatua*), which is pretty but not edible by any kind of food animal and being of a stronger growth than ordinary grazing grass supplants it wherever it is not rigorously kept down; and the sensitive plant (*mimosa pudica*), an imported nuisance, which rapidly covers all open and low lying places and is edible only by goats.

FAUNA AND ZOOLOGY.*

There are no dangerous mammals. The poisonous snakes include the cobra, the hamadryad, the blue karait, the sea snakes and two species of pit-viper; the last are very numerous, and frequently bite people working in the forests, though their bite is seldom fatal. A pig (*sus Andamanensis*), a paradoxurus ("wild cat") and an iguana of some size are hunted for food. The marine fauna is of unusual interest. On examination the marine life goes to show what other physiographical facts have proved—the close connection of the Islands with both Burma and Sumatra and the distant alliance with the Indian Peninsula. The land fauna, in several particulars, shows that the Andamans are closely allied zoologically with their neighbours, Arakan and Burma. The economic zoology of the Islands may be thus summed

* Much of the information here is based on notes by Major A. R. S. Anderson, I.M.S.

up:—Extensive coral reefs for lime; sea cucumbers (trepang) and the finest quality of edible birds' nests for the Chinese market; wax and rather poor honey in quantities; cuttle bones, ornamental shells, edible oysters, edible turtle and tortoise-shell, ornamental and pet birds, all plentiful.

CLIMATE.

Speaking generally, the climate of the islands may be described as normal for tropical islands of similar latitude. It is warm always, and though tempered by pleasant sea breezes, very hot when the sun is northing. The rainfall is irregular but the climate is usually dry during the north-east monsoon and very wet during the south-west. The islands are exposed to both monsoons and subject to violent weather with excessive rainfall, but cyclones are rare, though the Andamans are within the influence of practically every cyclone that blows in the Bay of Bengal, whence their value from a meteorological point of view.

Owing to the importance of the information to be obtained at the Andamans as to the direction and intensity of cyclonic storms and as to whether prognostications generally as regards the eastern and northern portions of India, a well appointed meteorological station has been established at Port Blair on Ross Island since 1868. Two very serious considerations for commerce are involved here: *viz.*, timely and reliable warnings of storms in the Bay of Bengal and reliable weather forecasts. Accuracy in storm warnings and weather forecasts depends on the establishment of a number of meteorological reporting stations all over a given area of sea and land. It is therefore not sufficient for accurate warnings and forecasts to have meteorological stations round the Bay; they must be also established if practicable within it. The Andaman and Nicobar Islands can provide a number of such stations right across the Bay from north to south.

The magnitude of the interests requiring accurate storm warnings can be gauged thus. In Bengal *excluding Madras and Burma*, about 4,400 vessels of a combined burthen of about 3¼ million carrying tons, conveying 300,000 passengers and cargoes to the value of upwards of R11¼ crores annually, leave and enter the Bengal ports in the coasting trade alone. The ever increasing size of the vessels carrying the trade implies an ever increasing number of passengers and size of cargoes in each bottom and a corresponding increasing value of each individual ship and increasing importance in saving it from loss or damage. So also the magnitude of the interests requiring accurate weather forecasts is very great. Of industries directly depending on the rainfall in the Bay of Bengal:—Jute exported from Bengal, raw and manufactured, has an average annual value of about R14¾ crores and the plant is grown on nearly 2 million acres; rice, as a staple food crop, in Bengal alone has an annual outturn of 20 million tons raised on between 30 and 40 million acres; tea has an average annual export in Bengal of about 7½ crores, and indigo of about three crores. Again the purchasing power of the native of Bengal depends on the state of the rice crop and hence the rate of piece-goods there depends so much on the rainfall that merchants closely watch it: this trade represents an average annual value of about 14 crores. The great importance to commerce therefore of weather forecasts has brought about repeated attempts to connect the Andaman Islands with the continent by telegraphs, as otherwise the meteorological observations have merely a scientific value, being received in India too late for practical purposes. In 1867 a serious attempt at a cable to Port Blair failed owing to initial and maintenance costs involved and also the hilly nature of the sea-bottom about the islands. In 1900 the question was reopened and a connection with the islands by wireless telegraphy established.

Calm weather can be counted on in February to April and in October. Fogs and chilly night winds are common in January to March in the valleys and inner harbour and also after excessive rain. Off shore breezes at night and on shore breezes in the day are most marked during the calm weather, due to the difference in temperature of sea and land. March and April are often hazy. Magnetic variation in the Andaman sea in 1904, 0° 40′ East, decreasing annually 2′. The normal barometric readings vary between 29·873 and 29·722, being highest in February and lowest in June.

Temperature.

The following official table gives the average temperature for 25 years ending with 1901:—

Port Blair.

Height of Observatory above sea level.	January.		May.		July.		November.	
	Mean.	Diurnal Range.*	Mean.	Diurnal Range.	Mean	Diurnal Range.	Mean.	Diurnal Range.
61 ft.	81·1	10·8	88·8	10·7	81·5	8·0	8 .·0	9·6

*Average difference between maximum and minimum temperature of each day.

The above table must, however, be received with caution, owing to the situation of the meteorological station on a bare islet surrounded by sea influences. The second average is also taken in May, a wet month, instead of in April, a dry month.

General meteorological statistics for Port Blair for five years are :—

	1897.	1898.	1899.	1900.	1901.
TEMPERATURE.					
Mean highest in shade	April 94·0	April 90·3	Mar. 91·8	April 94·1	April 95·1
Mean lowest in shade	Jany. 72·5	Jany. 70·5	Feby. 71·2	Dec. 72·9	Dec. 71·9
Highest in shade	April 96·8	April 93·8	April 95·8	April 97·0	April 97·1
Lowest in shade	Jany. 67·3	Mar. 63·2	Jany. 67·0	Jany. 68·0	Dec. 67·7
Dry bulb mean	85·2	84·3	[illegible]	90·6	91·7
Wet bulb mean	79·7	78·4	78·6	82·5	83·0
RAINFALL.					
Most wet days in a month	July 29	July 26	Sept. 7	June 27	Aug. 29
Heaviest fall in a month	July 30 97	May 40 58	Sept. 24·38	Sept. 15·44	May 20·8
Months without rain	January.	Feb. Mar.	Nil	February.	Nil.
Total wet days	196	160	177	162	188
WIND.					
N. N. E.	Jan., Feb., Dec.	Feb., Dec.	Feb., Nov., Dec.	Jan., Mar., Nov., Dec.	Jan., Feb.
E. S. E.	Mar. April Nov.	...	April, Oct.	...	...
W. S. W.	May, June, July, Aug. Sept., Oct.	May, June, July, Aug. Sept.	May, June, July, Aug. Sept.	May, June, July, Aug. Sept.	May, July, Aug., Sept Oct.
W. N. W.	...	...	...	April	June.
E. N. E.	...	Jan., Mar., April.	March	...	...
S. S. E.	...	Oct., Nov.	...	October	April, Nov.
N E.	...	...	January	February	Mar., Dec.
CLOUDS.					
Clouds are usually	P.K. & P.C. *	Cu. N. Acu. Ci *	Cu. N. Acu. Ci *	Cu. Acu. N. Ci *	Cu. Acu. N Ci *

* P. K.—Pallio-Cumulus : C & Ci—Cirrus : P. C.—Pallio—Cirrus : K.—Cumulus : Cu. N.—Cumulo-Nimbus : Acu.—Alto-Cumulus.

RAINFALL.

The rainfall varies much from year to year and to an extraordinary extent at places quite near to each other. The official meteorological station is situated in the driest spot in Port Blair. The official averages for 25 years ending with 1901 are as follows :—

January.	February.	March.	April.	May.	June.	July.	August.	September.	October.	November.	December.
1·04	0·73	0·48	8·02	16·64	18·71	15·06	14·40	18·84	11·61	9·44	6·52

The above monthly figures give a yearly fall of 116·43 inches. The fluctuations at the official station in these 25 years have been from 83·28 inches in 1900 to 137·67 inches in 1882. There are, however, altogether seven rain gaüges maintained at Port Blair within an area of 80 square miles with these results:—

	1895.	1896.	1897.	1898.	1899.	1900.	1901.
North Ross	133·34	108·73	126·52	116·89	78·63	88·50	121·37
South Ross	125·64	107·28	138·41	127·22	87·01	83·28	182·59
Anikhet	194·97	155·19	205·52	165·08	112·55	131·69	187·58
Goplakabang	158·26	145·10	184·92	151·70	122·88	115·48	158·56
Mount Harriet	154·66	117·08	166·62	148·14	88·95	98·40	115·89
Navy Bay	199·17	162·11	212·75	179·73	138·78	144·18	205·54
Viper	166·95	131·50	169·14	140·60	102·57	106·08	166·27
Mean of all stations	156·37	132·42	171·98	147·05	104·46	108·23	148·06

The combined results of the above table tend to show that the real average rainfall of the islands is about 140 inches per annum. The actual variation of the seven stations mentioned is very great, from an average in seven years ending with 1901 of 177·32 in. at Navy Bay to one of 111·14 in. on the North of Ross Island about two and a half miles distant. The difference in the fall on the North of Ross Island, half a mile from the South of Ross Island, the official station, is often as much as nine inches in one year.

Cyclonic Storms.

Accounts and records show that cyclonic storms struck Port Cornwallis in December 1792, the Archipelago in November 1844, and Port Blair in 1864 and November 1891. There are also abundant signs of a destructive storm between Stewart Sound and Port Cornwallis in 1893. The great storms of 1891 and 1893 travelled across the islands in a north-westerly direction creating havoc on both East and West Coasts. There is a full and valuable record of the disastrous storm of 1891 (*Cyclone Memoirs*, No. V, Government of India, 1893). Cyclones have been recorded in the Bay of Bengal in every month except February and heavy rain has fallen in the Andamans in every season of the year in consequence, but cyclones are unusual except from May to November, the early part of November being the most likely season for them, and much rain is not usual in the islands from December to May.

Earthquakes.

Although the Andamans lie along or at any rate are close to a recognised subterranean line of weakness, earthquakes of great violence have not so far in the short time of British occupation been recorded. Minor earthquakes occurred in August, 1868; February, 1880; and then shocks at times till December 31st, 1881; February,

1882; August, 1883; July, 1886; July, 1894; October, 1899. The sound of the great seismic disturbance in the Straits of Sunda on August 26th, 1883, was heard at Port Blair at 9 P.M. of that day and the extra tidal waves caused thereby were felt at 7 A.M. on the 27th. The great Assam Earthquake of 1897 was not felt at all. It is possible that the reason for the Andamans escaping violent earthquakes while the Nicobars are subject to them is that they are just off the line of greatest weakness, which may run from Sumatra through Great and Car Nicobar, Barren Island, Narcondam to the Arakan Yoma.

TIDE.

The tidal observatory with self-registering gauge on Ross Island, established in 1880, is in latitude 11° 41′ N., longitude 22° 45′ E. The Port Blair tide tables are printed by authority from local data. The heights are referred to the Indian spring low-water mark, which for Port Blair is 3·53 feet below mean sea level. The mean range of greatest ordinary springs is 6·6 feet. The highest high-water and the lowest low-water are 8·0 feet above and 0·8 feet below the datum abovementioned. The apparent time of high-water at the full and change of the moon is 9h. 36m. At various points of the great harbour of Port Blair the actual times for the tide depend on wind, strength of current, and distance from the open sea. The average variation in time of high tides at the several important points is from 18m. to 57m. later than Ross and in height it is from 20 inches less to 17 inches more than Ross. Wind and current will at these points affect time by as much as 29m. either way, and height by as much as 8 inches either way.

GENERAL HISTORY.

Owing to the ancient course of trade the existence of the islands now known as the Andamans has been reported from quite early times though which of Ptolemy's island names ought properly to be attached to them may still be regarded as a moot point. Gerini, in his ingenious paper, *Notes on the Early Geography of Indo-China* (*J. R. A. S.* 1897, p. 551 ff.), gives Bazakata for the Great Andaman, Khaline for the Little Andaman, Maniola for Car Nicobar, and Agathodaimonos for Great Nicobar. In the mediæval Latin editions of Ptolemy a remark somewhat as follows often appears opposite Bazakata:—"*cuius incolæ vocantur Aginatæ qui nudi semper degere feruntur, in hac conchæ sunt multæ.*" While it is on Maniola that the people are called *anthropophagi*. Even if one is inclined to accept Gerini's plausible theory, it is nevertheless probable that Yule is right in his conjecture that Ptolemy's *'Agathou daimonos nesos* preserves a misunderstanding of some sailors' term near to the modern Andaman, as perhaps does also the contemporary term Aginatæ (with its later corruptions Allegate, Alegada on maps) for the inhabitants. The old error that Ptolemy's maps were drawn by Agathodæmon, the grammarian of the 5th Century, A.D., is repeated in Portman's *History of our Relations with the Andamanese*, 1899, p. 50, and elsewhere.

Little Andaman, as a name, has a curious and obscure history on the old maps. In some of them we find Isle d'Andemaon (and Andaman) and also Isle de Maon (and Man), as if "Andaman" was the Great Andaman and "Man" the Little Andaman. Then in maps we have Chitre Andaman 1595, 1642: Chique Andemaon 1710: Cite Andemaon 1710, 1720 and Crita I. 1720 obviously corrupted out of Chitre, Chique and Cite. Cite d'Andaman is also to be found for a town or city in the Andamans which, of course, has never existed. And it is just possible that Chique Andemaon is responsible for the modern Cinque Islands between Great and Little Andaman, which are not five but obviously two islands. Chetty Andaman survived till 1858. Little Andaman, in its modern form, does not appear till the maps of Blair in 1790 and later.

The notices of the islands by the old travellers, Chinese, Asiatic and European, are continuous, and they regularly appear in some shape or other on all maps from the "Ptolemies" of the 15th-16th Century onwards, till we reach the middle of the 18th Century, when the East India Company's and Royal Naval commanders and surveyors began to make accurate reports of parts of the coast in charts preserved for us in the works of the indefatigable Dalrymple. In 1788, owing to piracies and ill-treatment of shipwrecked and distressed crews, the East India Company through Lord Cornwallis commissioned the great surveyor, Archibald Blair, to start a Settlement on the ordinary lines, to which convicts were afterwards sent as labourers. Blair fixed on Port Blair for his Settlement in 1789, but for strategical reasons it was moved to Port Cornwallis in 1792, where it perished miserably in 1796 from the effects of a bad unhealthy site and want of experience of the climate. Here it was under Major Kyd. Blair's and Kyd's reports have all been preserved in the *Bengal Consultations*, and are published in the *Indian Antiquary*, Vol. XXVIII onwards.

Thereafter notices of the Andamans are not numerous, but they must have occupied the Government attention, for a formal *résumé* of information was officially drawn up in 1802. In 1824 the fleet, formed for the attack on Burma, made its rendezvous at Port Cornwallis. In 1825 J. E. Alexander, *Travels from India to England*, gives an interesting account of a landing at the Little Andaman. In 1836, Malcolm, the missionary, notices the Andamans in his *Travels in Southern Asia.* In 1839 Dr. Helfer, the geologist, was murdered north of Port Cornwallis. In 1844 the transports *Briton* and *Runnymede,* from Sydney and Gravesend, respectively, were wrecked together on the Archipelago in a cyclone on 12th November. They contained detachments of the 10th, 50th and 80th Regiments, and the full record of the occurrence that has been left affords a fine example of pluck, endurance and resource in a great emergency. In 1850, a Mr. Quigley from Moulmein wrote a misleading and mischievous account of a visit to Interview Island. There is preserved an interesting account of the wreck of the *Emily* in 1849 off the West Coast and of the subsequent efforts to assist the crew. On this occasion the second mate was murdered by the aborigines, and there are records at this period of other murders dating before 1848 and continuing on till 1856.

These constantly recurring piracies and murders led to the second occupation of the Islands, a step which was hastened by the Mutiny of 1857. This event threw a large number of mutineers, deserters and rebels on the hands of the Government, with whom it was difficult to deal and in November of that year it was finally decided to send them to the Andamans to start a Penal Settlement. The Government sent the "Andaman Committee" to make a preliminary exploration, with Dr. Mouat as president, and this Committee, in a *Report* remarkable for its common sense, fixed upon Port Blair as the site of the Settlement. Upon this report and another equally able by Captain Hopkinson, Commissioner of Arakan in 1856, this great experiment in treating convicts was commenced in 1858, one of the last acts of the East India Company being the formal confirmation of the Indian Government's proceedings. In 1872 the Andamans and Nicobars were formed into a Chief Commissionership, and in that year occurred the one event of general importance that has made the Andamans well-known, the murder of Lord Mayo, Viceroy of India, by a convict, while on a visit of inspection to the Settlement, for the welfare of whose convict population he had worked so sympathetically.

Population.

In 1901 the total indigenous population was 1,882. No previous census of the aborigines had been taken, but their numbers are beyond doubt decreasing, owing to the introduction of disease, and in reading the following account of the people it must always be borne in mind that the statements therein made refer largely to a state of things practically already passed away and never likely to be revived. The reader can without difficulty use his discretion in separating what is from what has been in the course of his perusal.

Races and Tribes.

An Andamanese individual, as the people themselves recognise, belongs to a family, which belongs to a sept, which belongs to a tribe, which belongs to a group of tribes or divisions of the race. The first two of these, without being specifically named are recognised; the last two have specific names. There are twelve tribes in three groups as follows:—Northern or Yerewa Group, consisting of the Chariar, Kora, Tabo, Yere and Kede Tribes; Southern or Bojigngiji Group, consisting of the Bea, Balawa, Bojigyab, Juwai and Kol Tribes; Outer Group or Onge-Jarawa Tribes. All the tribes inhabit the Great Andaman, except the Balawa of the Archipelago, the Onge of the Little Andaman and the Jarawa of the North Sentinel and parts of the South Andaman and Rutland Island. Each Group has certain salient characteristics: the forms of the huts, bows and arrows, of the canoes, of ornamentation, female clothing, hair-dressing and utensils, of tattooing and of language, common generally to the Group, but differing in details and sometimes entirely from those of the other groups. The Onge-Jarawas differ from all the rest by not tattooing. Each tribe has a clearly defined locality or rather "run" with its own language and to a certain extent its own separate habits. The Septs are sometimes fairly well defined under headmen and have a local area of their own, but not under any separate designation. Portman in his *History* divides the Andamanese into twelve tribes, necessarily omitting the Kora and Tabo, but dividing the Jarawas into three tribes according as they inhabit South Andaman, Rutland Island, and the North Sentinel. It is to that painstaking and accurate observer, Mr. E. H. Man, that we are indebted for the true differentiation of the tribes.

In their present depopulated condition the friendly tribes have amalgamated, as so many savages have done before them elsewhere in other parts of the world in similar circumstances. Thus, though the Kora, Tabo and Yere still keep more aloof than the rest in the jungles of the North Andaman, the whole of the remainder are thoroughly mixed up at the Home and practically throughout the Great Andaman and the Archipelago. This is a matter of the generation now passing away, and it is only some thirty years ago when only the Bojigyab were known to us and the "coming in" of the first Balawa from the Archipelago and the first Chariar from the extreme North took place.

It is worth while bringing together here the remarkable series of differences dividing the Andamanese into three divisions; differences that more or less run through all matters concerning them. (1) *Tattooing.*—Bojigngiji; women are the tattooers cutting the skin slightly with small flakes of quartz or glass in patterns of zigzags or in straight vertical lines; face, ears, genitals, arm and knee pits are excepted. Men and women are tattooed alike. Yerewa; men are the tattooers, cutting the skin deeply with iron pig-arrow heads: short horizontal parallel cuts in three or five lines down the back and front of the trunk, round the anus and legs. Women are tattooed thus as life advances. Onge-Jarawa; no tattooing. (2) *Hair.*—Bojigngiji; partial to complete shaving of head. Yerewa; long matted ringlets touching the shoulders. Onge-Jarawas; closely cropped head to a mop. Onge-Jarawa women are not shaved. (3) *Ornaments and female clothing.*—Bojigngiji women wear a bunch of five or six leaves in front: Yerewa women a loose tassel of narrow strips of bark: Onge-Jarawa a bunching tassel of fibre. Bojigngiji women are most particular as to clothing: Yerewa women careless. Jarawa women are apt to be quite unclothed. Bojigngijis and Yerewas smear their faces with grey clay mixed with water, white clay in delicate patterns imitating the tottoo marks, red ochre mixed with turtle fat and almond oil in coarse undefined patterns. Onge-Jarawas, with yellow clay mixed with water in coarse patches, red ochre mixed with the above-mentioned oils on the head. Onge-Jarawas wear no bone ornaments. (4) *Ornamentation of utensils.*—Bojigngiji and Yerewas, slight: Onge-Jarawas delicate and elaborate. (5) *Pots.*—Bojigngijis, pots with rounded bottom: Onge-Jarawas and Yerewas with pointed bottom. (6) *Implements.*—Bojigngijis and Yerewas, coarse and rough in manufacture: Onge-Jarawas, often delicate and neat. (7) *Baskets.*—Bojigngijis and Yerewas have a 'kick' and stand well: Onge-Jarawas have uneven bottom and stand badly. (8) *Bows and arrows.*—Bojigngijis, *karama* bow and large arrows. Yerewas, *chokio* bow and small arrows. Onge-Jarawas, curved long bow and long arrows. (9) *Arrows.*—Generally common in type to all tribes: long with plain straight point, long with straight point and barbs, short with broad detachable barbed head for pigs.* Onge-Jarawas and Yerewas, multiple headed arrows for fish. (10) *Harpoons.*—For turtle, dugongs, and large fish among Bojigngijis and Yerewas: none among the Onge-Jarawas. (11) *Canoes.*—Bojigngiji and Yerewa, same pattern canoe; Onge-Jarawa pattern different from above. Both out-rigged, Bojigngiji has in addition a large dug-out without outrigger. (12) *Huts.*—Bojigngijis and Yerewas have temporary huts. Onge-Jarawas have large permanent communal dwellings. (13) *Dancing.*—Bojigngijis and Yerewas, sounding board and song and clapping in unison. Onge-Jarawa, standing in a ring and alternately bending and straighten-

* As the pig runs off, the trailing shaft is at once caught by something in the jungle and the animal is thus brought up short.

ing the knees: also on occasion kicking the buttocks with the flat of the foot. (14) *Beds.*—Jarawas sleep on the wood ashes of the fires. Onges on raised bamboo platforms. Other tribes on leaves and in sand-holes. (15) *Food.*—The staple food of the Onges is the mangrove fruit, boiled, and they preserve small fish dried after cooking. None of the other tribes do this.

The Andamanese race, besides its division into tribes and septs, is also divided into Aryoto or long-shore-men and Eremtaga or jungle-dwellers: the habits and capacities of these two differ, owing to surroundings, irrespective of tribe. Most tribes are Aryoto and Eremtaga, but some are entirely one or the other. Some tribes as the Tabo, Juwai, Kol, and the South Andaman Jarawas are entirely Eremtaga, while the Balawa, the Chairar, and the Jarawas of the North Sentinel are entirely Aryoto. The Aryoto holds himself to be better than the Eremtaga, but beyond this there seem to be no exclusive distinctions between them and an Aryoto will marry or adopt an Eremtaga. With the minuteness in matters concerning their surroundings that is characteristic of all entirely uneducated people, the Andamanese recognise a third division of themselves by habits into Adajig or creek-dwellers, *i.e.*, those who live on the shores of the many inlets of the sea on the coasts of the Islands. The habits of the Adajig, however, are practically those of the Aryoto. Distinctions by habits are quickly lost by the Andamanese. The Jarawas have now no canoes in the South Andaman and are quite incapable of constructing or using them, though all Onges have them and so have the Jarawas on the North Sentinel. So also had the Jarawas that Colebrooke met a century ago. And in 1902 it was ascertained that the young men brought up at the Duratang (Kyd Island) Home and occupied chiefly in market gardening could neither steer nor paddle a canoe, nor take up tracks in the jungles. In one generation, though there was no restriction in communication with their people, they had lost both sea and forest craft.

Before the arrival of the English, the tribes, excepting actual neighbours, may be said to have had no general intercourse with each other, and, excepting some individuals, were entirely unable to converse together, though it can be conclusively shown that all the existing languages are directly descended from one parent tongue. The tribes were in fact brought together and made definitely acquainted with each other's separate existence and peculiarities by the influence and exertions of Mr. Man between 1875 and 1880. Even septs had but little mutual intercourse and considerable differences in details of dialect and, as has occurred in other island abodes of savages, there must have been a change of dialect or language along about every 20 miles of coast.

The tribal feeling is friendly within the tribe, courteous to other Andamanese, if known, hostile to every stranger, Andamanese or other. The sympathy and antipathy exhibited are strictly natural and uncultivated, *i.e.*, savage, and are governed by descent. The feeling of friendliness lies in an ever-decreasing zone from the family outwards towards sept, tribe, group, hostility to all others. Even septs will fight each other and Aryoto and Eremtaga do not mix much. But there is no "caste" feeling, and tribes will, in circumstances favouring the actions (*e.g.*, living on the tribal borders), intermarry and adopt each other's children. Within the tribe there is so general a custom of adoption that children above six or seven rarely live with their own parents. It is an act of friendliness to give up or adopt a child and the custom has had the effect of making the various septs of a tribe hang together much better than would otherwise have been possible.

The Andamanese are bad fighters and never attack unless certain of success. During hostilities they never take any precautions as to their own safety, nor in the attack beyond taking advantage of cover. The only ideas of protection yet met with are among the Jarawas, who use trunk-armour consisting of a wide belt of bark and well devised sentry stations on the paths round their permanent communal huts. Jarawas and some Onges kill every stranger at sight, but at present the Jarawas are alone in being entirely hostile, as, on the whole, the Onges are friendly, the friendliness dating from the capture and subsequent judicious treatment of 24 men, women and children on the Cinque Islands in January 1885. The only positively dangerous people are thus the Jarawas, and this is to be accounted for in this way. The ancient (as proved by old separate kitchen-middens) incursion from the Little Andaman through Rutland Island of that section of the Onge tribe, which is now known as the Jarawas, into the South Andaman set up an implacable tribal hostility between them and the Beas, its other occupants, which has been extended to the foreign settlers in Port Blair, and has become an undying distrust of all strangers and an hereditary hostility towards them. All the other tribes are quite friendly, and, nowadays, shipwrecked mariners would find the people, not only friendly and helpful, but also likely to give notice to Port Blair at once of their predicament, except at the following points, South and West of Little Andaman, North Sentinel, South of Rutland Island and Hut Bay on its Western Coast, Port Campbell and a few miles North of it on the West Coast of the South Andaman.

Colebrooke, reporting in 1790, gives a vocabulary of a people, now identified with the Onge-Jarawa tribe by its speech, and, as theories have been built up on this fact, it is as well to see carefully when and where Colebrooke met the natives and who they were.

Colebrook left Diamond Island (Cape Negrais) on December 20th, 1789, and reached Port Cornwallis (*now* Port Blair) on December 23rd. Of the 24th, he went up the harbour and saw some natives (Jarawa Tribe) on Dundas Point. On the 26th, he went up the harbour with Commodore Cornwallis (brother of the Governor-General), accompanied by a native who had been wounded in a skirmish with his tribe, found to be very hostile by the people of the snow *Viper*, and was kept on board the *Ranger*, Cornwallis's ship. He is described as "very cheerful and quite reconciled to his captivity." They went up the Bumlitan Creek as far as Bumlitan and met another native (Jarawa) who ran away. They dined (lunched) on "Mount Pleasant," a hill on the harbour near Viper Island and met another Jarawa who exchanged his bow and arrows for a knife. On the 27th, the wounded native, who had been on the *Ranger* three weeks, was put ashore by the Commodore, who uniformly treated the savages with extreme consideration. On the 28th they met the Jarawa on Dundas Point, whom they had seen before, with a woman and a girl, and found him again friendly. On the 29th, there was trouble with the Bea Tribe at Phœnix Bay and with the Jarawas at Ariel Creek. Colebrooke then went to the Nicobars and returned to Port Blair on February 20th, 1790, starting up north on 21st February. On the 23rd March, at Port Meadows, he saw some of the Bea Tribe leaving Entrance Island and saw some more hostile Beas, whom the party frightened off, coming from the North. On the 26th, he went to the Archipelago, and met some hostile Balawas. On the 27th, he went into Colebrooke Passage and saw some Bojigyab huts and some more of the tribe, who ran away in Elphinstone Harbour, on the 29th. On the 30th, they met some hostile Kols in the east entrance to Homfray's Strait and some more on the 31st off the north end of Long Island. On the 3rd and 4th April, they found the Yere Tribe in Stewart Sound extremely hostile. On the 6th, Blair himself met some Koras at the foot of Saddle Peak, who ran away. On the 7th, Blair discovered the present Port Cornwallis and Colebrooke left for India. It is clear from this that the only native from whom Colebrooke could have procured his *Vocabulary* was the wounded man on the *Ranger* and that man, as the *Vocabulary* shows, was a Jarawa. The tribes of all sorts—Jarawa, Bea, Bojigyab, Balawa, Kol, Yere, Kora, whom Colebrook met, except in the case of one Jarawa and his family, exhibited either extreme fear or hostility.

The first word in Colebrooke's *Vocabulary*, the first ever made of any Andaman tongue, is Mincopie for "Andaman Island or native country," whence Mincopie has become a persistent book-name for the Andamanese. It has been a great puzzle to scientific men ever since, though it is now to be identified, as will be seen later, with "Möngebe, I am (an) Onge," a phrase, which was perhaps pronounced and, at any rate, sounded in Colebrooke's ears as "Minggobie." His informant, in using it, apparently meant to explain that he was an Onge, or as the Jarawas seem to pronounce the name,—an Inggo.

Language.

The Andamanese languages are extremely interesting from the philological standpoint on account of their isolated development, due to the very recent contact with the outer world on the part of the speaker. No connection with any other group has yet been clearly traced. These languages exhibit the expression only of the most direct and simplest thought, show few signs of syntactical, though every indication of a very long etymological, growth, are purely colloquial and wanting in the modifications always necessary for communication by writing. The Andamanese show, however, by the very frequent use of ellipsis and of clipped and curtailed words, a long familiarity with their speech.

The sense of even Proper Names is usually immediately apparent, and the speakers invariably exhibit difficulty in getting out of the region of concrete into that of abstract ideas, though none in expanding or in mentally differentiating or classifying ideas, or in connecting several closely together. Generic terms are usually wanting, and specific terms are numerous extremely detailed. The following are examples of the extent to which the use of specific terms to describe details of importance to the Andamanese is carried by them. Stages in the growth of fruit:—*Otdereka*, small: *chimiti*, sour: *putungaij*, black: *chebada*, hard: *telebich*, seed not formed: *gad*, seed forming: *gama*, seed formed: *tela*, half-ripe: *munukel*, ripe: *roichada*, fully ripe: *otyobda*, soft: *chorurė*, rotten. Stages of the day: *waingala*, first dawn: *elawainga*, before sunrise: *bodola doatinga*, sunrise: *lilti* (*dilma*), early morning: *bodola kagalnga*, morning: *bodola kagnga*, full morning: *bodo chanag*, forenoon: *bodo chau*, noon: *bodola loringa*, afternoon: *bodo l'ardiyanga*, full afternoon: *elardiyanga*, evening: *dila*, before sunset: *bodola lotinga*, sunset: *elakadauya*, twilight: *elaryitinga*, dark: *gurug chau*, midnight.

Narration almost always concerns themselves and the chase. Only the absolutely necessary is usually employed and the speech is jerky, incomplete, elliptical and disjointed. Introductory words are not much used and no forward references are made. Back references by means of words for that purpose are not common, nor are conjunctions, adjectives, adverbs and even pronouns. An Andamanese will manage to convey his meaning without employing any of the subsidiary and connecting parts of speech. He ekes out, with a clever mimicry, a great deal by manner, tone and action; and this habit he abundantly exhibits in the form of his speech. His narration is, nevertheless, clear, in proper consecutive order and not confused, showing that he possesses powers of co-ordination.

The following account of a story, abstracted from Portman, of an imaginary pig hunt as told by a Bea, *eremtaga* (forest-man), for the amusement of his friends, will go far to explain the Andamanese mode of speech, and the form that its grammar takes. The narrator sits on the ground, facing a half circle of lounging Andamanese. After a short silence he leans forward with his head bent down. Suddenly he sits erect with brightening eyes and speaks in a quick, excited way, acting as if carrying on a conversation with another person. "After how many days will you return?" And then answering as if for himself: "I will come back to-morrow morning, I am off pig-hunting now." A pause. "I am going." Very suddenly. "You stay here." Moving as if going away. "I am going to another place." Squeaking like a young pig with pantomime of shooting it. "It is only a little pig. I will take it to the hut." Moving his shoulders as if carrying. "They roasted it there." Wave of the hands, signifying that the pig was of no account. Pause. "I started in the early morning after a big one,—a big pig." Motions of hands to show length and breadth of pig. To an imaginary friend. "I will sharpen pig arrows to take with me. Come after me and we will hunt together." Imitation with the hands of a pig running, shooting arrows, slap on the left breast, squeals of several wounded pigs and so on. A pause. "You take them in front of me." Directions by pantomime to other persons as to the pigs. "They were cooking them for me in the hut, cooking them well." Brightens up and begins again. "I will bring several more." Pretends to listen. "We have got them. The dogs are barking." And so on, for hours.

The actual expressions for such a story are:—

Ba kichika arla—l'—eate ngo on? Wainga——len do
How many day———past you come? Morning——in I
on. Ña do reg dele. Kam wai dol. Kam wai
come. Now I pig hunt. Away indeed I. Away indeed
do on. D'–arlog–len ka. Wai do jala———ke
I come (go). Me-behind-in there. Indeed I go-away—do
Reg—ba. Kam wai do ik on. Wai ka eda
Pig—little. Away indeed I take come. Indeed there they
otjoi. Do lilti doga————lat. Reg doga.
roast-d. I (in the)——early morning big–(pig)——for. Pig big.
Do ela l'igjit——ke. D'-okanumu—kan. Kaich
I pig-arrow sharpen—do. I——go————do. Come.
d' -arolo. Do—ng' –igdele. D'—okotelema ik on. Wai
me-after. I——you-hunt. Me——before take come. Indeed

d'a—be objoi——— ka bud-len. Tun roicha-beringa-ke. Ña
me—for cooking——were hut-in. Very ripe——good——do. Now
do- ikpagi—ke. Ikre ka. Wai eda ikkenawa.
I several—do. Getting—were. Indeed they barked.

Nothing could show more clearly how "savage" the speech is in reality, how purely colloquial, how entirely it depends on concurrent action for comprehension. When the party, who were out with Mr. Vaux, when he was killed by the Jarawas in February 1902, returned, they explained the occurrence to their friends at the Home in Port Blair by much action and pantomime and few words. The manner of his death was explained by the narrator lying down and following his movements on the ground.

The characteristics of speech exhibited in the above story are visible throughout the languages as may be seen from the following five versions of the Fire Legend culled from Portman's works:—

Bea Version.

Tol l'oko -tima-len Puluga-la mami——ka. Luratut-la chapa
(a Place)———in God asleep——was. (a Bird) fire
tap—nga omo——re. chapa-la Puluga-la pugat——ka
steal-ing bring-did. fire God burning—was
Puluga-la boi———ka. Puluga-la chapa emi————ka. a ik
God awake—was. God fire seizing—was. he taking
chapa-lik Luratut l'ot-pugari-re. jek Luratut-la emi————ka
fire—by (Bird) burn—t. at-once (Bird) taking—was
ai Tarcheker l'ot-pugari-re. Wota-Emi-baraij—len Chauga-tabanga
he (a Bird) burn—t. Wota-Emi-village-in The—ancestors
oko—dol-re. Tomolola.
made-fires. Tomolola.

Translation.—God was sleeping at Töl-l'okotima. Luratut came, stealing fire. The fire burnt God. God woke up. God seized the fire; He took the fire and burnt Luratut with it. Then Luratut took (the fire); he burnt Tarcheker in Wota Emi village. (where then) the Ancestors lit fires. (The Ancestors referred to were the Tomolola.)

Balawa Version.

Dim-Dôra—le rita Keri-l'ong-tôwer—te Puluga l'i toago choapa
(a Man) long-ago (a Place) —by God his platform fire
l'—omo—kate | ong ik akat-pora puguru—t l'—a—re |
bringing —was | he taking all—men burn —t di—d |
(Bolub ka Tarkôr ka Bilichau ongot oto—jurugmu
a Man) and (a Man) and (a Man) they in-the-sea
— t —ia | ongot at—yôkat mo —nga | ongot oaro—tichal-
wen— t —did | they fish becom—ing | they carry-

ena — te Rokwa-l' ar-tonga-baroij— a oko — dal — nga l' — a —re
taking— by (a Place) -village - in fire-mak —ing di — d

Translation.—Dim-Döra, a very long time ago, at Keri-l'ong tôwer, was bringing fire from God's platform. He taking the fire, burnt everybody with it. Bolub and Tarkôr and Bilichau fell into the sea and became fish. They took the fire to Rokwa-l'ar-tonga village and made fires there.

Bojigyab Version.

Tôl-l'oko-tim— an Bilik l'ong — pat — ye | *Luratut* | *l'ong at—*
(a Place) — in God sleep — did | (a Bird) | he fire
ab— lechi — nga | *Luratut l'ong — di — ye* | *kota ong Bilik*
bring ing | (a Bird) seiz — ed | then he God
l'ab — biki — ye | *kota Bilik l'ong — konyi — ye* | *Bilik* | *l'on*
burn — t | then God awaken — ed | God | he
at li — ye | *ong e Luratut l'oto - toi-chu—nga* | *kota kol*
fire seiz — ed | he then (a Bird) (with) — fire-hit-ing | then again
ong e Tarchal l'ote — toi-chu — ye | *Chalter l'ong — di —ye*
he then (a man) (with) fire-hit — did | (a Bird) seiz —ed
ong Lau-Cham — len da — nga | *Wôta-Emi — en ota Lau-Cham* | *n'ong*
he ancestors — to giv — ing | Wôta-Emi — in then ancestors | they
o — kadak — nga.
fire-mak-ing.

Translation.—God was sleeping in Tôl-l'oko-tima. Luratut went to bring fire. Luratut caught hold of the fire, then he burnt God. Then God woke up. God seized the fire. He hit Luratut with the fire. Then again he hit Tarchal with the fire. Chälter caught hold of it. He gave it to the ancestors. Then the ancestors made fire at Wôta-Emi.

Juwai Version.

Karo-t'on-mik — a Mom Mirit — la | *Bilik l'ökö — ema — t* | *peakar at—*
(a Place) ——in Mr. Pigeon | God sl p— t | wood fire—
lo top — chike at laiche Lech — lin a | *kotak a*
with stealing —was fire the-late (a Man) — to he | then he
öko — kodak — chine at - lo Karat tatak—emi —in
fire-make — did fire—with (a Place) —at

Translation.—Mr. Pigeon stole a fireband at Kuro-t'on-mika, while God was sleeping. He gave the brand to the late Lech, who then made fires at Karat-tatak-emi.

Kol Version.

Tôl-l'oko-tim—en Bilik —la pat —ke | *Luratut— la Oko-Emi—t*
(a Place) —in God asleep —was | (a Bird) (a Place)—in
at kek — an | *Kölotat —ke* | *lin l'—a—chol — an Min-tong-t*
fire too — k | (a Man) —was | by (he) —wen — t (a Place)

—kete | *Min-tong-ta-kete-lak l'—ir—bil—an* | *Kôlôtat l'ir— pin l'ir—dôk—an* |
— to | (a Place)-to -by (it) —out-wen—t | (a Man) charcoalbreak—did |
k'irim—kodak — an | *n'a n'otam—tepur—an* | *at ke n'ote*
fire-make-did | they alive—became | fire— by (they)
—tepur—an | *Min-tong-tôk-pôroich — in Jangil* | *n'a l'oko—*
—alive—became | (a Place) village — in ancestors | they
kôduk — an |
fire-make—did |

Translation.—God was sleeping at Tôl-l'oko-tima. Luratut took away fire to Oko-Emi. Kôlotat went to Min-tong-ta (taking fire with him from Oko-Emi). At Min-tong-ta the fire went out. Kôlotat broke up the charred firewood and made fire again (by blowing up the embers). They (the people there) became alive. Owing to the fire they became alive. The ancestors thus got fire in Min-tong-tôk village.

The general indications that the languages give of representing the speech of undeveloped savages are confirmed by the intense anthropomorphism exhibited therein. The Andamanese regard not only all objects, but also every idea associated with them, as connected with themselves and their necessities, or with the parts of their bodies and their attributes. They have no means of expressing the majority of objects and ideas without such references; *e.g.*, they cannot say "head" or "heads," but must say "my, your, his, or————'s, this one's, or that one's head" or "our, your, their, or————'s, or these ones', those ones' heads."

But though they are "savage" languages, limited in range to the requirements of a people capable of but few mental processes, the Andamanese Languages are far from being "primitive." In the evolution of a system of pre-influxion, in order to intimately connect words together, to build up compounds and to indicate back references and in a limited exhibition of the idea of concord by means of post-inflexion of pronouns, they indicate a development as complete and complicated as that of an advanced tongue, representing the speech of a highly intellectual people. These lowest of savages show themselves to be, indeed, human beings immeasurably superior in mental capacity to the highest of the brute beasts.

The Andamanese Languages all belong to one Family, divided into three Groups, plainly closely connected generally to the eye on paper, but mutually unintelligible to the ear. They are agglutinative in nature, synthesis being present in rudiments only. They follow the general grammar of agglutinative languages. All the affixes to roots are readily separable and all analysis of words shows a very simple mental mechanism and a low limit in range and richness of thought and in the development of ideas. Suffixes and prefixes are largely used, and infixes also to build up compound words. As with every other language, foreign words have lately been fitted into the grammar with such changes of form as are necessary for absorption into the general structure of Andamanese speech. A detailed grammar of the languages will be found in the Census Report for 1901, pp. 98-121; or in the *Indian Antiquary* for 1907.

RELIGION.

The religion is simple animism and consists of fear of the evil spirits of the wood, the sea, disease and ancestors, and of avoidance of acts traditionally displeasing to them, and this in spite of an abundance of mythological tales told in a confused, disjointed manner that is most instructive to the student of such things. There is neither ceremonial worship nor propitiation. There is an anthropomorphic deity, Puluga, the cause of all things, whom it is not, however, necessary to propitiate, though sins, *i.e.*, acts displeasing to him, are avoided for fear of damage to the products of the jungle. Puluga dwells now in the sky, but used to live on the top of Saddle Peak, their highest mountain. The Andamanese have an idea that the "soul" will go under the earth by an aerial bridge after death, but there is no heaven nor hell nor any idea of a corporeal resurrection in a religious sense. There is much active faith in dreams, which sometimes control subsequent conduct, and in the utterances of "wise men," dreamers of prophetic dreams, gifted with second sight and power to communicate with spirits and to bring about good and bad fortune, who practise an embryonic magic and witchcraft to such personal profit by means of good things tabued to themselves as these people appreciate. There are no oaths, covenants and ordeals, nor any forms of appeal to supernatural powers.

Puluga, who is fundamentally with some definiteness identifiable with the storm (*Wuluga*) mixed up with ancestral chiefs, has so many attributes of the Deity that it is fair to translate the term by "God." He has a wife and a family of one son and many daughters. He transmits his orders through his son to his daughters, who are his messengers, the Morowin. He has no authority over the evil spirits and contents himself with pointing out offenders against himself to them. The two great evil, *i.e.*, harmful, spirits are Erem-chauga of the Forest and Juruwin of the Sea. Like Puluga both have wives and families. The minor evil spirits are Nila and a numerous class, the Chol, who are practically spirits of disease. The Sun is the wife of the Moon and the stars are their children dwelling near Puluga, but there is no trace of sun-worship, though they twang their bows and "chaff" the moon during an eclipse, and a solar eclipse frightens them, keeping them silent.

The Andamanese idea of the soul arises out of his reflection in water and not out of his shadow which follows him about. His reflection is his spirit, which goes after death to another Jungle world, Chaitan, under the earth, which is flat and supported on an immense palm tree. There the spirit repeats the life here, visits the earth occasionally and has a distinct tendency to transmigration into other beings and creatures. Every child conceived has had a prior existence and the theory of metempsychosis appears in many other superstitions, notably in naming a second child after a previous dead one, because the spirit of the former babe has been transferred to the present one, and in their recognition of all Natives of India and the Far East as *chauga*, or persons endowed with the spirits of their ancestors.

The superstitions and mythology of the Andamanese are the direct outcome of their beliefs in relation to spirits. Thus, fire frightens Erem-chauga, so it is *always* carried. They avoid offending the Sun and the Moon by silence at their rise. Puluga shows himself in storms, and so they appease him by throwing explosive leaves on the fire, and deter him by burning beeswax, because he does not like the smell. Earthquakes are the sport of the ancestors. There are lucky and unlucky actions, but not many, and a few omens and charms. Animals and birds are credited with human capacities, *e.g.*, convicts murdered by Jarawas have been found with heavy stones placed on them and stones have been found placed along their pathways. Every Andamanese knows that this is a warning to the birds not to tell the English that the men had been murdered and that the murderers had passed along the path in front.

The great bulk of the Andamanese mythology turns on Puluga and his doings with Tomo, the first ancestor, to whom and his wife he brought fire and taught all the arts and for whom he created everything. This line of belief is still alive and everything natural that is new is attributed to Puluga. Thus when the Andamanese were introduced to the volcano, Barren Island, on seeing the smoke from the top they at once christened it Molatarchona, Smoke Island, and said the fire was Puluga's. The next most important element in the mythology is in the story of the cataclysm, which engulfed the islands and was of course caused by Puluga. It separated the population and destroyed the fire, which was afterwards stolen by Luratut, the kingfisher, and restored to the people. The population previous to the cataclysm became the *chauga* or ghostly ancestors. Others stories relate, in a fanciful way, the origin of customs, *e.g.*, tattooing and dancing.

of the arts, articles of food, harmful spirits, and so on. An important ethnological item in these stories is the constant presence of the ideas of metempsychosis and of metamorphosis into animals, fish, birds, stone and other objects in nature. Indeed the fauna chiefly known to the Andamanese are ancestors changed supernaturally into animals.

Rudimentary initiatory customs for both males and females, connected with arrival at puberty and nubility, point to a limited tabu. On reaching puberty or thereabouts, between 12 and 16 years of age, abstention from about 6 kinds of food, each in turn, is voluntarily commenced and continued for some years. At the end of each abstention there are a few ceremonies and some dancing and the youth of both sexes become "grown up." There is nothing else to mark this period beyond the application of an honorific name while it lasts, no secret to be communicated, no religious ceremony. In after-life, however, men who have gone through the initiatory period together will not fight, quarrel, nor call each other by name. They will assume great friendship, while avoiding each other with a mutual shyness. The women also practise a limited tabu as to food during menstruation and pregnancy. The idea of tabu does undoubtedly exist as to food and every man has his own tabued articles through life, which is, however, usually something observed to disagree with him in childhood or to be unpalatable. The tattooing is partly ceremonial, as a test of courage and endurance of pain, and so is painting the body with clays, oils, etc. By the material and design is shown sickness, sorrow or festivity and the unmarried condition.

Death Ceremonies.

Deaths occasion loud lamentation from all connected with the deceased. Babies are buried under the floor of their parents' hut. Adults are either buried in a shallow grave, or, as an honour, tied up in a bundle and placed on a platform in a tree. Wreaths of cane leaves are then fastened conspicuously round the encampment, and it is deserted for about three months. Burial spots are also sufficiently well marked. Mourning is observed by smearing the head with grey clay and refraining from dancing for the above period. After some months the bones of the deceased are washed, broken up and made into ornaments, to which great importance is attached, as mementos of the deceased and as they are believed to stop pain and cure diseases by simple application to the diseased part. The skull is worn down the back tied round the neck, usually, but not always, by the widow, widower or nearest relative. Mourning closes with a ceremonial dance and the removal of the clay. The ceremonies connected with the disposal of the dead are conventional, reverential and by no means without elaboration in detail.

PHYSICAL CHARACTERISTICS.

The physical characteristics of the Andamanese have been considerably studied by Mr. M. V. Portman and Major W. S. Molesworth, and as their work has never been published, the following account thereof may serve to draw attention to it. It is to be found in 15 volumes, copies of which are deposited at the India Office, the Home Department Library in Calcutta, and the British Museum. Volumes 10, 11, 14 and 15 contain anthropometric measurements, and medical details of 200 Andamanese: thus—volume 10 of 50 South Andaman males, volume 11 of 50 South Andaman females, volume 14 of 50 North Andaman males, and volume 15 of 50 North Andaman females. The remaining volumes are platinotype photographs with explanatory letterpress of Andamanese. Volumes 1 and 2, typical heads: volume 3, heads, full face and profile: volume 4, adze and bow-making: volumes 5 and 6, bow and arrow-making: volume 7, rope-making and hut-building: volume 8, eating and drinking, packing and carrying bundles, utensils, attitudes, torch-making, greeting: volume 9, painting, tattooing, counting: volume 12, full length, full face and profile, view of males: volume 13, of females. The following table summarises the results of this elaborate enquiry for general information, and shows that the women are slightly smaller than the men:—

	Height in inches.	Temperature Fahr.	Pulse beats per minute.	Respiration per minute.	Weight in lbs.
Men	58½	9 °	82	19	96 lbs. 10 oz.
Women.	54	99 5°	93	16	87 lbs.

The high bodily temperature may be an indication of the low vitality characteristic of the race. The cause is obscure, unless it is to be traced to their largely carbonaceous diet or to saturation with malaria producing a condition of masked fever. It has been observed that they do not feel themselves to be otherwise than quite well when the temperature is over 100° Fahr., and that that condition does not affect their appearance or actions.

In view of the experiments made in European countries and the United States as to the relative breathing of the sexes, it is of interest that the breathing of both sexes among the Andamanese is abdominal or upper abdominal, the women showing scarcely any indication of their breathing, though the men show it well. In the healthy younger Andamanese the breath is sweet and there is no distinctive smell from the body when clean, though they perspire freely. The older people with decayed teeth and tissues, have foul smelling breath and bodies, partly due to a mild form of scurvy, caused by absence of vegetable food at certain times of the year.

The Andamanese male matures at about 15, attains full growth at about 18, and marries at about 26, he begins to "age" at about 40 and lives on to about 60 to 65, if he reaches "old age." Except as to marriage at an earlier age, about 18, these figures apply fairly to the women also, who, however, live somewhat longer than the men, retaining in old age both health and mental faculties. The marriages are infructuous, though barrenness is uncommon, a couple rarely producing families of even moderate size and many none at all. The child-bearing age is from 16 to 35; weaning is much delayed.

Left to themselves the Andamanese go stark naked and with head uncovered, except that the women wear, as clothing and not ornament, one or more leaves in front and a bunch of leaves tied round the waist behind, or a tassel of leaves all round. Jarawas, however, of both sexes have been seen entirely naked. They dislike and fear cold, but not heat, though they avoid exposure to the sun; and being accustomed to gratify every sensation as it arises, they endure thirst, hunger, want of sleep, fatigue and bodily discomfort badly. Want of sleep, such as occurs at their dances for occasionally as much as four days and nights, exhausts them greatly. A man's load is 40 lbs. and his distance 15 miles for a day or two only. After that he will rest, whatever the urgency.

The skin, which is smooth, greasy and satiny, varies in colour from an intense sheeny black to a reddish brown on the unexposed parts and also on the collar bones, cheeks and other prominences of the body. Its general appearance has been likened to a "black-leaded stove." The scalp, the lips and nostrils are black, and there are black patches on the palate. The soles of the feet are brownish yellow. The Bojigngiji Group (South Andaman) are the darkest, and among the Onges parts of the face are a light reddish-brown. The Jarawas are distinctly fairer than the rest, the general colour being a deep reddish brown. Leucoderma occurs on the fingers and lips.

The hair varies from a sooty black to dark and light brown, yellowish brown and red. The general appearance of it is sooty black or yellowish brown. Except on the head the hair is scanty, but not absent: on the head it grows in small rings, which give it the appearance of growing in tufts, though it is really closely and evenly distributed over the whole scalp. Limited baldness is unknown, but temporary general baldness after disease occurs with a weak growth of the hair afterwards. The hair is not shaved, except on the head and eyebrows, and each tribe has, with many fantastic individual variants, its own method of wearing it. It turns grey at about 40, but white hair is not common. Shaving is "woman's work" and was performed by small flakes of quartz, but nowadays flakes from the kicks of glass bottles are substituted. It is effective and close, but a painful operation on an European's face, as I proved by personal experience many years ago.

The mouth is large, the palate hard and highly arched, the lips well formed. The hands and feet are small and well made. The ears are small and well shaped, the eyes are generally dark to a very dark brown, bright, liquid and clear, but prominent with slightly elevated outer angles and become dulled with age. The teeth, in the young, except amongst the Onges, are white, good and on the whole free from disease. Those of the Onges are irregular and discoloured. As age advances the teeth generally lose their whiteness and become worn, but without much caries. The teeth are roughly used without any care whatever. Dentition is early.

The muscular strength is great, but the vitality is low, and the apparently robust quickly die after sickening or severe injury. However, like many of the lower mammals, they recover quickly from illness when they overcome it. Idiocy, insanity and natural deformities are rare. Epilepsy is however recognised and homicidal mania occurs sometimes with concomitants of insanity such as eating raw flesh or earth and drinking the blood of the murdered. No parts of the body are intentionally pierced, injured, or deformed for the wearing of ornaments and other purposes, though the skin is extensively tatooed. An unintentional artificial depression of the forehead and sides and top of the skull is produced in some women, chiefly among the Onges, caused by using a strap to carry loads on the back when young.

The data at present available as to the relative prevalence of diseases among the Andamanese and their relative fatality are unsatisfactory, but the following appears to be a fair statement of the case in order of importance :—

I.—Fevers	45	per cent.	of all	cases.
II.—Respiratory organs	35	„	„	„
III.—Digestive organs	18	„	„	„
IV.—Other diseases	2	„	„	„

These classes may be further divided up more specifically thus :—

1.—Malaria	40	per cent.	of all	cases.
Other fevers	5	„	„	„

II.—Chronic bronchitis	21	per cent. of all cases.
Pneumonia	12	,, ,, ,,
Other chest diseases	3	,, ,, ,,
III.—Diarrhœa	15	,, ,, ,,
Other abdominal diseases	3	,, ,, ,,
IV.—Other diseases	1	,, ,, ,,

Without placing too much reliance on the above table, it serves to bring out the fact that among the Andamanese, as among the alien immigrants, malarial fevers are the overwhelming prevalent causes of sickness. As also in the case of immigrants, malarial fevers are not nearly so fatal in proportion to cases as the diseases of the respiratory and digestive organs. Thus it may be said that deaths from malarial fevers occur in 8·5 per cent. of the cases, while those from diseases of the respiratory organs in 90 per cent., and of the digestive organs in 74 per cent. These considerations prepare us for the old statement that the prevalent diseases among the Andamanese are climatic and the same as those of the foreign immigrants.

Going a little further into detail, it has been noticed that malarial fevers are commonest in June, at the commencement of the monsoon and during heavy bursts of rain thereafter. Malarial fevers commence as usual in their intermittent form and prove fatal as remittent fever. Other zymotic fevers are uncommon, though the Andamanese will drink the filthiest water. A short rainfall in the Andamans is usually accompanied by high dry winds and then is the high time of the chest diseases. But though the Andamanese are susceptible to bronchial catarrh, and though chronic bronchitis is common, it is not fatal; pneumonia is however extremely fatal. Pleurisy, hæmoptysis and phthisis are comparatively rare. Abdominal diseases, though comparatively uncommon, are very fatal, diarrhœa, including probably dysentery, claiming most victims. Dyspepsia and colic are both common. In health the stools are regular, but inclined to looseness. They have been likened to those of the lower mammals when in good health. Of other diseases sunstroke is dreaded and always fatal. The brain and spinal cord are not often affected, though curvature of the spine is occasionally seen. Scurvy occurs at the seasons when vegetable diet, *i.e.*, such as fruits and roots afford, is too scanty. Elephantiasis occurs among the Onges, but is limited to the Little Andaman. Chronic muscular rheumatism occurs among the older people, leading to loss and withering of limbs. Ulcers, generally the result of wounds in the jungles, are common and, as with the immigrants, slow to heal. Abscesses are also common. Considering that personal uncleanliness is often extreme, skin diseases are curiously infrequent, except ringworm and exfoliated dermatitis, sometimes leading to destruction of finger and toe nails, due either to scurvy or exposure. Excluding malaria, endemic disease has not been recognised among the Andamanese, and the only epidemics that have been known to attack them are imported pneumonia (1868), syphilis (1876), measles (1877), and influenza (1892), in that order: unhappily with disastrous effect. Exposure to the sun and wind in the cleared spaces, the excessive use of tobacco and over-clothing, as results of contact with civilisation, are also said to have undermined their health as a body of human beings. Intoxicants are forbidden to them by local rules and are not easily or commonly procured by them.

The diseases which the Andamanese distinguished by name are malarial fever, catarrh, coughs and rheumatism. Phthisis and heart disease are recognised, but are spirit caused and so are all internal maladies, which of course are not understood. Medicine and surgery are almost absent from the Andamanese purview. They will bleed on the forehead for fever and headache and round abscesses to alleviate pain. They scarify for rheumatism and internal pain as a last resort. Red ochre and various herbal concoctions are both swallowed and applied as all-healers, in which they have great faith. Certain leaves are sometimes applied to local affections and beds made of them for the sake of their supposed medicinal odour. Cinctures, sometimes of human bones, are used to alleviate pain, but no other charms are employed. Occasionally the diet is slightly changed to relieve illness and they are quick to avail themselves of the hospital provided for them. They are extremely afraid of European surgery and will tremble violently at the sight of the operating knife. They smear themselves with white clay and water against the heat of the sun and with red ochre and oil after dark as a protection against cold. The sick are sympathetically and very kindly, but superstitiously, treated. There are no pregnancy customs and those at childbirth are sensible and without superstition, difficult delivery being practically unknown. Snakebite is uncommon and seldom fatal. Ligatures above the bite and scarifying are applied, both operations showing observation and common sense. Bites of centipedes, scorpions, leeches and ticks cause little inconvenience to the Andamanese, though very much to immigrants.

The figures of the men are muscular and well formed and generally pleasing; often a young man is distinctly good looking, for, though there is a tendency to prognathism, it is not commonly pronounced, while a straight and well formed nose and jaw, accompanied by superior intelligence and an irritable temper indicating a nervous temperament, are by no means rare. The natural good looks of many of the people are injured by the habit of shaving and smearing themselves with greasy red and white pigments.

The pleasing appearance of the men is not a characteristic of the women, whose habits of completely shaving the head and profusely smearing themselves, with an early tendency to stoutness and ungainliness of figure and sometimes to pronounced prognathism, frequently make them unattractive objects to Europeans.

The voice of the Andamanese, though occasionally deep and hoarse, is usually pleasant and musical. The mode of speech is gentle and slow, and among the women a shrill voice is used in speaking; but though the tendency is towards a drawled pronunciation, they can express their meaning quickly enough on occasion, too quickly, indeed, for a foreigner to clearly follow the minutiæ of pronunciation without very close attention. The general tone of the voice in speaking is low.

The nerve development of the Andamanese is low, pain is not severely felt and wounds quickly heal. The sense development is normal and instances of unusual acuteness observed are the result of personal training in certain directions and not of heredity, *e.g.*, they will recognise one of themselves at a great distance, but not an unaccustomed object such as a European: they can smell a fire or hear the sound of dancing also at a great distance, but this is because they are always on the look-out for these things and their discernment is a matter of habit and of much consequence to themselves. They can, in short, do well such things as they pay particular or habitual attention to. The Andamanese are naturally far sighted, and any near sight observed will be found to be due to leucoma or other disease. The colour sense is hardly developed at all and they are what would be called in Europe colour-blind to most colours. Black, white and red are distinguished, but green and blue are not. This is due apparently to want of observation only, as they distinguish between white paint and the white European skin. A good deal of blindness was caused by imported epidemic ophthalmia in 1877. In the jungles hearing is not abnormally acute, but is highly trained in matters pertaining to jungle craft. Touch seems to be undeveloped. The sense of smell is highly developed in matters necessary to their existence, but they have no appreciation of artificial scent or of that of flowers which do not denote food, nor can they distinguish by smell that which they cannot see unless it be an object of food. Taste is strongly developed as to honey, distinguishing that deposited from different flowers. They care nothing for scenery and do not decorate themselves with flowers. In the jungles all shooting with arrows is necessarily at very short distance, and generally the Andamanese are good shots at short distances only, judging direction very well but distance hardly at all. They can, however, at the very short distance required for shooting fish allow accurately for refraction in moving water and will shoot their fish successfully, even in the surf, in a manner that is inimitable: this is really due to accurate judgment of direction.

Mental Characteristics and Capacities.

In childhood, the Andamanese are possessed of a bright intelligence, which, however, soon reaches its climax and the adult may be compared in this respect with the civilised child of ten or twelve. He has never had any sort of agriculture, nor until the English taught him the use of dogs, did he ever domesticate any kind of animal or bird, nor did he teach himself to turn turtle or to use hook and line in fishing. He cannot count and all his ideas are hazy, inaccurate and ill-defined. He has never developed unaided any idea of drawing or making a tally or record for any purpose, but he readily understands a sketch or plan when shown him. He soon becomes mentally tired and is apt to break down physically under mental training.

He retains throughout life the main characteristics of the child: of very short but strong memory, suspicious of, but hospitable to, strangers, ungrateful, imitative and watchful of his companions and neighbours, vain and, under the spur of vanity, industrious and persevering, teachable up to a quickly reached limit, fond of undefined games and practical jokes, too happy and careless to be affected in temperament by his superstitions, too careless indeed to store water even for a voyage, plucky but not courageous, reckless only from ignorance or inappreciation of danger, selfish but not without generosity, chivalry or a sense of honour, petulant, hasty of temper, entirely irresponsible and childish in action in his wrath and equally quick to forget, affectionate, lively in his movements and exceedingly taking in his moments of good temper. At these times the Andamanese are gentle and pleasant to each other, considerate to the aged, the weakly or the helpless and to captives, kind to their wives and proud of their children, whom they often over-pet; but when angered, cruel, jealous, treacherous and vindictive, and always unstable. They are bright and merry companions, talkative, inquisitive and restless, busy in their own pursuits, keen sportsmen and naturally independent, absorbed in the chase from sheer love of it and other physical occupations and not lustful, indecent or indecently abusive.

As the years advance they are apt to become intractable, masterful and quarrelsome. A people to like but not to trust. Exceedingly conservative and bound up in ancestral custom, not amenable to civilisation, all the teaching of years bestowed on some of them having introduced no abstract ideas among the tribesmen, and changed no habit in practical matters affecting comfort, health, and mode of life. Irresponsibility is a characteristic, though instances of a keen sense of responsibility are not wanting. Several Andamanese can take charge of a large steam launch through dangerous channels, exercising, then, caution, daring and skill, though not to an European extent, and at one time the dynamo-man of the electric lighting on Ross Island was an Andamanese, while the wire-man was a Nicobarese. Both of them exhibited the liveliest sense of their responsibilities, though a deeprooted unconquerable fear of the dynamo and wires when at work. The Nicobarese showed, as was to be expected, the higher order of intellect. Another Andamanese was used by Portman for years as an accountant and kept his accounts in English accurately and well. The highest general type of intelligence yet noticed is in the Jarawa tribe.

The intelligence of the women is good, though not as a rule equal to that of the men. They are, however, bright and merry even in old age and are under no special social restrictions, have a good deal of influence, and in old age are often much respected, exhibiting then a considerable mental capacity. They nevertheless readily and naturally acquiesce in a position of subordination, slavery and drudgery to the men, and are apt to herd together in parties of their own sex. Several women trained in a former local Mission Orphanage from early childhood have shown much mental aptitude and capacity, the "savagery" in them, however, only dying down as they grew older. They can read and write well, understand and speak English correctly, have acquired European habits completely, and possess much shrewdness and common sense: one herself taught her Andamanese husband, the dynamo-man abovementioned, to read and write English, and induced him to join the Government House Press as a compositor. She writes a well expressed and correctly spelt letter in English and has a shrewd notion of the value of money. Such women, when the instability of youth is passed, make good "ayas," as their menkind make good waiters at table.

The Andamanese divide the day by the position of the sun and can roughly divide the night, though they have no idea of steering by the sun or stars. The year is known by the three main seasons of the climate and the months rudely by the flowering and fruiting of trees of economic value to them. Tides are understood and carefully noted, a necessary accomplishment to a people largely living on shell-fish and navigating shallow tidal creeks and shores. They are aware of the connection of the phases of the moon with the tides and have names for the four phases of each lunation. They know the four quarters of the compass in reference to the daily position of the sun and have names for the four chief winds that blow (N. W., N.E., S.E., S.W.). They differentiate three kinds of clouds:—Cumulus, stratus, nimbus. The only constellation they have distinguished is Orion and they have discovered the Milky Way for which they have a name, and also call it "the way of the angels" (*morowin*, the daughter-messengers of Puluga).

SOCIAL CHARACTERISTICS.

Food.

The food consists of fish, pork, turtle, iguana, "wild cat" (*paradoxurus sp.*), shell-fish, turtle eggs, certain larvæ, and a great variety of fruit, seeds, roots, and honey and is plentiful both by sea and land. They never starve, though they are habitually heavy eaters. The food is always cooked and commonly eaten very hot. As much as possible of an animal is eaten and the Andamanese, like most hunters, have found out the dietary value of tripe. The Andamanese are expert cooks and adepts at preparing delicacies from parts of animals and fish. The charge of cannibalism seems to have arisen from three observations of the old mariners. The Andamanese attacked and murdered without provocation every stranger they could on his landing; they burnt his body (as they did in fact that of every enemy); and they had weird all-night dances round fires. Combine these three observations with the unprovoked murder of one of themselves and the fear aroused by such occurrences in a far land in ignorant mariners' minds, century after century, and a persistent charge of cannibalism is almost certain to be the result.

Dwellings.

Except in the Little Andaman and among the Jarawas there are no fixed habitations, the search for easily obtained food and insanitary habits obliging the people to be nomads, for they have no practice of cultivation and domesticate no animal whatever, except dogs obtained from the English. They thus dwell in various customary encampments, situate within their respective territories. At these encampments usually fixed in sheltered spots, they erect about 14 temporary huts capable of holding up to 50 to 80 persons, arranged facing inwards on an oval plan always more or less irregular. The central space is the dancing ground. A hut is merely a thatch about 4 feet long by 3 feet wide, sloping from 8 inches behind to 4½ feet in front, placed on four uprights and some cross-pieces without walls. In unsheltered spots and at the head-quarters of Septs large circular huts are built with a good deal of ingenuity, having eaves nearly touching the ground. These will be as much as 15 feet high and 30 feet in diameter.

For hunting purposes mere thatched shelters are erected for protection from the wind. The use of the flimsy hunting shelters and camp huts of the Andamanese is rendered possible in the wet and stormy weather so common in the Islands by the deneseness of the jungle, which prevents the winds from reaching them even when close to the sea-beach and causes the rain to fall vertically upon them. Close to every hut is a very small platform for surplus food about 18 inches from the ground, and in it at least one fire is carefully preserved. This is the one thing that the Andamanese are really careful about for they do not know how to make fire, though they show much skill in so carrying smouldering logs with them by land or sea that they are not extinguished. Their ignorance of this fundamental requirement of civilization is shown in their fire-legend that fire was originally stolen from their deity Puluga and has never been allowed to become extinct since. Excepting guns, nothing has more impressed the Andamanese with European power and resources than the use of matches, *i.e.*, of making fire whenever required with ease.

In the Little Andaman and among the Jarawas of the South Andaman, large permanent huts for use in the wet season are built up of solid materials to 30 feet in height and 60 in breadth to hold the fires of 7 to 8 hunting parties, say 60 to 70 people, *i.e.*, they contain 7 to 8 fires with about 8 persons to each "fire." The Jarawa hunting camp is much the same as that of any other Andamanese and his great communal hut is built on the same principle as the larger huts of the other Andamanese.

Games.

The Andamanese are childishly fond of games and have an indigenous blind-man's-buff, leap-frog and hide-and-seek. Mock pig and turtle hunts, mock burials, and "ghost" hunts are favourite sports. Matches in swinging, swimming, throwing, skimming (ducks and drakes), shooting (archery), and wrestling are practised.

Amusements.

The great amusement of the Andamanese, indeed their chief object in life, after the chase, is the formal evening or night dance, a curious monotonous performance accompanied by drumming the feet rythmically on a special sounding board, like a Crusader's shield and mistaken for a shield by several observers, singing a song more or less impromptu and of a compass limited to four semitones and the intermediate quarter tones, and clapping the hands on the thighs in unison. The dance takes place every evening whenever there are enough for it, and lasts for hours and all night at meetings of the tribes or septs for the purpose. It then becomes ceremonial and is continued for several nights in succession. Both sexes take allotted parts in it. This and turtle hunting are the only things which will keep the Andamanese awake all night long. There are five varieties of the dance among the tribes: that of the Onge-Jarawas being an entirely separate performance.

Music and Song.

The Andamanese appreciate rhythm and time, but not pitch or tune. They sing in unison, but not in parts, and can neither sing in chorus nor repeat or even catch an air. The key in which a solo or chorus is started is quite accidental. They can be readily taught any dance step and can teach it themselves from observation. Every man who respects himself is a composer of songs, always consisting of a solo and refrain, and sings without action or gesticulation and always to the same rhythm. The songs relate only to travel, sport and personal adventures, never to love, children and the usual objects of poetry, and very rarely to beliefs and superstition. The wording is enigmatic and excessively elliptic, the words themselves being in grammatical order, but shorn of all affixes as a rule. As in all poetry unusual words are employed. But clipped as the wording is and prosaic as the subjects are, the Andamanese are far from being unable to give a poetic turn to their phraseology and ideas. The women have lullabies for their babies.

Family System.

The salient points in the Andamanese family system may be described thus:—The duties of the men and women are clearly defined by custom, but not so as to make those of the women comparatively hard. The women have a tacitly acknowledged inferior position, but it is not such as to be marked or to leave them without influence.

Family relations in daily life are subject to sexual limitations. Only husband and wife can eat together. Widows and widowers, bachelors and maidens eat with their own sex only. A man may not address directly a married woman younger than himself, nor touch his wife's sister, nor the wife of a younger relative, and *vice versâ*. All this creates a tendency towards the herding together of the women.

Marriage Relations.

The Andamanese are monogamous, and by preference, but not necessarily, exogamous as regards sept and endogamous as regards tribe or more strictly group. Divorce is rare and unknown after the birth of a child, unfaithfulness after marriage, which entails the murder of both the guilty parties if practicable, is not common, and polyandry, polygamy, bigamy and incest are unknown. Marriages are not religious, but are attended with distinct ceremonies. Marriage after death of one party or divorce is usual. Before marriage free intercourse between the sexes within the exogamous limits is the rule, though some conventional precautions are taken to prevent it. Portman tersely describes the marriage ceremony thus:—" When the elders of a sept are aware that a young couple are anxious to marry, the bride is taken to a newly made hut and made to sit down in it. The bridegroom runs away into the jungle, but after some struggling and pretence at hesitation, is brought in by force and made to sit in the bride's lap. This is the whole ceremony. The newly married couple have little to say to and are very shy of each other for at least a month after marriage, when they gradually settle down together."

Marriages are the business of parents or guardians and they have a right of betrothal of children, the betrothal being regarded as a marriage. Marital relations are somewhat complicated and quite as strictly observed as among civilised communities. Old books on this point generally ascribe bestiality and promiscuity to the race, but quite wrongly. There is no "caste" feeling and tribes will, in circumstances favouring it, intermarry and adopt each other's children. Within the tribe there is so generally a custom of adoption that children above six or seven rarely live with their own parents.

Social Emotions.

The social emotions are not generally expressed. The Andamanese have no words for ordinary salutations, greeting or for expressing thanks. On meeting they stare at each other for a lengthened period in silence, which the younger breaks with a commonplace remark and then follows an eager telling of news, which an Andamanese always delights in hearing. Relatives however sit in each other's laps, huddled closely together at *meeting*, weeping loudly and demonstratively, and after a long separation this may last for hours. The Onges are less demonstrative and on such occasions shed a few silent tears only and caress each other with their hands. At *parting* they take each other by the hand and blow on it, exchanging sentences of conventional farewell. Undemonstrative though they are, the Andamanese are readily roused to emotion, finding that difficulty in separating the real from the assumed observed in other savages. At Government House, Calcutta, in 1895, when a party was told to sit down and weep to show the custom at meetings, in a few moments the weeping became genuine, and when after a short time they were told to stop and get up, tears were streaming down their faces.

Nomenclature.

Every child is named for life after one of about twenty conventional names by the mother, of course, without reference to sex, immediately upon pregnancy becoming evident. To this is subsequently added a nickname, varying occasionally as life proceeds, derived from personal peculiarities, deformities, disfigurements, or eccentricities and sometimes from flattery or reverence. Girls are also given "flower names" after one of sixteen selected trees which happen to be in flower at the time they reach puberty. The "womb-name" is called the *teng-l'ar-ula* and on the child being born, the words distinguishing sex by the genitals, *ota*, male, and *kata*, female, are prefixed to it in babyhood. The woman's "flower name" precedes the *teng-l'ar-ula* till motherhood or advancing years, but is often used alone. As the "flower names" are of much interest, the following list of them is given in the Bea language. There are eleven of them and the flowers they represent, regarded as identical by the Andamanese, belong to trees sometimes widely differing in species: a mistake that is made by people of much higher mental development. The people are now ignorant of the origin of the flower names or of the cause of the selection of the trees mentioned in the list.

Flower name.	Tree.	Flowering month.
Moda	(1) Semecarpus (Sp.) (2) Odina wodier	March.
Ora	Chickrassia tabularis	March.
Jidga	(1) Unidentified (2) Croton argyratus	April.
Yeri	Sterculia (Sp.)	April.
Pataka	(1) Moliorma simplicifolia (2) Terminalia procera	May.
Reche	(1) Eugenia (Sp.) (2) Rubiaceæ	June. July.
Chagara	Pterocarpus dalbergioides	August.
Charapa	Unidentified	September.
Chenra	Leea sambucina	October.
Yulu	(1) Unidentified (2) Eugenia (Sp.)	November.
Chilip	Diospyros densiflora	November, December, January and February.

The honorifics *maia* and *mam* are prefixed out of respect to the name of elderly males and *chana* to all names of married women. Girls are addressed by the flower name and the elders by the honorific. Names are not much used in addressing, but chiefly for naming the absent or in calling.

Arts and Industries.

The great objects of Andamanese life are hunting for food and dancing at night. All other occupations arise out of the necessities of their personal lives. In general terms it may be said that they make their own weapons, bows and arrows, harpoons and spears, string and nets of string, baskets and mats, unglazed circular cooking pots, bamboo baskets and canoes hollowed out of trunks. The ornamentation is crude, but customary and conventional. Their implements are quartz flakes, *cyrena* valves and natural stones, and latterly ends of glass bottles and iron from wrecks. Excellent information with illustrations on the domestic and other arts is to be found in a minutely accurate work, Man's *Aboriginal Inhabitants of the Andaman Islands*.

The only stone cutting implement known to the Andamanese is the quartz flake chipped off, never worked, and held between the fingers for shaving and tattooing, and shells and fish bones are used for the small blades of the peculiar adze of this people, and for arrow points, scraping and cutting. A *cyrena* valve is the ordinary knife and scraper. Hammers, anvils, hones and oven-stones consist of natural stones. They have never made celts. The ends of glass bottles for some years, and iron from wrecks for a long time past, have been substituted for the indigenous implements, when and where procurable. The object of the long series of murderous raids made by the inland Jarawas on the outlying parts of the Penal Settlement has now been proved to have been made in search for iron. The implements on the whole are coarsely and roughly made.

The weapons of the Andamanese are bow and arrow, harpoon, fish spear, pig spear, and they have never had any notion of poisoning the blades, which however sometimes inflict dangerous septic wounds from dirt, though as a rule they are kept bright as a matter of pride. Barbed arrows and harpoons with loose heads are used for catching and pulling up game in the jungles and marking where turtle or large fish are sinking.

String for nets and all purposes is twisted, often neatly, from the inner bark of creepers. Large nets of this string are made for driving turtle and hand-nets for prawns and small fish and for wallets. Stout cord is made from the inner bark of the *melochia velutina*. Whole, split and scraped canes are used as binders. The weaving is good, neat and stout, and baskets and mats are thus well made from strips of canes.

The unglazed circular clay cooking pots with rounded or pointed bottoms, to the Andamanese very valuable, are built up by hand, sun-dried and then baked, but not thoroughly, in the fire. They are often encased in basket work for safety. Their manufacture, form and ornament are typical of the Stone Age generally. Buckets are hollowed out of wood or cut from the joints of the bamboo. Canoes are hollowed out of whole trunks of light, soft timber by the adze without the use of fire, do not last long and are only fair sea boats. They are, however, capable of holding many people and a good deal of light cargo.

The personal ornaments made are—bunches and strips of fibres and leaves scraped, cut and hammered, fringes of dentalium shells and straw-coloured wreaths of hammered and roasted dendrobium bark. The bones, skulls and jawbones of deceased relatives are also used whole, or broken and scraped to fancy or requirement, as ornaments, besides necklaces of the bones of animals. Tattooing and painting the body are only ornamental to the extent that, in the latter case especially, deviations from the conventional designs are due to personal taste. The only ornaments to dwellings and huts are the heads of turtle, pigs, iguana, paradoxurus killed in hunting. These are hung up partly as ornaments and partly as trophies, but not with any idea of record. Every manufactured article has its own customary conventional line ornament in one or more of three colours and in one or more of eleven patterns approximately achieved only. The colours are red, white and brown from natural earths. The patterns are (1) chevrons, (2) close cross hatch, (3) wide cross hatch, (4) parallel lines, (5) parallels and chevrons combined, (6) lozenges, (7) plait or guilloche, (8) herring-bone, (9) cross cuts, (10) hoops, (11) vandyke with scolloped bands and cross lines.

COMMUNICATIONS.

The Andamanese modes of communication by land and sea are "natural." They are good climbers, and rapid walkers and runners, moving with a free and independent gait, and can travel considerable distances at a time. The Jarawas turn their toes in, due to the necessity of stooping to pass along their paths through the tangled jungle. The Eremtaga are good but not remarkable trackers. The Aryoto are good swimmers and are much at home in the water. The Andamanese generally show a dexterity in getting about their thick and tangled jungles which baffles all immigrants, though in this respect the Eremtaga quite out-distance the Aryoto, and the Jarawas apparently all the others. They are unadventurous seamen, poling and paddling their canoes with small spade paddles at considerable speed, faster than that of an ordinary ship's boat for a little distance though they could not paddle away from one in even a short chase, but they never go out of sight of land, have never been even to the Cocos (30 miles), nor to Narcondam and Barren Island, nor had they ever any knowledge of the existence of the Nicobars till the British occupation.

Tribal Administration.

There is no idea of Government, but to each tribe and to each sept of it there is a recognised head, who has attained that position by tacit agreement on account of some admitted superiority, mental or physical, and commands a limited respect and such obedience as the self interest of the other individual men of the tribe or sept dictates. There is a tendency to hereditary right in the natural selection of chiefs, but there is no social status that is not personally acquired. The social position of a chief's family follows that of the chief himself and admits of many privileges in the shape of tribal influence and immunity from drudgery. His wife is among women what he is among men and at his death, if a mother and not young, she retains his privileges. Age commands respect and the young are deferential to the elders. Offences, *i.e.*, murder, theft, adultery, mischief, assault, are punished by the aggrieved party on his own account by injury to the body and property or by murder, without more active interference on the part of others than is consistent with their own safety, and without any fear of consequences except vengeance from the friends of the other side, and even this is usually avoided by disappearance till the short memory of the people has obliterated wrath.

Property is communal, as is all the land, and ideas as to individual possessions are but rudimentary, accompanied with an incipient tabu of the property belonging to a chief. An Andamanese will often readily part with ornaments to any one who asks for them. Theft, or the taking of property without leave, is only recognised as to things of absolute necessity, as arrows, pig's flesh, fire. A very rude barter exists between tribes of the same group in regard to articles not locally obtainable or manufactured. This applies especially to cooking pots, which are made of a special clay found only in certain parts of the islands. The barter is really a gift of one article in expectation of another of assumed corresponding value in return, and a row if it is not forthcoming. The territory of other tribes is carefully respected without however there being any fixed boundaries.

Relations with the English.

Since the establishment of the Penal Settlement in 1858 an Andamanese Home has been created in Port Blair for the use of the aborigines, a free asylum to which every Andamanese that likes is admitted. He may stay as long as he pleases and go when it suits him. While there he is housed, fed and taken care of, and for the sick there is a good and properly maintained hospital. From the Home, too, are taken such little necessaries and luxuries as the people desire to friends at a distance and during each of the many tours taken round the coasts by the officials. In return the Andamanese of the Home are employed to help in catching runaway convicts, in collecting edible birds'-nests and trepang and other natural produce, and in making "Andamanese curios," from which a small income is derived and expended on them. They have never succeeded in acquiring any true idea of money for themselves and all their earnings have to be administered for them. It is indeed against local rules to give them money, as it is at once spent in intoxicants. The present policy, in short, is to leave them alone and to do what is possible in the conditions to ameliorate their lives. The administrative objects gained by establishing friendly relations with the tribes are the cessation of the former and much too frequent murder of shipwrecked crews, the external peace of the Settlement and the creation of a jungle police to prevent escapes of convicts, and secure the recapture of runaways.

In the days of Blair and Kyd, 1789-96, the tribes showed themselves to be practically uniformly hostile, despite the conspicuous consideration these early officials exhibited, and remained continuously so after the commencement of the re-establishment of the Settlement in 1858, attacking the working parties of convicts, just as the Jarawas do still, for iron and articles suitable to them and robbing the gardens started for food supplies. These practices had to be repressed by force, and efforts towards friendly relations had to be postponed until respect for the settlers was established. The procedure officially then adopted and carried out with such success in the end by Messrs. Corbyn, Homfray, Man, Godwin-Austen, and Portman in succession was the simple one of providing the Home and visiting the people in their own haunts, as opportunity arose, with suitable presents.

CHAPTER III.

THE NICOBARS.

Physical Aspects.

The Nicobar Islands lie in the Bay of Bengal between Sumatra and the Andaman Islands. Geographically, they are situated between the 6th and 10th parallels of north latitude, and between

92° 40′ and 94° of east longitude. The extreme southern point is 91 geographical miles from Pulo Brasse off Achin Head in Sumatra, and the extreme northern point 75 miles from the Little Andaman. They consist of twelve inhabited and seven uninhabited islands running in a rough line from Sumatra to the Andamans. The extreme length of the sea-space occupied by the Nicobars is 163 miles, and the extreme width is 36 miles.

The geographical names of the Nicobars are nearly all foreign, and are not used by the inhabitants. Their names and dimensions are as follows from north to south, the Islands having an aggregate area of about 635 square miles:—

Geographical Name.	Native Name.	Area in square miles.
Car Nicobar . . .	Pu	49·02
*Batti Malv . . .	Et	0·80
Chowra	Tatat . .	2·80
*Tillanchong . . .	Laok . . .	6·50
Teressa	Taihlong . . .	34·00
Bompoka	Poahat . . .	3·80
Camorta . . .	Nankauri . . .	57·91
Trinkat	Laful . . .	6·40
Nancowry	Nankauri . . .	19·32
Katchall	Tehnyu . . .	61·70
*Meroe	Miroe . . .	0·20
*Trak	Fuya . . .	0·10
*Treis	Taan . . .	0·10
*Menchal	Menchal . . .	0·50
Little Nicobar . . .	Ong	57·50
Pulo Milo	Miloh . . .	0·40
Great Nicobar . . .	Loong . . .	333·20
Kondul	Lamongshe . .	0·50
*Cabra	Konwana . . .	0·20

* Uninhabited.

Origin of the Name.

The situation of the Nicobars along the line of a very ancient trade has caused them to be reported by traders and sea-farers through all historical times. Gerini has fixed on Maniola for Car-Nicobar and Agathodaimonos for Great Nicobar as the right ascription of Ptolemy's island names for this region. This ascription agrees generally with the mediæval editions of Ptolemy. Yule's guess that Ptolemy's Barussæ is the Nicobars is corrected by Gerini's statement that it refers to Nias. In the 1490 edition of Ptolemy the Satyrorum Insulæ, placed to the south-east of the Malay Peninsula, where the Anamba Islands east of Singapore, also on the line of the old route to China, really are, have opposite them the remark:—*qui has inhabitant caudas habere dicuntur*—no doubt in confusion with the Nicobars. They are without doubt the Lankhabalus of the *Arab Relations* (851 A.D.), which term may be safely taken as a misapprehension or mistranscription of some form of Nicobar (through Nakkavar, Nankhabar), thus affording the earliest reference to the modern term. But there is an earlier mention of them by I-Tsing, the Chinese Buddhist monk, in his travels, 672 A.D., under the name of the Land of the Naked People (Lo-jen-kuo) and this seems to have been the recognised name for them in China at that time. "Land of the Naked" translates Nakkavaram, the name by which the islands appear in the great Tanjore inscription of 1050. This name reappears in Marco Polo's Necuveran 1292, in Rashiduddin's Nakwaram 1300, and in Friar Odoric's Nicoveran 1322, which are the lineal ancestors of the 15th and 16th Century Portuguese Nacabar and Nicubar and the modern Nicobar. The name has been Nicobar since at least 1560. The fanciful story of the tails is repeated by the Swede Kjoeping as late as 1647.

The modern geographical names of these islands have not yet been traced to their sources, except in a few cases, and the old maps do not help much. Nicobar turns up as a general name in maps of 1560, 1688, and 1710, but this name is separately traced out. Nicobar, and corruption Nicular means, however, on the maps the Great Nicobar (1595, 1642, 1710, 1720, 1764). It did so to Dampier in 1688. Car Nicobar has a variety of names; some through misprints—Carecusaya, 1560, for Carenicaya? Caremcubar, 1595, for Carenicubar. Carenicubar, 1642. Cara Nicobar, 1710. Cornalcabar, 1720, for Cornaccabar? Curnicubar, Carnicular and Carnioubas, 1720, all for Carnicubar. Carnicobar, 1764, 1785. Chowra appears as Jara, 1764, 1785, and all the other names for it are corruptions of *sombrero*, from the remarkable umbrella-shaped hill to the south of it whence the existing (Canal de Sombreiro) Sombrero Channel in these islands:—Dosombr 1595 for Dos Sombros? Somebrero, 1642, 1710, 1720. Dos Sombreros, 1686. Sombrera, 1720. Teressa was always distinguished and shows its origin in the village of Tras, with which, no doubt, trading was done. Rasa, 1595, 1642. Raya, 1686, for Rasa. Rasa, 1710. Possa, Rasa, and de Richo, 1720, all for Rasa. I. Roses, 1764, for Rasa. Terache, 1764, 1785. Bompoka appears as Pemboc, 1764, and Perboc, 1785 (misprint for Pemboc). Camorta was called the Isle of Palms.

Thus, Das Palmeiras, 1642; Des Palmas, 1720. But later by its native name Nicavari (= Nancowry) 1764, 1785. Tillanchong is Talichan, 1764, 1785. Trinkat is Sequinte in 1710. Nancowry is Souri in 1764, 1785 (and in all reports up to 1800 and some time after). Katchall is de Achens in 1710. And Great Nicobar is Seneda for some reason in 1710.

Geology.

Geological knowledge of the Nicobars depends mainly on the observations of three scientific visitors, who did not, however, explore the islands, Dr. Rink of the *Galathea* (Danish) Expedition in 1846, Dr. von Hochstetter of the *Novara* (Austrian) Expedition in 1858, and Dr. Valentine Ball in 1869. These observers are not in entire agreement. The sandstones and shales of the Southern Islands are apparently similar to those distinguished as the Port Blair series in the Andaman Islands, and in both areas poor lignitic coal is found in the series. The clay stones and associated conglomerates of Camorta, Nancowry and Trinkat are probably the same formation as that recognised in the Andaman (Ritchie's) Archipelago.

It will be sufficient here to note that Dr. Rink of the *Galathea* expedition notices, that though the Islands form part of a submarine chain known for its volcanic activity, he found no trace of true volcanic rocks, but features were not wanting to indicate considerable upheavals in the most recent periods. The connection of the Islands with the principal chain is exhibited in the strike of the oldest deposits, from south-south-east to north-north-west, *i.e.*, coincident with the line between Sumatra and the Little Andaman. The hilly islands consist partly of these stratified deposits, which occupied the level bottom of the sea before their appearance, and partly of plutonic rocks which pierced the former and came to the surface through the old upheaval. The age of the stratified rocks generally indicates that of the islands, which Dr. Rink takes to be tertiary. The undulating hilly land of the islands he considers to be due to an old alluvium upheaved by a movement subsequent to that which caused the principal upheaval of the islands. In addition to this there is a distinct new alluvium on the flat lands due to the disintegration of coral reefs, which still surround the islands as a circular flat.

Dr. von Hochstetter, of the *Novara* expedition, classifies the most important formations, thus:—eruptive, serpentine and gabbro; marine deposits,—probably later tertiary,—consisting of sandstones, slates, clay, marls and plastic clay, recent corals. He connects the whole group geologically with the great islands of the

Asiatic Archipelago further south. From his observations the following instructive table has been drawn up as to the relation of geological formations to soil and vegetation and showing how the formations have affected the appearance of the islands:—

Geological character of the underlying rock.	Character of the soil.	Character of the forest vegetation.
1. Salt and brackish swamp, damp marine alluvium.	Uncultivable swamp . .	Mangrove.
2. Coral conglomerate and sand; dry marine alluvium.	Fertile calcareous soil carbonate and phosphate of lime.	Cocoanut.
3. As above, with dry fresh water alluvium.	Fertile calcareous sandy soil	Large trees.
4. Fresh-water swamp and damp alluvium.	Cultivable swamp . .	Pandanus.
5. Plastic and magnesian clay, marls, partially serpentine.	Unfertile clay; silicates of alumina and magnesia.	Grassy, open land.
6. Sandstone, slate, gabbro, dry river alluvium.	Very fertile; loose clay and sand, rich in alkalis and lime	Jungle; true primeval forest.

Small traces of copper have been found in the igneous rocks, the presence of tin and amber has been reported, but not confirmed scientifically. The white clay or marls of Camorta and Nancowry have become scientifically famous as being polycistina marls like those of Barbadoes.

Botany and Forest.

Although the vegetation of the Nicobars has received much desultory attention from scientific observers, it has not been subjected to a systematic investigation by the Indian Forest Department like that of the Andamans. In economic value the forests of the Nicobars are quite inferior to the Andaman forests, and, so far as known, the commercially valuable trees, besides fruit trees such as the *cocoanut* (*cocos nucifera*), the betel-nut (*areca catechu*), the mellori (*pandanus leeram*), are a thatching-palm (*nipa fruticans*), and the timber trees *myristica irya, mimusops littoralis, hopea odorata, artocarpus lakoocha, calophyllum inophyllum, calophyllum spectabile, podocarpus neriifolia, artocarpus chaplasha.* Of these only the first would at the Andamans be classed as a first class timber, the last would be a third class timber and the rest second class. The minor forest products are limited to dammer (obtained from *dipterocarpus sp.*) and rattans. The palms of the Nicobars are exceedingly graceful, especially the beautiful *ptychoraphis augusta.* The large clumps of *casuarina equisetifolia* and great tree-ferns (*alsophila albo-setacea*) are also striking features of the landscape in places.

In the old missionary records are frequently mentioned instances of the introduction of foreign economic plants. In this matter the people have been apt pupils indeed and nowadays a number of familiar Asiatic fruit-trees are carefully and successfully cultivated; pumelos (the largest variety of the orange family), lemons, limes, oranges, shaddocks, papayas, bael-fruit (wood-apple), custard apples, bullock's hearts, tamarinds, jacks, and plantains; besides sugar-cane, yams, edible collocasia, pine-apples, capsicum, and so on. A diminutive orange, said to come from China and to have been introduced by the Moravian missionaries, is now acclimatised (and at the Andamans). It is quite possible also that with the missionaries came the peculiar zigzag garden fence of the Northern Islands. With the long commerce of the people a number of Indian weeds (*malvaceæ* and *compositæ*) have been introduced, *datura, solanum, flemmingia mallotus, mimosa,* and so on.

The Hills.

The hills in the Nicobars vary greatly in the several islands. The chief summits are on Teressa, Bompoka, Tillanchong, Camorta, Nancowry, Katchall, Great and Little Nicobar. The only hills over 1,000 feet are on Tillanchong, Great and Little Nicobar. The more prominent hills with names are on Great Nicobar, Mount Thullier (2,105); on Little Nicobar, Mount Deoban (1,428), Princess Peak (1,353), Empress Peak (1,420); on Camorta, Mount Edgecumbe (251) near to and south of Dring Harbour, west coast of Camorta, so called from the likeness to the scenery of Plymouth.

Rivers and Streams.

The Nicobars generally are badly off for fresh surface water: on Car Nicobar there is hardly any, though water is easily obtained by digging. The only island with rivers is Great Nicobar, on which are considerable and beautiful streams: Galathea (Dak Kea), Alexandra (Dak Anaing) and Dagmar (Dak Tayal).

Harbours.

There is one magnificent land-locked harbour formed by the Islands of Camorta, Nancowry and Trinkat, called Nancowry Harbour, and a small one between Pulo Milo and Little Nicobar. There are good anchorages off east, south and west of Kondul, in some seasons in Sawi Bay in Car Nicobar, East Bay in Katchall and in Castle Bay in Tillanchong: but the overgrown coral interferes with the usefulness of the otherwise large and land-locked Expedition Harbour, west coast of Camorta, Dring Harbour, west coast of the same island, Campbell Bay and Ganges Harbour east and north respectively of Great Nicobar, and Beresford Channel between Trinkat and Camorta. Galatea Bay and Laful Bay, south and east of Great Nicobar, are too open to be much better than roads, and the other usual points of anchorage are merely open roadsteads. The coasts are coral-bound and dangerous, but there are many points at which small craft could find convenient shelter. The other usual anchorages are off Car Nicobar, Mus, north-east, and Kemios, south: off Chowra, Hiwah, east: off Teressa, Bengala, Kerawa, Kolarue, all west, Hinam, east: off Bompoka, Poahat, east: off Katchall, west, good for small boats: between Menchal and Little Nicobar, west; inside Megapod Island, Great Nicobar, east,—good for small boats: Tillanchong, Novara Bay.

The Scenery.

There is a considerable variety in the appearance of the several islands of the Nicobar groups. Thus from north to south, Car Nicobar is a flat coral-covered island; Chowra is also flat, with one remarkable table-hill at the south end (343 feet); Teressa is a curved line of hills rising to 897 feet, and Bompoka is one hill (634 feet) said by some to be volcanic; Tillanchong is a long, narrow hill (1,058 feet); Camorta and Nancowry are both hilly (up to 735 feet); Trinkat is quite flat; Katchall is hilly (835 feet), but belongs to the Great and Little Nicobars in general form, differing much from the others of the Central Group; the Great and Little Nicobars are both mountainous, the peaks rising to 1,428 feet in the Little, and to 2,105 feet in the Great, Nicobar. Car Nicobar is thoroughly tropical in appearance, showing a continuous fringe of cocoanuts, but a high green grass is interspersed with forest growth on Chowra, Teressa, Bompoka, Camorta, and Nancowry, giving them a park-like and, in places, an English look. It is also found on Car Nicobar in the interior. Katchall, Great and Little Nicobar have from the sea something of the appearance of Sardinia from the Straits of Bonifacio, and are covered with a tall dense jungle. Rocky, though heavily wooded, Tillanchong is entirely unlike the rest. The scenery is often fine and, in some places, of exceeding beauty, as in the Galathea and Alexandra Rivers and in Nancowry Harbour.

Fauna and Zoology.

There are no indigenous dangerous wild animals, but on Camorta there are buffaloes and some cattle left by the Missionaries, which have become wild. On Great and Little Nicobar and elsewhere in places crocodiles are found in the rivers and monkeys on Great and Little Nicobar and Katchall, but not elsewhere. The marine and land fauna of the Nicobars take generally the character of those of the Andamans, though while the Andamans fauna are closely allied to Arakan and Burma, the Nicobars display more affinities with Sumatra and Java. The land fauna, owing to greater ease in communications, have been better explored than the Andamans. The economic zoology of the Nicobars is also mainly that of the Andamans. Coral, trepang, cattle bones, sea-shells, oysters, pearls, pearl-oysters, turtle and tortoise-shell, edible birds'-nests are equally found in both groups of islands. And in the Nicobars a somewhat inferior quality of bath sponge is obtainable.

Climate.

The climate generally is that of the islands of similar latitude; very hot except when raining, damp, rain throughout the year, generally in sharp heavy showers, unwholesome for Europeans, in places dangerously subject to malaria. The weather is generally unsettled, especially in the south. The islanders are exposed to both monsoons with easterly and north-easterly gales from November to January, and south-westerly gales from May to September, smooth weather only from February to April and in October. The normal barometric readings (five years in Nancowry Harbour) vary between 29·960 and 29·797, being highest in January and lowest in June.

Temperature.

Statistics are scanty as regards temperature. They were kept up for 15 years (1874-88) in Nancowry Harbour while the Penal Settlement lasted and were commenced on Car Nicobar during 1898. From the returns the following tables give the main features:—

Nancowry Harbour.

	1884.		1885.		1886.		1887.		1888.	
Mean highest in shade	May	91·3	April	91·6	April	91·9	July	86·5	April	91·2
Mean lowest in shade	Dec.	74·5	Dec.	73·3	Dec.	71·8	Feb.	72·2	Jan.	72·2
Highest in shade	May	92·2	May	95·4	Aug.	96·2	April	90·6	May	97·4
Lowest in shade	July	70·3	Sept.	71·0	Dec.	64·0	Mar.	66·4	Jan.	68·8
Dry bulb mean		83·3		84·4		84·0		82·7		83·9
Wet bulb mean		77·5		78·1		76·6		77·2		7·8

CAR NICOBAR.

	1898.*		1899.		1900.		1901.†	
Mean highest in shade	Sept.	84·4	May	88·7	July	88·6	April	91·6
Mean lowest in shade	,,	76·7	April	77·8	Feb.	77·6	Oct.	74·6
Highest in shade	,,	88·0	Mar.	92·2	April	93·5	April	92·3
Lowest in shade	Nov.	70·7	Feb.	66·0	Mar.	66·8	Jan.	71·6
Dry bulb mean	,,	79·3	,,	83·2	,,	83·8	,,	84·2
Wet bulb mean	,,	77·2	,,	73·6	,,	73·0	,,	74·0

* The observations in 1898 are only available from September 1st to December 31st, 1898.

† In 1901 the observations available are only up to October 31st, 1901.

RAINFALL.

The rainfall varies much from year to year. The following statistics are available:—

NANCOWRY HARBOUR.

	1884.		1885.		1886.		1887.		1888.	
Most wet days in a month	May	21	July	23	Nov.	23	May	27	Sept.	22
Heaviest fall in a month	May	21·75	Dec.	17·90	Nov.	25·23	Nov.	20·41	Oct.	27·63

CAR NICOBAR.*

	1898.		1899.		1900.		1901.	
Most wet days in a month	Oct.	18	June	26	May	20	Sept.	22
Heaviest fall in a month	Sept.	11·38	,,	20·96	,,	15·79	,,	19·77

* The same remarks apply to this table as to the temperature table for Car Nicobar.

Between 1874 and 1888 the wettest year in Nancowry Harbour was 1887 with 165·44 inches and the driest 1885 with 93·04 inches. The two full years of observation at Car Nicobar (1889-1900) showed 104 and 106 inches of rainfall, respectively.

CYCLONIC STORMS.

Cyclones occasionally visit the islands. Recorded instances in 1885 in May and 1892 in March.

Earthquakes.

As the Nicobar Islands apparently lie directly in the local line of greatest weakness, severe earthquakes are to be expected and have occurred at least three times in the last 60 years. Earthquakes of great violence are recorded in 1847 (31st October to 5th December), 1881 with tidal wave (31st December), and milder shocks in 1899 (December). The tidal waves caused by the explosion of Krakatoa in the Straits of Sunda in August 1883 were severely felt.

General History.

Like the Andamans, the existence of the Nicobars has been known from the time of Ptolemy onwards, but unlike the Andamans, there is as long a history of European occupation as of other parts of the Eastern seas. In the 17th Century at least, and probably much earlier, as the Missionary Haensel speaks of *pater* = sorcerer and Pere Barbe of *deos* and *reos* = God as survivals of Portuguese missionaries, the Nicobars began to attract the attention of a variety of missionaries. As early as 1688 Dampier mentions that two (probably Jesuit) "fryers" had previously been there "to convert the Indians." Next we have the letters (in *Lettres Edifiantes*) of the French Jesuits, Faure and Taillandier, in 1711. And then in 1756 the Danes took possession of the islands to colonise, the previous possession being a shadowy French one, but employed the wrong class of men sent by the Danish East India Company. The colony, affiliated to Tranquebar, had perished miserably by 1759. The Danes then in 1759 invited the Moravian Brethren to try their hands at conversion and colonisation, and thus in due time commenced the Moravian (Herrnhuter) Mission which lasted from 1768 to 1787. It did not flourish and the Danish East India Company losing heart, withdrew in 1773 and left the missionaries to a miserable fate. In 1778, by persuasion of an adventurous Dutchman, William Bolts, the Austrians appeared, but their attempt failed in three years. This offended the Danes and from 1784 till 1807 they kept up a truly wretched little guard in Nancowry Harbour. In 1790 and 1804 fresh attempts by isolated Moravian missionaries were made. From 1807 to 1814 the islands were in English possession during the Napoleonic wars and were then handed back by treaty to the Danes. During this time an Italian Jesuit arrived from Rangoon and soon returned. In 1831 the Danish pastor Rosen from Tranquebar again tried to colonise, but failed for want of support and left in 1834, and by 1837 his colony had disappeared, the Danes officially giving up their rights in the place. In 1835 French Jesuits arrived in Car Nicobar (where the Order claim to have succeeded 200 years previously) and remained on in great privation in Teressa, Chowra and elsewhere till 1846, when they too disappeared. In 1845 the Danes sent Busch in an English ship from Calcutta to resume possession, who left a good journal behind him, and in 1846 the scientific expedition in the *Galathea* with a new and unhappy settlement scheme. In 1848 they formally relinquished sovereignty and finally removed all remains of their settlement. In 1858 the Austrians again arrived scientifically in the *Novara* with a scheme for settlement which came to nothing. In 1867 Franz Maurer, an officer, strongly advised the Prussian Government to take up the islands, but in 1869 the British Government, after an amicable conversation with the Danish Government, took formal possession, and established in Nancowry Harbour, under that at the Andamans, a Penal Settlement which was withdrawn in 1888. In 1886, the Austrian corvette *Aurora* visited Nancowry and produced a *Report* and also a series of well-illustrated articles by its surgeon, Dr. W. Svoboda. At present there are maintained native agencies at Nancowry Harbour and on Car Nicobar, both of which places are gazetted ports. At Car Nicobar is a Church of England mission station under a native Indian catechist attached to the Diocese of Rangoon; the only one that has not led a miserable existence. The islands since 1871 have been included in the Chief Commissionership of the Andaman and Nicobar Islands.

The long story of the European attempts to colonise and evangelise such a place as the Nicobars is a record of the extreme of useless suffering that merely well-intentioned enthusiasm and heroism can inflict, if they be not combined with practical knowledge and a proper equipment. Nevertheless the various missions have left behind them valuable records of all kinds about the country and its people: especially those of Haensel (1779-1787, but written in 1812), Rosen (1831-1834), Chopard (1844), Barbe (1846). Scattered English accounts of the islands are also to be found in many books of travel almost continuously from the 16th Century onwards.

British Penal Settlement.

Despite the nominal occupation of the country by Europeans for so long, the inhabitants, even of Nancowry Harbour, have been systematic pirates, and there is a very long list of authentic cases in which traders and others of all nationalities have been murdered, wrecked and plundered by them even to quite recent times. Complaints of piracy and murder of crews made in the records left behind by missionaries and seamen occur up to 1848, and in 1852 there commenced formal official complaints and correspondence on the subject, which continued at intervals, until in 1867 the question already mooted of annexation of the islands to stop piracy, some cases of which had been especially atrocious, was formally taken up, and in 1869 they were annexed to the British Crown and attached to the Andamans for administration and the establishment of a Penal Settlement. This was maintained for nineteen years and succeeded effectually and there is now no fear of a recrudescence of the evils it was designed to eradicate.

The Penal Settlement in Nancowry Harbour consisted on the average of 350 persons: 2 European and 2 other officers; garrison, 58; police, 22; other free residents, 35; convicts, 235. They were employed on public works similar to those of the Andamans. The health was never good but sickness was kept within limits by constant transfer to the Andamans. Individual health, however, steadily increased with length of time and there is no doubt that in time sanitary skill and effort would have made the sick rate approach without special efforts that of the Andamans. The first year of residence was always the most sickly, partial acclimatisation being quickly acquired. Some officers stayed two to three years. Mr. E. H. Man was in actual residence on and off six and a half years. Some of the free people remained on several years: convicts usually three, and sometimes voluntarily from five to fifteen without change. As a matter of fact, with the precautions taken, the sick rate at the Nicobar Penal Settlement did not compare unfavourably with that at the Andamans at its close in 1888. The story of the Settlement was well told by Mr. E. H. Man in a final Report on its being broken up in 1888, and this will be found in p. 188 of the Census Report for 1901.

British Colonisation.

Like all the other Governments who had had an interest in the islands, the British tried a colony, Chinese, in 1884, which failed. But the attempt drew from the most experienced officer there, Mr. Man, the following advice of value, considering the perennial interest in these islands betrayed by European speculators and would-be colonisers:—"To colonise the Nicobars employ Chinese; send them to Great Nicobar: employ agriculturists who are not opium users: maintain quick and frequent communication with the Straits Settlements: assist the colonists in transporting their families: provide them with ready means of procuring food, clothing, medicines, tools and implements." A large capital and much perseverance would always be necessary for exploiting the Nicobars with any hope of success.

The People.

The indigenous population increased slightly from 5,942 in 1883, to 5,962 in 1901, when the total population was 6,511. There is a strong local idea that, like the Andamanese, the Nicobarese, too, are rapidly decreasing in population, but there is no real ground for this opinion. Island by island, the Census gave figures, which can be compared with those procured by Messrs. Man and de Roepstorff in 1883, showing the population to be stationary, as one would expect it to be on the theory already expounded, with reference to the Andamanese, as to the causes which govern the growth and maintenance of the population of savage and semi-savage peoples. The compared figures also go to corroborate what is known as to the movement of the population amongst themselves. There has lately been an emigration from over-crowded Chowra to Camorta North, and many people both in Nancowry and Camorta own property in Katchall East, and villages and cocoanut plantations are owned both in Trinkat and Nancowry by the same men. Hence it is quite a chance on which of adjacent islands owners of property on both will be found on any given day. There is also communication between the coast men of the Southern Group and Katchall West, and, similarly, the people of Great Nicobar will bodily "visit" Kondul, and so will those of Little Nicobar visit Pulo Milo, and *vice versâ*. Indeed, Kondul is an appanage of Great Nicobar East, and so is Pulo Milo of Little Nicobar. So, though by the dialect test the Nicobarese can be divided into six varieties, by habits of intercommunication they may be well divided into Northern or Car Nicobarese, the Central Nicobarese (Chowra to Nancowry), Southern or Great Nicobarese, and the isolated Shom Pen of Great Nicobar. Taken thus the population has been stationary between 1883 and 1901. Stationary in Car Nicobar, slightly increased in the Central Groups, and slightly decreased in the Southern Groups by internal movement. As regards individual islands, those with stationary population may be taken as Car Nicobar, Bompoka, Nancowry, Little Nicobar, Pulo Milo. Those with an increased population are Teressa, Camorta, Trinkat, Katchall, Kondul. Those with a decreased population are Chowra and Great Nicobar.

Race and its Divisions.

The Nicobarese are not divisible into tribes, but there are distinctions, chiefly territorial. Thus, they may be fairly divided into the people of Car Nicobar, Chowra, Teressa with Bompoka, the Central Group and the Southern Group. In the Great Nicobar there is the one inland tribe of the Shom Pen. The differences to be observed in language, customs, manners, and physiognomy of the several kinds of Nicobarese may be with some confidence referred to habitat and the physical difficulties of communication. There is, however, nothing in their habits or ideas to prevent admixture of the people, for both intermarriages and mutual adoptions are as freely resorted to as circumstances will admit.

In the matter of differences between islands and communities, the information available is neither complete nor certain, but it is nevertheless worth while to note down such as have been ascertained or reported. Abbreviations are here necessary in referring to Islands. N. = North : S. = South : C. = Central : C.N. = Car Nicobar : Ch. = Chowra : T. = Teressa : S.P. = Shom Pen. *Devil murders.*—C. N. common Ch. and T. rare : C. and S. very rare. *Lying-in.*—Ch. and T. couvade : C.N. Special lying-in hut with uncleanliness of the woman. *Bodily malformation.*—C. and S. except S. P. flatten the occiput. *Hair.*—C. N., Ch., C., cut level to below the ears, oiled, parted in the middle : T. cropped to a mop : S. untidy to the shoulders : S. P. unkempt, long and matted. *Female Dress.*—Ch. and T. cocoanut-leaf petticoat : S. P. and S. bark-cloth petticoats : C. blue calico petticoats : C. N. red calico petticoats. *Fighting helmets.*—C. and S. of padded cloth : N. of cocoanut husks. *Weapons.*—S. P. wooden-head spears only : N. cross bows : C. and S. toy bows for children. *Days of rest.*—C. N. 7th, 14th and 22nd in five of the lunar months of the S.W. monsoon, in two of the N.-E. monsoon, perhaps copying the Ubokne of the Burmese traders. *Funeral Customs.*—N. ossuaries : N., C., and S. P. special customs : Ch., T., and Pulo Milo in S. aërial "burial" : C. N. special burial of the revered dead in coffins. *Position of corpse in grave.*—C. and C. N. feet to shore at right angles to it : Ch. and S. males, feet to shore, females, head to shore : T. parallel to shore : S. P. squatting and facing the nearest stream. *Position of grave.*—C. and S. in cemetery between village and jungle with family divisions : Ch. and T. near the huts : C. N. on sea-shore near the village. *Spirit scarers.*—*C. kareau* human images, numerous : S. and Ch. few : T. scarce and made of the skull of a deceased priest with wooden trunk filled with his bones : C. N. none. *Priests and novices.*—*Mafai* or novices on C. N. only. *Locomotion.*—C. bamboo and light wooden stilts for crossing muddy foreshores at low tide. *Cocoanut climbing.*—C. N. loops round the ankles and a dah. Elsewhere, men without assistance, women with a cocoanut-leaf in place of dah. *Government.*—N. chiefs, elders and council of three in each village : C. and S. no chiefs, except vaguely of groups of huts and cocoanut lands. *Villages.*—C. N. and S. clean : elsewhere dirty. *Huts.*—Ch. pent roofs tabued. *Food.*—Ch. eat dogs. *Drink.*— C. N. cocoanut-milk, no water (never at all except a little as medicine). N. toddy is sucked up through a tube from the storage vessel : C. and S. drink from a cup or out of a hole in the storage vessel. *Drink materials.*—C. cocoanut vessels blackened with oil and soot. *Cook-*

ing utensils.—S.P. on bark: elsewhere of pottery. *Pottery.*—Made only on Ch.

The ethnological interest attaching to the Shom Pen lies in the fact that, owing to their fear of the coast people of the Great Nicobar and indeed of each other at a little distance from their houses, and the sterility of known crosses between them and the coast people, they probably represent the race in its purest form. It is also necessary to state distinctly that they are Nicobarese pure and simple, as so lately as in Yule's edition of Marco Polo it is stated—partly on the authority of one of my own predecessors based on local enquiry—that they were an aboriginal people like the Andamanese. There is no radical difference between a Shom Pen and any other Nicobarese. The differences are merely such as exist between islands and as are to be expected among people living an almost isolated existence.

Antiquity.

The Nicobarese in Ptolemy's day were reported by sailors to be "tailed" men, a statement due to the long, waggling end of the narrow loin-cloth still looked on by the Nicobarese themselves as representing the tail of their "dog" first ancestress. In the 7th Century A.D., I-tsing, in his travels, describes them as a naked people, whose women wore girdles of leaves, whose coasts were lined with cocoanuts and betel-palms, who came off in canoes in large numbers eager to barter cocoanuts, plantains and articles of cane and bamboo for iron, which they valued beyond all things, who had "not much rice," who were of middle height and not black, who were skilled in cane and bamboo basket work, who apparently understood the trade language of the day. In the 9th Century A.D., in the *Arab Relations* they were described as a naked people, the women wearing a girdle of leaves, who came off to passing ships to barter ambergris and cocoanuts for iron. Such generally is the description of the Chinese (and Japanese) travellers and traders who actually visited the islands in the first millenium A.D. Such, too, is generally the description of the travellers from the West that speak from personal experience up to Dampier, who was stranded in Great Nicobar in May 1688 and lived there for a time actually on "mellori" [a term for which he is apparently responsible, though Fontana (1795) calls it a Portuguese word], *i.e.*, pandanus paste, and that of the "fryer" who was living in his time as a missionary in Nancowry Harbour. Dampier's description of the people will be found on p. 221 of the Census Report. The story is always the same:—Unclothed men, women with short petticoats, possession of cocoanuts, betel and ambergris, manufactures in cane and bamboo, eagerness to trade for iron with passing vessels, meeting strangers in canoes, isolation from the world except for passing ships. And it is a fair inference that the Nicobarese have been a very long time, at least two thousand years, on their present site, with the same civilisation and the same habits as they possess at the present day. In this view a study of them should be of great ethnological value, as it must be their habits that can explain those of the general Indo-Chinese race, to which it will be seen from the following pages that they presumably belong, rather than the other way round.

Language.

The Nicobarese language in the Central Dialect has been long since studied. Vocabularies, collections of sentences and partial Grammars of this Dialect have been made at intervals by various missionaries and others from 1711 onwards:—the two Jesuit Fathers Faure and Bonnet in 1711; Surgeon Fontana of the Austrian vessel *Josef und Theresia* in 1778 (pub. 1795); G. Hamilton in 1801; the Danish missionary Rosen in 1831-7; Fathers Chabord and Plaisant (in Teressa) in 1845; Fathers Barbe and Lacrampe in 1846; Dr. Rink in the Danish vessel *Galathea* in 1846; the Austrian *Novara* Expedition in 1857 (pub. in 1862), with additions by de Roepstorff and others under Colonel H. Man; Maurer in 1867; Mr. A. C. Man in 1869; comparative statement by V. Ball of all information up to 1869; Mr. E. H. Man in 1871 onwards; F. A. de Roepstorff in 1876 onwards; Dr. Svoboda of the Austrian *Aurora* Expedition, 1886 (pub. 1892). Ten Vocabularies and a translation into the Central Dialect of 27 Chapters of the Gospel of St. Matthew were made by the Danish Moravian missionaries (Herrnhuter) in 1768-87. These are still preserved in manuscript at Herrnhut, and were partially embodied in de Roepstorff's posthumous *Dictionary of the Nancowry (Central) Dialect*, 1884; a capital book with valuable appendices, requiring, however, retransliteration for English readers. But the latest and best attempt to reproduce this Dialect is Mr. E. H. Man's *Dictionary of the Central Nicobarese Language*, 1889. This contains also a brief and valuable attempt at the Grammar and a Comparative Vocabulary of all the Dialects. The system of transcription adopted is the very competent one of the late Mr. A. J. Ellis. Mr. Man had the advantage of all the labours of his predecessors, together with a much longer residence in the islands than any of them and better means of locomotion. To these he has added the accuracy and care which distinguish all his work. The other Dialects only find a place in Mr. Man's studies and are still but little known, no one with sufficient scholarly equipment or inclination having ever resided on any of the islands for the time necessary to study them to the extent that has been possible at Nancowry.

The Nicobarese speak one language, whose affinities are with the Indo-Chinese Languages, as represented nowadays by the Mon Language of Pegu and Annam and the Khmer Language of Cambodia amongst civilised peoples and by a number of uncivilised tribes in the Malay Peninsula and Indo-China. It has affinities also with the speech of the tribes in the Peninsula, who are generally classed as "wild Malays" (Orang-utan and Orang-bukit), so far as that speech has come under the old influence of the Indo-Chinese Languages. The Nicobarese language is thus of considerable importance philologically, as preserving, on account of isolation and small admixture with foreign tongues for many centuries, the probable true basis for the philology of the Languages of the Indo-Chinese Family. The argument here is as follows:—The Nicobarese have been on the same ground for at least two thousand years, and they have a tradition of migration from the Pegu-Tenasserim Coast. They have been quite isolated from the coast people, except for trade, for all that period. Their language has been affected by outside influences almost entirely in trade directions, and then not to a great degree. It has been subjected to internal change to a certain degree by the effects of tabu. Yet we find roots in the language of the kind that remain unchanged in all speech, which are apparently beyond question identical with those that have remained unchanged in the dialects of the wild tribes of the Malay Peninsula; these very roots owe their existence among the wild tribes to the effect on them of the influence of the Indo-Chinese Languages, civilised and uncivilised. Considering then the long isolation of the Nicobarese, it is a fair inference that these islanders probably preserve a form of the general Indo-Chinese speech that is truer to its original forms than that of any existing people on the Continent. We may, therefore, find in the Nicobarese speech the real foundation on which to build up the philology of the whole Indo-Chinese Group of Languages. In this view the Nicobarese dialects are of great scientific value and well worth a thorough investigation.

The language is spoken by 6,300 people in six dialects, which have now become so differentiated in details as to be mutually unintelligible, and to be practically, so far as actual colloquial speech is concerned, six different languages. These dialects are limited in range by the islands in which they are spoken:—Car Nicobar (3,451); Chowra (522); Teressa and Bompoke (702); Central Camorta, Nancowry, Trinkat, Katchall (1,095); Southern, Great Nicobar Coasts and Kondul, Little Nicobar and Pulo Milo (192);

Shom Pen, inland tribe of Great Nicobar (348). Although it can be proved that the Nicobarese Language is fundamentally one tongue, yet the hopeless unintelligibility of the dialect of one island to the ear of the people of another may be shown by the following example:—

Car Nicobar.

om	*paiakua*	*dra*	*chain*	*ka*	*tarik*
don't	afraid	not	I	eat	man

Central.

wot	*men*	*pahou*	*chit*	*ohngok*	*ten*	*paiyuh*
don't	you	afraid	I-not	eat	to	man

Sense of both.

Don't be afraid ! I don't eat men ! (I am not a cannibal.)

In spite of the aptitude of the people for picking up such foreign tongues as they hear spoken, quite a few foreign words have been adopted into their speech. Examples are:—

From Portuguese.

English.	Nicobarese.	English.	Nicobarese.
boot	shapato	cask	pipa
book, paper	lebare	elephant	lifonta
hat	shapeo	rupee	rupia
copper money	Santa Maria	shaman, sorcerer	pater
"God"	Deuse, Reos		

From Hindustani.

salt	shal, sal

From Malay.

cup	mongko	cat	koching
buffalo	kapo	fowl	haiyam

The Nicobarese are natural linguists. Only a century ago Portuguese was the trade language of the Islands with a sprinkling of Danish, German and English. Malay and Chinese were both so before the Portuguese day and now English, Burmese and Hindustani are well understood. Indeed, the nature of the trade at any given island can be tested by the foreign languages best understood there. *E.g.*, on Car Nicobar, Burmese is best understood, and then English and Hindustani: Malay and the other Nicobarese dialects not much. On Chowra, Hindustani, Tamil, Malay, and

English are spoken, and generally also the other Nicobarese dialects, except Shom Pen. On Teressa, Malay, Burmese, and English are the languages with the dialects of Chowra and the Central Group. In the Central Group they talk Hindustani, Malay, Burmese, English, and Chinese with the dialects of the South and Teressa. In the Southern Group they talk Malay, Hindustani, Chinese, and English with the Central Dialect. In the Nicobars generally as elsewhere among polyglot peoples, natives of different islands have to converse in a mutually known foreign tongue (*e.g.*, Hindustani, Burmese, Malay or English) when unable to comprehend each other's dialects. The women know only their own language and are dumb before all strangers.

There is a custom of tabu, which in the Nicobars, as elsewhere when it is in vogue, has seriously affected the language at different places, at least temporarily. Any person may adopt any word, however essential or common, in the language as his or her personal name, and when he or she dies it is tabued for a generation, for fear of summoning the ghost. In the interval a synonym has to be adopted and sometimes it sticks, but that this is not very often the case is shown by a comparison of the Vocabularies published or made in 1711, 1787, 1876, and 1889, which prove that the language possesses a stability that is remarkable in the circumstances of its being unwritten and therefore purely colloquial, spoken by communities with few opportunities of meeting, and subject to the changing action of tabu.

Nicobarese is a very highly developed Analytical Language, with a strong resemblance in grammatical structure to English. It bears every sign of a very long continuous growth, both of syntax and etymology, and is clearly the outcome of a strong intelligence constantly applied to its development. Considering that it is unwritten and but little affected by foreign tongues, and so has not had extraneous assistance in its growth, it is a remarkable product of the human mind. There is no difference in the development of the different dialects. That of the wild Shom Pen is as "advanced" in its structure as the speech of the trading Car Nicobarese. The growth of the language has been so complicated, and so many principles of speech have been partially adopted in building it up, that nothing is readily discoverable regarding it. The subject and predicate are not at once perceptible to the grammarian, nor are principal and subordinate sentences. The sentences, too, cannot at once be analysed correctly, nor can the roots of the words without great care be separated from the overgrowth. Neither syntax nor etymology are easy, and correct speech is very far from being easily attained. Grammatically the point to bear in mind is the order of the words, which is practically the English order, especially as functional inflexion is absent to help the speaker to intelligibility, and there is nothing in the form of the words to show their class, whether nouns, verbs, adjectives, and so on. Prepositions, conjunctions, auxiliaries, adverbs, and the "particles" of speech are freely used, and so are elliptical sentences. Compound words and phrases, consisting of two or more words just thrown together and used as one word, are unusually common, and the languages show their Far-Eastern proclivities by an extended use of "numeral coefficients."

The great difficulty in the language lies in the etymology. Words are built up of roots and stems, to which are added prefixes, infixes, and suffixes, both to mark the classes of connected words and to differentiate connected words when of the same class, *i.e.*, to show which of two connected words is a verb and which a noun, and to mark the difference in the sense of two connected nouns, and so on. But this differentiation is always hazily defined by the forms thus arrived at, and the presence of a particular classifying affix does not necessarily define the class to which the word belongs. So also the special differentiating affixes do not always mark differentiation. Again the affixes are attached by mere agglutination, in forms which have undergone phonic change, and by actual inflexion. Their presence, too, not unfrequently causes phonic change in, and inflexion of, the roots or stems themselves. The chief peculiarity of the language lies in a series of "suffixes or direction," indicating the direction (North, South, East, West, above, down, below, or at the landing place) action, condition or movement takes place. But even suffixes so highly specialised as these are not by any means only attached to words, the sense of which they can and do affect in this way. It is just possible that "North = up there: South = down there: West = below: East = in towards" have reference to the original migrations of the people, because the general direction of a migration, still in steady progress, of half civilised tribes of considerable mental development on the Northern Burmese frontiers is North to South regularly. But this point would require proof. It is thus that only by a deep and prolonged study of the language, one can learn to recognise a root, or to perceive the sense or use of an affix, and only by a prolonged practice could one hope to speak or understand it correctly in all its phases. It is, in this sense, indeed a difficult language. The Nicobarese, moreover, speak in a deep monotonous tone and with open lips, thus adding to the many difficulties presented by their language by giving it an exceedingly indistinct sound. The pronunciation is guttural, nasal, drawled and indeterminate, *i.e.*, the Nicobarese speak slowly from the throat with the flat of the tongue and open lips. Final consonants are habitually slurred, especially labials, palatals and gutturals. All this is the result of the habit of betel-chewing till the lips are par[illegible]he teeth greatly encrusted and the gums distended, rendering [illegible] articulation of speech most imperfect. There is however no abnormal dependence on tone, accent or gesture to make the meaning clear. The dialects are, as might be expected, rich in specialised words for actions and concrete ideas, but poor in generic and abstract terms. A detailed Grammar of the Dialects will be found in the Census Report, pp. 255-284.

Religion.

The religion of the Nicobarese is an undisguised animism, and the whole of their very frequent and elaborate ceremonies and festivals are aimed at exorcising and scaring spirits ("devils," as they have been taught to call them). Fear of spirits and ghosts (*iwi*) is the guide to all ceremonies, and the life of the people is *very* largely taken up with ceremonials and feasts of all kinds. These are usually held at night, and whether directly religious or merely convivial, seem all to have an origin in the overmastering fear of spirits that possesses the Nicobarese. It has so far proved ineradicable, for two centuries of varied and almost continuous missionary effort has had no appreciable effect on it: indeed, apparently none at all, if some of the "Creation" stories recorded from the Southern Group by de Roepstorff and the term *Deuse* learnt from the missionaries and still surviving among some of the Central Group islanders for a vague idea of an embodied "chief of the spirits," be excluded. A few rosaries still existed a generation ago in Nancowry Harbour. The one outcome of their religion of political import is the ceremonial murder of one of themselves for grave offences against the community, *e.g.*, for murder, habitual theft or public annoyance. Such a one is regarded as "possessed," and is, by a sort of lynch law, formally put to death with great cruelty. This is the "devil murder" of the Nicobars, now being gradually put down. Witches and of course witch-finders abound. It follows that the mind of the Nicobarese is largely occupied with superstitions, which cover the ancestors, the sun and the moon. The funeral ceremonies show that human shadows are the visible signs of the spirits of the living, and on Car Nicobar there is a special ceremony for "feeding shadows." Every misfortune and sickness is spirit-caused or witch-caused, especially so is that scourge of Chowra, elephantiasis, and the remedy in every case is special exorcism by means of the *menluana*, *i.e.*, doctor-priests, or general exorcism performed privately. Of this last class of remedy is the libation which is poured out before drinking always and at spirit feasts. Lucky and unlucky actions and conditions naturally [illegible]und, *e.g.*, it is lucky to get a pregnant woman and her husba[illegible] plant seed in gardens. Uneven numbers are unlucky, and n[illegible] are allowed at funerals.

The superstitious and animistic beliefs of the Nicobarese explain a good many articles to be seen prominently about their houses and villages. Of these may be taken as a sample the *henta*, in its various forms, the forms and purposes of which have thus been described by Mr. Man:—

The *henta* are paintings, punctured sketches on *areca* spathe screens, or carvings on boards. They are somewhat ambitious in design, containing some seven or eight pictures on a single screen, but ordinarily three or four. In the former, a representation of the sun surmounts the whole, or the sun and moon are represented at the top right and left corners. *Deuse* is depicted as standing dressed in some quaint garb; on either side of him are usually shown various weapons, implements and articles in daily use. In the sketch below him are seen huts, cocoanut trees, birds, and sometimes men and women; below these domestic animals and poultry; below these again a row of men and women dancing; next come ships and canoes in full sail; and lowest of all are represented various descriptions of fishes, with the invariable merman or mermaid, and crocodile. When first made, and at subsequent times of sickness, the *henta* is called *henta-koi-henta*. They are made and used in the Central and Southern Groups and at Teressa; but only in the Central Group are representations of *Deuse* ever introduced. The object supposed to be served by the *henta* is, as in the case of the other similar carvings and paintings, to gratify the good spirits (*iwi-ka*), and frighten away the demons (*iwi-pot*). Varieties of the *henta* are:—(*a*) The *henta-koi* are carved figures, or painted wooden or spathe screens, representing real or mythical animals, birds, or fishes, also models of ships, canoes, ladders, etc. The execution of these and other carvings and paintings by the Nicobarese, though crude, not unfrequently displays a fair amount of talent. *Kareau* at certain periods also serve as *henta-koi*. They are made at times of sickness at the direction of the Shaman (*menluana*), with the object of discovering and frightening away the bad *iwi* (*i.e.*, the evil spirits), which have caused the sickness. If the patient recovers the *henta-koi* is regarded with favour and retained for future service; but if the patient dies, it is thrown away into the jungle. The figure of a ladder (*halak*), when carved for this purpose, is intended for the use of the *menluana's* spirit to climb up and discover whether the malicious spirit is in the air; while the model of a canoe or ship is to enable his spirit to search among the neighbouring coast-villages or islands. The figures usually carved, punctured, or painted, are a mermaid (*shawala*), merman (*shamiral*), gar-fish (*ilu*), iguana (*huye*), fish-eagle (*kalang*), a mythical animal with human face and back like a tortoise (called *kalipau*, and declared to exist in certain portions of the jungle of Katchall Island), and various others. They are generally placed or suspended in the hut, but a few are sometimes to be seen in front of the huts. The object of these representations of animals, birds, and fishes is to invoke their assistance and good-will in the endeavour of the *menluana* to discover the whereabouts of tho offending spirits, and to alarm the latter with the appearance of these effigies in the event of their venturing to repeat their visits. *Henta-koi* are to be seen principally in the Central Group, less commonly in the Southern Group, and rarely at Teressa and Chowra, and never at Car Nicobar, where the models of ships stuck on posts on the foreshore during the trading seasons must not be mistaken for an analogous practice, those effigies being used with the object of attracting trading vessels to their coasts at such times as they have accumulated large quantities of cocoanuts for export. (*b*) The *henta-koi-kalang* is a carved fish eagle; one of the most common effigies used for the above purposes. (*c*) The *henta-ta-oinya* is a single representation on a board or *areca* spathe of *Deuse*, and serves the purpose of a *henta*. Its name implies that the carving is carried through the board or spathe and does not consist of mere puncturing, or paintings, on one side of the surface of the material employed. (*d*) The *henyuingashi-heng* is a *henta* representing the sun with a human face and eight "arms," between which are shown his children (called *moshaha*), to whom is attributed the faint light at dawn. The object of this and the next item (*henyuingashi-kahe*) is the same as that of other *hentas*. (*e*) The *henyuingashi-kahe* is a *henta* representing the moon, in which *Deuse* is depicted as holding a wine glass in the right hand: on his left side are usually shown a pair of cocoanut-shell water-vessels, a lantern, *pandanus*-paste board, a basket, an *areca* spathe mat and pillow, also weapons, spoons, table, chairs, etc.: on the right side of the central figure are generally shown a watch, telescope, boatswain's whistle, various spears, spathe, mat, table, and decanters. Only in the Central Group is *Deuse* depicted in the above manner. This is probably due to the fact of missionaries in this and the last century having laboured longer in that portion of the islands than elsewhere.

There seems to be an embryonic invocation of supernatural punishment— an idea so much developed in the *traga* and *dharna* of India—in some of the actions of the people. Thus setting fire to their own huts and property is one way of showing shame or disgust at the misconduct of relatives and friends, and Offandi, the chief of Mus, in Car Nicobar, once attempted to dig up his father's bones before they were transferred to the ossuary, and to throw them into the sea, because an important villager had called his father a liar.

The spirit feast is a family (including the friends) general exorcism with the aid of the *menluana*. The men sit smoking and drinking, and the women bring from the family stock, provisions, implements, weapons and curiosities, which last, after a good howl, they break up and throw outside the house. A large specially fattened pig is then roasted whole and divided between the ancestors and the party, chiefly the latter. By this the spirits are mollified. The *menluana* now commence to work, worked up to an ecstasy by drink and their mysteries. Their faces are painted red and they are rubbed over with oil. They sing dolefully in a deep base voice, and rush about to catch the *iwi* or spirit of harm, and coax, scold and abuse him, to a tremendous howl from the women, till after a struggle he is caught and put into a small decorated model of a boat, and towed far out to sea. Being now safe from the spirit, the fun is kept up long with eating, drinking, singing and dancing.

Evil spirits, especially those that cause sickness or are likely to damage a new hut, can be caught by the *menluana* and imprisoned in special cages which are placed on special rafts and towed out to sea. It is when the raft lands at another village and transfers the spirit there that those quarter-staff fights take place that are described later on, under the section on Social Characteristics. In the North, elaborate feasts and ceremonies are held to confine the spirits and ghosts to the *elpanam*, public ground and cemetery, and to keep them away from the cocoanut plantations during the trading season. High poles are to be found in the Central Group, attached to most landing places, and placed there at a fixed season for each village, to ward or scarce away evil spirits. These poles are run up to 60 or 80 feet. In Great Nicobar palm stalks similarly adorned are used to ward off fever. These are not to be mistaken for the very lofty poles with flags, 100 feet and much more, put up as examples of skill at the great quinquennial feasts (etkaitni).

TABU.

Tabu, light or serious in its consequences, enters largely into the funeral customs, and appears again in a tabu of warning fires, light in houses, smoking and speech for a month after sweeping the spirits out of the cemetery of Car Nicobar. There is also a strongly marked tabu of the names of deceased relatives and friends which lasts for a whole generation. Tabu further affects the forms of the huts in some villages and islands. Among the Shom Pen the hut in which a death has occurred is tabued for an uncertain period. The making of pottery is tabued except on Chowra, and certain large kinds of pots are tabued to certain old people at the memorial feasts. Making shell lime for betel chewing is tabued except on Car Nicobar, Katchall, Nancowry, Southern Group and parts of Camorta. One kind of fish trap is tabued for every place, except Nancowry Harbour in the rainy season. There is a common kind of private tabu of much interest, and the persons undergoing it are termed *saokkua*, dainty, fastidious. It amounts to an embryonic asceticism. These people will not eat any food cooked by others, nor drink well-water. They will not eat domesticated fowls and pigs, and their drinking water must be rain or running water. They will only drink water drawn by themselves at a distance from the village, and rum out of a cocoanut shell. Bread, biscuits and rum are the only food and drink they will accept from others. There is, of course, also a good deal of pretence about observing the highly inconvenient funeral tabus. The late Okpank or Captain Johnson, a well-known chief in Nancowry Harbour, once refused rum on board a visiting steamer because of the tabu consequent on the death of a near relative, but was eager to get beer in its place. The Nicobarese, and indeed the general human, attitude towards an inconvenient superstition is well illustrated by the following story from the Agent at Car Nicobar:—"The Chief Offandi, Friend-of-England, and a few other notables of Mus came and asked my permission to expel from the Beacon the ghost of the boy who had died the other day. I told them that the Beacon was a standard erected in honour of Her Majesty the Queen-Empress, and that no ghost could go into it. I also told them that if they defiled the Beacon, they must not expect the usual presents from the Queen (*i.e.*, the Indian Government). They then went into the nearest jungle, and caught the ghost in a thick bush and threw it into the sea."

Funeral Customs.

The funeral customs, the whole object of which is spirit-scaring, are distinct in the North and South and are noteworthy, but everywhere extravagant grief is displayed at all deaths for fear of angering the ghost. In the Central and Southern Groups, notice is given to all friends and relatives, who are expected to be, and in the latter case must be, present if possible at the funeral ceremonies with presents in order to appease the ghost. Relatives unavoidably absent are tabued the village until the first memorial feast (*entoin*) a few days later. The eyes of the dead are closed to prevent the ghost from seeing, the body is laid out, feet to the fire place, head to the entrance of the hut, and washed in hot water continually once to five times according to the length of time intervening before interment. Then follow eight obligatory duties:—(1) Removal of all food, as it is tabued to the mourners till after the ceremony of purifying the hut, only hot water and tobacoo being allowed: (2) the destruction of the movable property of the deceased and placing the fragments on the grave as a propitiatory sacrifice to the ghost: (3) the collection of a little food at the head of the corpse for the ghost, the "remains" of this are thrown on its removal to the dogs and pigs: (4) the construction of a bier made out of the deceased's or a mourner's broken up canoe: (5) the digging of the grave five feet deep and putting up the two head posts and the foot post: (6) the making of the fire to "bar the ghost" on the ground at the hut entrance out of chips from the bier and cocoanut husks: (7) the completion of the grave by placing the sacrificed articles on the ground or in the deceased's destroyed basket: (8) the throwing of the pig-tusk trophies, some *kareau* and pictures (*henta-koi*) into the jungle.

The deceased is buried in or with all the clothing and ornaments possessed in life to appease the ghost, and "ferry-money" is placed between the chin-stay and the cheek. The corpse is entirely swathed, except as to a small portion of the face, in new clothes of any colour, except black, presented by the mourners for the purpose. Burial takes place at sundown, before midnight or early dawn in order to prevent the shadows (*i.e.*, spirits) of the attendants from falling into the grave and being buried with the corpse. Before removal to the grave, the body is taken to the centre of the hut and placed cross-wise to the entrance, where it is mourned a short while and then carried down the entrance ladder head foremost. Some of the mourners occasionally make a feint of going to the grave with the deceased, and the priest (*menluana*) exhorts the ghost to remain in the grave until the memorial feast and not to wander and frighten the living. When in the grave the body is pinned into it by special contrivances to prevent the *mongwanga* or body-snatching spirits from abstracting it. The spirits even of those present are finally waved out of the grave by a torch and it is quickly filled in. After the burial the family return to their hut, in which they are bound to sleep, and about 24 hours after the interment, the hut is purified by mere brushing and washing, and the mourners by bathing, anointing on the head and shoulder by the priest, and the waving of a lighted torch to drive away the spirits. The family then disguise themselves by shaving the head and eyebrows and assuming new names, with the object of deceiving the ghost of the deceased. They then take a meal in silence with all the mourners, consisting of every variety of food procurable, in order that each person present may then and there choose the article that is to be tabued for him till firstly the *entoin* feast, three to seven days after the funeral, and secondly the *laneatla* feast, two to three years later. The balance of the food is placed on the grave. The vows of abstinence on these occasions may be therefore very light or very serious, as they consist in tabuing for self, intoxicants, tobacco, betel, pigs, fowls, fish, turtle, ripe cocoanuts, vegetables, plaintains, and rice; ornaments, new clothing and paint; singing, dancing, and music. For a few days the tabu is nothing; for three years it is most serious. Sham fights with the quarterstaff are in vogue at these feasts to gratify the departed spirit. Pretty necklaces of plaintain leaves are also worn at the memorial feasts to please the ghost and friendly spirits. A custom at most places connected with funerals is worth further investigation. It is customary after the funeral to cut through or severely notch a supporting post of the house so that it requires renewal. G. Hamilton (1801) reports this to be a vicarious sacrifice of one of the widow's finger joints, inferring a survival of the actual sacrifice of the finger joint. It would be desirable to know how far this is really the case.

At the *laneatla* feast the skeleton is exhumed and thoroughly cleaned, together with the ferry-money and silver ornaments, and reinterred, a custom which is a survival apparently of the still existing Northern custom of reinterment in communal ossuaries. On Chowra and Teressa the dead are swathed in cloths and leaves and put into half a canoe cut across for the purpose and placed in the forks of a pair of posts about 6 feet from the ground. These canoes are in Chowra kept in a cemetery in a thick grove about 50 yards from the "public buildings" of the village, in Teressa on the sea-shore, till they fall out and are partly devoured by the pigs. The bodies rapidly decompose and become skeletons without apparently much effluvia arising from them. Children are put into small half canoes. Every three or four years the bones are thrown at a feast into a communal ossuary. An account of the great ossuary feast by Mr. V. Solomon, Agent at Car Nicobar, is to be found at p. 226 of the Census Report, 1901.

On Car Nicobar there is serious wrestling over the corpse on its way to the grave: one party being for the burial and the other against it. This goes on till the corpse falls to the ground and several of the carriers are injured. It is then sometimes just thrown into the grave with the sacrifice of all the deceased's livestock. On Car Nicobar there is only one short head-post, but this is carefully made in a conventional pattern, and there is also a special ceremonial for the burial of highly revered personages, which is a distinctly Indo-Chinese custom. The following is an account of the scene at a funeral on Car Nicobar by the Government Agent there:—"Information about the death of a man at Lapati received. The man died on the previous evening at about 3 o'clock. He was an old man of about hundred years of age...... the landlord of a third portion of the village. The burial ceremony was performed in a curious way; a short account thereof will be somewhat interesting. The body was neatly wrapped in cloths under a curtain in the dead-room. An open sort of coffin, about 7 feet long and 4 feet wide, was made on the spot, and was fastened by six long, thick, green canes, three on the front side and three on the rear side; each cane was about 60 yards long. When everything was ready the coffin was drawn inside the dead-room on a sloping plank. The corpse was placed in the middle of the coffin and two women lay on either side of the corpse with their hands embracing it, and thus it was dropped below the house; when the coffin had fallen on to the ground, two stalwart men fell upon the corpse and lay together in the coffin. The large *elpanam* (public ground) of that village was filled by about a thousand people, both young and old, including those who came from all other villages of the island. Of these about a hundred men of the Southern villages and about a hundred of the Northern villages, caught hold of the long cane on either side and dragged the corpse up and down in competition. The canes were broken several times. Thus they occupied themselves until the grave was ready. At last they buried the body at about 6 o'clock. It appears that this ceremony is performed only when they bury those in the highest repute among them."

The "devil murders" of Car Nicobar are serious and cases occasionally occur on Chowra, Teressa, and the Central Group. The missionary Haensel (1779-87) reports them from the Central Group. "They commit, when there is, as they say, a necessity for it, murder." At p. 232 of the Census Report, 1901, will be found notes on every case that has come to light during the last twenty years. They are true ceremonial murders of men and women and sometimes even of children undertaken for the public benefit by a body of villagers after a more or less open consultation to get rid of persons considered dangerous and obnoxious to the community. The actual immediate causes of the murders have proved to be the following at trials:—Possession by an evil spirit; witchcraft to the public harm; danger to the community (a "bad man," incendiary), homicidal proclivity; fear of homicide (threat to kill); failure to cure (murder of a "doctor" *menluana*); theft. But the root cause is always spirit possession—the victim is bad and dangerous because he is possessed. The orthodox method is very cruel. The legs and arms are broken or dislocated so that the victim cannot fight; he is then strangled and his body sunk at sea. But it will be seen from the details above referred to that there is a good deal of variation from this practice in actual fact. The victims are usually taken unawares, but sometimes they make a fight and struggle for life.

The *menluana* is a Shaman or doctor-priest of a sort that is common to many half-civilised peoples, but there is an interesting variety of him at Car Nicobar in the *mafai* or novice, the word actually meaning one undergoing sacerdotal instruction. Any one that feels himself inspired may become a *mafai*, but does not necessarily pass on to the state of a *menluana*. He can give up the position at any time. The ordinary cause of becoming one is recovery from severe illness. The ceremony of making a *mafai* is to place round his bed spirit-scaring articles and plenty of toddy. He is then profusely adorned with spirit-scaring articles and silver or platedware and many spelter rings are put on his arms and legs. He is then placed in a chair, given a *menluana's* silver-mounted sceptre, a spirit slaying dagger, and a bottle of toddy with a straw to suck through. He is now inspired, is highly fed at the public expense and liberally supplied with toddy and danced round every night. He is carried about from village to village in his chair carefully sheltered from the sun. His use is to cure the sick by touch and shampooing. If he resigns his position as *mafai* he goes through a special ceremony for the purpose. It is acknowledged that some *mafais* are impostors. Temporary mafaiship is hardly distinguishable from convalescence. In 1899 Offandi, Chief of Mus in Car Nicobar, was persuaded by *menluanas* for their own benefit that he was possessed. They extracted, by conjuring, bits of iron and stone from his body, *beat* the devil out of him by a rope's end, adorned his limbs with spelter wire, put a *mafai* sceptre in his hand, and kept him like that for several days before he was released by the resignation ceremony.

Tales of origin and the like, told in a jerky, disjointed fashion, the Nicobarese share with the civilised and semi-civilised world. Chowra is their holy land, the cradle of the race where the men are wizards. A belief that the inhabitants of Chowra turn to good account for keeping the control of the internal trade chiefly in their own hands. The Car Nicobar story of origin is that a man arrived there from some unknown country on the Pegu-Tenasserim Coast with a pet dog. By her he had a son, whom the mother concealed in her *ngong* or cocoanut leaf petticoat. The son grew up, killed his father, and begot the race on his own mother. The end of the long bow tied round the foreheads of young men is to represent the dog ancestress's ears, and the long end of the loin cloth, her tail. They treat all dogs kindly in consequence, whence perhaps we may trace a lost totemism among them. At Car Nicobar, too, cocoanuts originally grew out of the head of a man who was beheaded for procuring water out of his elbow by magic. Water is scarce in Car Nicobar. The people, however, were afraid to touch a cocoanut till one was given to a dying old man who at once recovered. Cocoanut trees are therefore valuable spirit scarers and at every death some are cut down, the nuts placed in the grave-yard and the leaves round the house, and the body is washed with the milk,—all to scare the ghost. The moon at an eclipse is eaten by a serpent and a great deal of noise is made on such occasions to frighten off the serpent. Their other tales are full of magic and mythical animals and supernatural occurrences. In them appears the *pait*, an ophiophagus, snake-eating snake, which is *not* indigenous: the *tekari* which (?) is a tiger or lion, *not* indigenous: the *akafong*, a pure myth nowadays with a flame for a tongue. In the Census Report, p. 230, will be found de Röepstorff's pretty tale of Shoán and the Mermaid. The latter is the whale's daughter, the cachalot being indigenous to the Nicobar seas. It is given as an instance of the receptivity of the Nicobarese to *foreign stories*, and hence the practically certain missionary and Biblical origin of the Great Nicobar tale of the Creation, in which *Deuse*, God, appears, also Eve and her birth, the forbidden fruit, and the temptation.

PHYSICAL CHARACTERISTICS.

Physically there is little difference between the inhabitants of the various islands, except that the Shom Pen are about an inch shorter and are less robust than the coast tribes, are anæmic in complexion and have protuberant bellies, all due probably to diet, surroundings and mode of life. Mr. E. H. Man's measurements show that the Nicobarese are a fine well developed race.

AVERAGE MEASUREMENT IN INCHES.

Height.	Full span.	Seated height.	Foot.	Chest.	Weight in lbs.	
63¾	67	33⅓	9¾	34⅓	186	Men.
60	61⅓	81⅓	8¾	...	118	Women.

The following may be taken to be the prominent external physical characteristics of the people:—The forehead is well-formed, the lips are normal and the ears of medium size, the eyes are obliquely set, the nose wide and flat, rarely aquiline, the cheek bones prominent, the face somewhat flat and the mouth large. The complexion is yellowish or reddish brown. The figure is not graceful, the waist being square and the back bending inwards sharply. The legs are extraordinarily developed, and the foot long. Such prognathism as is observable is due to habits: prolonged lactation, sucking green cocoanuts and betel chewing until the incisors of both jaws are forced forward in a revolting manner.

Owing to their habit of dilating the lips by constant betel-chewing the Nicobarese adults of both sexes are often repulsive in appearance.

The skin is smooth throughout life and perspires freely, in the Car Nicobarese much about the nose. The people claim to tell the inhabitants of each group by their odour, but this is doubtful, as there appears to be no distinctive odour when the body is free from dirt and unguents, though the odour of these is often sufficiently repugnant to Europeans.

The hair of the Nicobarese is of the straight tough type, growing to about 20 inches in length and is a dark rusty brown in colour, though from being oiled it seems to be black. Occasionally among the Shom Pen it is curly. The hair on the body is scant, but by no means absent. Beards are not approved and are plucked out. When cropped the hair is stiff and brush-like. The middle aged are often bald but not grey till over 50. The women's heads are sometimes shaved and generally kept close cropped.

The recuperative powers of the Nicobarese are good, much better than those of the natives of India, and equal to those of Europeans. Life is not regarded as precarious after five years of age. Wounds, cuts and contusions heal with great rapidity. Childbirth is easy, but not to an abnormal extent, and the women are proud of a large family. The child-bearing age is 15 to 40 and the children are suckled two years. There is no partiality for male children, girls being as greatly if not more valued. During pregnancy the man and wife do not work and pass the time in visiting and feasting. Lying-in custom vary a good deal, but do not appear to be cruel in their nature.

Living in for them such a land of plenty, the Nicobarese endure hunger and thirst badly, and will eat and drink and chew betel at short intervals all day long whenever practicable. So little will they endure hunger that they will eat raw fish if delayed out fishing. They avoid the sun which is apt to give them headaches, and they thoroughly appreciate the virtues of a *sola topi*. Want of sleep is however borne with ease on occasion, though the sleepiness of the people in the daytime has deceived visitors. This is due to their habits of fishing and holding their ceremonies at night. They can carry heavy weights, the average man's load being about 1 to 1½ cwt. and a woman's about ¾ cwt. A full man's load is 3 score husked or 4 score unhusked cocoanuts slung in pairs on a pole, or 20 pair of water vessels filled. The former weight works out to 160—180 lbs. and the latter 110—120 lbs. Both sexes climb cocoanut trees with great skill and ease, and the men paddle their canoes long distances, and will walk up to 15 miles at 3 miles an hour with a load up to 30 lbs. without undue fatigue.

The gait is sluggish, slouching and inelastic, but extreme agility is shown in climbing the cocoanut tree and activity generally when there is anything important to be done. The Nicobarese on the whole do well what they are obliged to do. The daily necessary work is done regularly and systematically and with a strict division of tasks between the sexes, and they are then industrious and diligent. They are expert in paddling and sailing boats, but not good swimmers. They are skilful and persevering sea fishermen, spearing fish by torch-light from canoes and catching them in sunken baskets, but not in nets or with stakes. Fishing lines are, however, well understood.

The gait betrays the nature. The Nicobarese will not exercise or tax his powers of endurance if he can help it, resting with his loads every few hundred yards, and he is an adept in lessening the weights of cocoanuts when obliged to carry them. He will not walk more than five miles without a rest. Both sexes understand the advantage of working together at heavy tasks to the accompaniment of the voice. The women never go far from their homes. The racial laziness is explainable by the climate and the ease with which all their wants are supplied by nature. The cocoanut tree is their great stand-by. It supplies them with a wholesome drink, goes far to feed themselves, and altogether feeds their domestic animals, supplies them with oil, spirits, vessels of every description and cloth, poles and thatching, sails for canoes, torches for fishing and means of trade and by trade of procuring all iron, luxuries, foreign articles and food they require. Fish and pigs are everywhere caught: pigs, fowls, and dogs are domesticated. Pandanus and cycas provide abundant farinaceous food, though no kind of cereal crop is even grown. The areca-nut and betel-leaf and a great number of fruits are easily cultivated. Posts and planks for houses and boats are readily made from trees in the surrounding jungle. Twine binders and baskets and shafts for weapons are procured without difficulty from barks, bamboos, canes, and creepers. Thatching material is everywhere abundant from the nipa (*dhani*-leaf) palm and the tall coarse *lalang* grass.

The Nicobarese boys attain puberty at about 14, girls at about 13; they attain full height at about 18 and 17 and full growth about 22 and 21; the men marry at about 24 and the women much earlier, 14 to 15; they age at about 50 and live on to 70 and even 80. There are more old women than old men, and length of life is apparently greater than in India or Indo-China.

Insanity is unknown, epilepsy almost so, and bodily abnormalities are rare. The great epidemics of the neighbouring continents, cholera, typhoid, small-pox, measles and beri-beri, are usually absent and never endemic. Leprosy is unknown. Syphilis and cholera as epidemics have been imported, apparently since 1800. Small-pox of a mild and presumably therefore of an old type existed in 1800, but devastating epidemics of it in 1834 and 1856 were introduced by Malay vessels in the Central Group. In the second case, the introducer, a Nicobarese passenger, was killed and the people took "precautions" to prevent its spread. In 1836 a virulent outbreak of cholera or more probably poisoning in Camorta occurred from devouring looted salt meat from an English barque off Expedition Harbour, but it was confined to the villages in and about the place. Malarial fevers are rampant everywhere, but worst in the Central Group, and though the inhabitants of localities resist them, to all aliens they are specially deadly. A residence of three months in Nancowry Harbour was sufficient to bring on severe attacks. Of the 25 Danish Moravian (Herrnhuter) Missionaries, living under native Nicobarese conditions between 1768 and 1787, who spent from a few days to seven years there, 13 died in the place and 11 others soon after their return to Tranquebar. Elephantiasis, as a mosquito-borne disease, has an interesting history. On Chowra, 522 people in 3 square miles, about 20 per cent., are attacked with it, but it is unknown on Car Nicobar, and is rare everywhere else. The other diseases, asthma, bronchitis and other diseases of the respiratory organs, are climatic and occur chiefly, as do the fevers, at the change of the monsoons. An anæmic condition, with its concomitants, splenic and liver complaints, tumours, swollen glands, is common on Chowra and the Central Group. Skin diseases are common, but not severe. Itch and pityriasis are the commonest and are "cured" by sea-bathing. The people are constant bathers and rub themselves over with cocoanut oil.

The medicine of the Nicobarese is almost wholly exorcism and belongs to the domain of superstition. The Nicobarese "doctor" cures by a spiritual fight with the spirit who has possessed the sick man and includes conjuring tricks in his practice, such as pressing damaging articles, like pigs' teeth, stones, etc., out of the body. Medicine is, however, practised to a slight extent, and the Government Agent's efforts to help a dying friend with medicine at Car Nicobar were refused on the ground that the people had their own. Haensel in the 18th Century speaks of decoctions of herbs. Aphrodisiacs are sometimes sought to the profit of Burmese and other native traders. Some unguents, gum resin, beeswax and ambergris are applied to the forehead for headache and there is a mixture, dammer, cocoanut, gum resin, ambergris, and beeswax, used for the same purpose. Hog's lard is rubbed on in cases of fever. Certain simple foreign remedies are understood and prized, *e.g.*, the virtues of rum, Epsom salts, Eno's fruit salt, turpentine, camphor, quinine. Bathing in sea water and rubbing in cocoanut oil are also practised as preventives of skin diseases. Under foreign influence the "doctors" are now learning to prescribe. On 14th April 1896, a "doctor" at Kenuaka, on Car Nicobar, prescribed as follows:—"Mix Eno's fruit salt in water. Add to it a little powdered camphor and turpentine. Give twice a day for colic and stomach-ache. Add a little quinine to the above in fever cases." Of surgery the Nicobarese know nothing. Indeed, one of the main desiderata of the people is the teaching of simple medicine and surgery and the simple methods of differentiating and diagnosing diseases. G. Hamilton (1801) reports a case of surgery, which consisted of hammering the jaw of a fish with sharp spiked teeth into a swelling till it bled profusely.

Mental Characteristics and Capacities.

The sense development is normal, any excellence being due to special development for daily requirements. Their sight is good, but not exceptional, though blindness and "old sight" are rare. The power of smell is normal, and they are fond of sweet scents and object strongly to certain others, *e.g.*, carbolic acid. Young men will bring home sweet scented leaves to gratify sweethearts and wives. The power of taste is, though extremely un-European, also normal, and they are able to distinguish flavour in food and drink at once. As to touch they can feel the points of a compass at from ¾ to 1 inch apart. The hearing is good, but not abnormally so.

Taken as a whole, the Nicobarese, though for a very long while they were callous wreckers and pirates and then very cruel, and though they show great want of feeling in the "devil murders," are a quiet, good natured, inoffensive people, honest, truthful, friendly, helpful, polite and extremely hospitable towards each other and not quarrelsome. By inclination they are friendly and hospitable towards, and not dangerous to, foreigners, though sometimes suspicious of and surly toward them, especially on Chowra and Katchall West. They are kindly to children, the aged, and to those in trouble, even when foreigners, respectful and kindly to women, the wife being a help not a slave, and deferential towards elders. They are very conservative and bound down by custom in all things, changing, however, with the times in certain respects, *e.g.*, they have abandoned since 1840 leaf tobacco for China tobacco twisted dry into cigarettes, Burmese fashion.

Their mental capacity is considerable. It is lowest in the South and highest in the North, and there is a marked difference between the sluggish inhabitants of Great Nicobar and the eager trader of Car Nicobar.

The Nicobarese divide the day and night by the position of the sun and moon when the latter is visible, using the same terms for both; and by means of watching and stating their position they manage to roughly express nearly every hour of the day and night. The islands being so close to the equator, there is but little difference in the length of the day and night at any period of the year. Even on dark nights they can express most of the hours. There are of course, for the day, the usual forenoon, noon and afternoon —and then sunrise, morning, advanced morning, noon, afternoon, advanced afternoon, toddy-drawing time, sunset, twilight, dusk. For the night, dark, roosting time, supper time, after supper time, near midnight, midnight, deep sleep, near dawn. Distance in movement is expressed in terms of the time it takes to perform certain habitual actions. The chew of a betelquid is about a quarter of an hour and roughly a mile on land. So a cocoanut drink is about two miles in a canoe. Nancowry Harbour to Chowra, 12 miles, is six cocoanut drinks. So a few moments is one holding of the breadth: an hour is a stage of the sun: three hours by night is one small bundle of firewood and six hours is one large one.

A noteworthy mental characteristic of the Nicobarese is their capacity for picking up after a "pigeon" fashion any foreign language with which they come into contact. The former Portuguese trade has left its mark in several terms: the records show that some of the Danish, French, German and English-speaking officials and missionaries did not acquire a working colloquial knowledge of a Nicobarese language, and communication must have been in these languages or some form of Tamil or Hindustani: at present English and Hindustani are readily understood almost everywhere, and also Tamil, Burmese, Malay and Chinese are spoken and understood.

Social Characteristics.

Food.

The food of the Nicobarese is firstly the cocoanut and next the pandanus pulp, fish and imported rice. Pigs and fowls are kept for feasts. Dogs are eaten in Chowra. Cultivated fruits of many Oriental kinds are eaten everywhere. They are very fond of stimulants and smoke a great deal of cultivated tobacco. *Pan*, *i.e.*, betel-nut and betel-leaf and quicklime, is the usual stimulant and is in perpetual use. They make toddy from the cocoanut palm, constantly use it and often get very drunk on it. Any kind of foreign spirit is acceptable, rum and arrack of any sort being in much request. This is their great trouble with traders and foreigners, and has led to many disputes and crimes.

Dwellings.

The people are well housed, the houses being often of considerable size and containing an entire family. The house is raised on piles some 5 to 7 feet from the ground, and consists of one large boarded floor, with mat and sometimes boarded walls, but without divisions. It is approached by a movable ladder. The houses are usually circular with a high thatched pent roof, but they are sometimes four-cornered oblongs. The thatching is of grass or palm leaves. Underneath are often large four-square platforms for seats or food. There is much rude comfort about such a dwelling, and inside it everything has its place and all is kept clean and in order. The cooking place is in a separate small hut in which are kept the cocoanut water-vessels, and the *larom* or prepared pandanus. Besides the dwelling houses there are, in the Northern villages, special houses for the moribund and the lying-in women: The interior of the villages and the immediate surroundings of houses are, in the North, kept well swept and clean. Nicobarese villages vary in size from one or two houses to about fifty or more, and are situated in all sorts of sides, but usually on or near the sea-shore. When on a back-water or site safe from a heavy sea the house piles are at times driven into the sand below high and even low-water mark. In the house are kept all the utensils, weapons, ornaments, and belongings of the family, in chests on the floor, on platforms built into the roof, about the walls and roof. In places the most striking objects to the visitor are the *kareau*, or spirit-scarers: up to life-size figures of human beings often armed with spears, of mythical animals based on fish, crocodiles, birds, and pigs, and pictorial representations of all kinds of things in colours on areca spathe stretched flat, all connected with their animistic religion. There is often an armed figure just above the ladder. Outside the houses, too, will be seen similar "very bad devils," *i.e.*, spirit-scarers. Of common objects, also, that can easily be mistaken as to use, one is the row or rows of pigs' lower jaws with tusks. These are not mementos of sport, but of the skill of the housewife in rearing large pigs for food. Also bundles of wood, neatly made, are kept under the house, not for domestic use, but ready to place on the next grave that it will be necessary to dig. So, again, models of ships outside houses in Car Nicobar are not spirit-scarers, but signs to traders that the people are ready to trade in cocoanuts.

On Car Nicobar and Chowra, near each village by the sea-shore, is the *elpanam*, where are the public buildings of the village, consisting of a meeting house, a lying-in house, a mortuary and the cemetery. Village affairs, canoe races, etc., are settled at the Assembly-house; a woman must be confined in and go through a probationary period of uncleanliness in the lying-in house and everyone ought to die in the mortuary: a dying person is removed thither if possible. At the *elpanam* are provided places for all foreign traders to set up their houses, shops and *kopra* factories.

Occupations.

The Nicobarese busy themselves firstly with household duties, the care of their fruit gardens and making articles for use and sale, secondly with religious ceremonies and feasts, and thirdly with trade external and internal. Special occupations are pottery and ceremonial ironwork on Chowra, basket-work on Car Nicobar, canoes and iron spears in the Central Group, baskets, matting, wooden spears, and jungle produce in the Southern Group. Car Nicobar grows half the cocoanuts in the Islands.

Games and Amusements.

The great pastime of the Nicobarese is feasting and besides the numerous religious feasts and ceremonies they are constantly giving each other private feasts, of which the following is a description from Car Nicobar. A week before an intended feast, a Nicobarese sends friends or dependants decorated with garlands to those he wishes to invite. When they arrive, they are entertained with betel, cheroots and toddy, and, if possible, a sucking pig. After this the invitation is given, and the intended guest is asked to bring some food with him to help out the feast. If he can he accepts: if he cannot he declines. On the night before the feast the guests are reminded by messenger. At the fixed time, usually at night, the guests arrive with baskets of food which they deliver to the housewife. These consist of pork (roasted or boiled) cut into thick pieces; yams of different kinds; plantains and papayas (all boiled); *kuwen* or bread fruit pudding—all fastened to strings, in such a manner that each string may be given to one guest: one or two bamboos filled with toddy; betel-nut neatly folded and fastened to thin bamboo sticks; and China tobacco (*sannoi am*, or dog's hair as they style it) twisted in dry pandanus leaves and arranged in bamboo holders. The food brought by one guest can be shared with about ten or fifteen other persons. The host slaughters one or two pigs and prepares other things according to his ability. When all the guests have arrived, toddy is served out first in a small bamboo vessel or in a clean cocoanut shell, and then the food is distributed in basket plates made of cane. The chiefs and elders sit in a row in the middle of the room and the others here and there scattered about, and while they are eating they smoke cheroots and chew betel nut at intervals. After finishing the food the elders commence to sing jovial songs followed by the younger men. Thus it will be seen that the Nicobarese dinner party costs the host very little; but, on the other hand, he must be prepared to return the obligation to help his friends when his turn comes.

The people do not seem to play games much, their leisure time being so occupied with religious and other festivals. But wrestling and playing with the quarter-staff are favourite amusements. For children spinning tops are ingeniously made out of the betel nut and a bit of stick and so is a toy windmill, of the fashion well known in Europe, out of the seed of a creeper. Models of all kinds of articles are also made as toys, and toy imitations of the articles a dead child would have used in later life are pathetically placed on its grave.

The Nicobarese dance is a circular dance performed inside or outside near the houses and in the North at the Assembly-house. They lay their arms across each other's backs, with the hands resting on the next person's shoulder, and form a circle or as near as may be. Both sexes join, but in separate groups. There is a leader in a monotonous concerted song and then they step right and left under his direction, and jump in unison coming down on both heels. The Nicobarese are a musical people and sing clearly and well in unison. They compose songs for special occasions and are adepts at acrostic songs. They have flageolet and a stringed musical instrument, made of bamboo, on which they accompany themselves.

Family System.

The size of the Nicobarese family can be gauged by the population in each hut, and the figures show that it is normal.

Car Nicobar	5	Trinkat	4
Chowra	4	Katchall	4
Teressa	5	Great Nicobar	4
Bompoka	4	Little Nicobar	3
Camorta	5	Kondul	4
Nancowry	5	Pulo Milo	4

These figures should help at the next Census to get at an approximate estimate of the Shom Pen by simply going through their country and counting and mapping huts and then multiplying them by 4 for the population.

Families are patriarchal and are apt to live jointly. In such a joint household the father is the head of the family and after his death the mother. When both parents are dead the eldest brother.

Houses and especially cocoanut and vegetable gardens are private property passing from life to life by heredity. The latter are carefully marked off and each owner has distinct notions as to the extent of his holding, which is carefully denoted by his private mark.

On the death of the parents all real property, *i.e.*, cocoanut and pandanus trees, fruit trees and all cultivated gardens, is equally divided among the brothers except that the lion's share of the cocoanut trees passes to the eldest brother. Practically all the father's personal property, *i.e.*, what he has purchased with cocoanuts in the way of clothing and luxuries of every kind, is destroyed at his death on his grave, a custom that keeps the people perpetually poor. The sisters inherit nothing at the death of the father. Their shares are allotted on marriage by the father or the brothers and consist of trees and pigs. The whole subject of proprietary rights is still however most obscure and requires much more investigation than has hitherto been possible. According to the two Censuses of 1883 and 1901, in the Central Group the proprietary rights, that is village or grouped ownerships, in cocoanuts has apparently changed in the last twenty years, as shown in the map attached to the Census Report. It must be understood, however, that this map was put forward as a definite groundwork for investigation rather than as a statement of established fact.

Girls are free to choose their husbands, but as is the rule where female freedom of choice in marriage exists, the questions of trees and pigs, *i.e.*, wealth, influence relatives, who then bring pressure on the girls in favour of certain suitors. There is no marriage ceremony, and though dissolution of marriage by mutual consent is common, unfaithfulness during marriage is rare. On separation the children go to relatives and step-children are not kept in the house. That is, children being valuable possessions in a thinly populated land, are looked on as belonging to the families of the persons who produced them.

Social Emotions.

There is a distinct expression of the social emotions by exclamations of the usual kind and a great deal of politeness in language, though the high degree of social equality among the people prevents the use of honorifics of any kind or titular forms of address. This is shown in such conventional expressions as the following and in the use of the term *pehari* (all right), as the obligatory reply to all polite expressions :—

Kâbatore, (mutually), never mind ; no matter.

Anri-chüä, (another still), the same to you.

Expressions demanding the reply pehari.

ta yait ta chaká (in respect of beat in respect of face), I beg your pardon *Pehari*, don't mention it.

Kóangúté me kăt (thank you now), thank you. *Pehari*, don't mention it.

chakâ hĕ kifĕ yól (face we you? all), Here's to us all, friends? *Pehari*, to us all (toast at convivial meetings).

met (*indĕt, ifĕt*) *chuichachâkā* or *chaicharăkăt* (you greet-face-indeed, or greet-face-now), How d'you do? (you, you two, you all). *Pehari*, very well.

Expressions on departure.

yishe me (*indĕ, ifĕ*) *ra* [part from you (you two, you all) now], Good bye (said by guest).

tawâtse me (*indĕ, ifĕ*) *rukăt* [just so you (you two, you all) now], Good bye (said by host).

The conventions on visiting are thus described by Mr. Solomon, the Agent at Car Nicobar. "At noon (24th May 1896) to-day four young women came from Malacca to Mus on some affair of their own, and came to my hut and asked me, 'Where is Solo?' ('Solo' being my name to the Nicobarese). I replied in Nicobarese fashion, 'I don't know.' 'Then who are you?' they asked. 'I am a man.' 'What is your name?' they asked. I said, 'I have no name.' All this is in tone with Nicobarese manners. I then said, 'Tell me your name and I will tell you mine.' They complied and then I revealed the fact that I was Solo." The above remarks show that the social emotions are strongly felt and a fact to this point is that James Snooks, an elder and landholder at Mus in Car Nicobar, committed suicide by hanging himself on the 5th October 1902, owing to domestic troubles with his children, whom his ghost will no doubt exceedingly trouble.

Quarrels are nearly always settled by mutual friends and seldom get beyond angry words, the final settlement being concluded by a feast given by the party adjudged to be in the wrong. Quarrels of a sort however arise over superstitions. When a family evil spirit has been caught and sent to sea in a model canoe and this canoe lands at another village or house site, the evil spirit has been transferred to a new house and vengeance results. This is taken secretly by the aggrieved party and all its friends, who collect and on a dark night attack the offenders, while asleep, with quarter-staves steeped in pig's blood and covered with sand. They wear helmets consisting of a cocoanut husk and smear their faces with red paint, so as to look savage. There is however not much real savageness in it. The sticks are so long that they cannot be used in the houses and so the attacked party has to come out, which it does readily. As every village is liable at any time to such an attack, it is always prepared and keeps quarter-staves and cocoanut helmets ready for the purpose. There is a great deal of noise and some vigorous hammering till one party is getting the worst of it and then the women interfere and with cutlasses part the combatants. Sore limbs, bruises and broken fingers, but no broken heads are the results, of which the heroes are proud. When all the trouble is over, the aggressors remain as the guests of the other party and after a couple of day's feasting return home. This procedure is adopted also when serious general offence is given by any particular person.

NOMENCLATURE.

A child is named immediately after birth by its father and an additional name is granted as a mark of favour by a friend. This name is frequently changed in after life, which causes trouble when identity is sought by officials. A chief cause of the change is the tabu of the name of deceased relatives and friends for a generation, for fear of summoning their spirits, and the obligatory assumption of the name of the deceased grandfather by men and grandmother by women on the death of both parents. Also any person may invent and adopt a name out of any word in the language, a custom which combined with the tabu on death here, as elsewhere, has a serious effect on the stability of the language in any given locality and has caused the frequent use of synonyms. There is a feast on the occasion of naming a child and a ceremony before it, directly bearing on spirit scaring. On the name being given the women start crying and then collect round a trough, crying all the time, into which they throw specimens of all the food of the feast, each with a good wish for the babe's good luck in life. When this is over the trough is thrown into the sea and all spirits of harm are exorcised.

The Nicobarese have for a long while had a great fancy for foreign, chiefly English, names, with an extraordinary result, for traders and others have for generations allowed their fancy play in giving unfortunate Nicobarese ridiculous names, which have been used in addition to their own by the people in all good faith. Many persons also bear Indian, Burmese and Malay names in a corrupted form. A chief, or headman, is usually styled "Captain," a title they regard as lofty from observing the position of a ship's commander on board.

INDUSTRY AND COMMERCE.

MANUFACTURES.

The Nicobarese are good carpenters and can make good models of most of their larger articles. They can work in but not make iron, and are adepts in constructing all sorts of articles for domestic use: *vide*—Man's elaborate *Catalogue of Objects made and used by the Nicobarese.* Harpoons and spears of all sorts are made well, with detachable heads for pigs. All the heads are of iron, except for small fish and among the Shom Pen, who use hard wooden spears with notched heads. They make and use a cross-bow in some places, and everywhere quarter-staves (in the play of which they are adepts) and helmets, made of padded cloth or cocoanut husk. The pottery of Chowra is manufactured up to a large size and turned by hand, not on the wheel, and every maker has his own distinctive mark under the rim. The use of the pottery is for food that is cooked, *i.e.*, pork, pandanus, and cycas paste, fowls, rice, vegetables, cocoanut oil (for which however they have besides a special press). Fish is cooked in pots procured by trade from India. Rain-water is also ingeniously caught in Indian pots.

A large portion of their manufactures is of articles connected with their superstitions, but in addition they are very expert and neat in articles made from the leaves and spathes of palms, the leaf of the pandanus and the shell of the cocoanut. The shells, with and without spouts, are used for storing every kind of liquid and small articles, for drinking cups, bowls, basins and lamps, for funnels, filters, for mortars in preparing powered food, for scrapers and rings for pet parrots' feet. The leaf of the cocoanut is used for sails, thatch, skirts, and loin-cloths. Its stem-sheath for strainers; the spathe as a slow match, torch or light for cigarettes and fires.

The nipa palm is used thus: leaves for screens, spathe for mats, screens, fans, receptacles of many kinds, buckets, baskets, dishes. Pandanus leaves are used for receptacles of several kinds, ornaments for the head, brushes, brooms and foot-wipers and covers of pots. Out of wood, for preparing their food they make scoops for serving rice, pestles, graters, boards, spits. And a great number of domestic articles, including rakes, scrapers, pillows, poles, and so on. They make iron scoops for cutting out cocoanut kernels, hoes, and tools for scooping out logs for canoes. Shells of fish are used for many domestic purposes, chiefly as scrapers, and, at Chowra, in the manufacture of pottery. Fibres of several kinds are used for thread, bow strings, fastenings for spears and harpoons, and fishing lines. Bamboos and canes are used for many purposes. Of bamboo are made receptacles of all sorts, blow-pipes, betel-crushers, flageolets, lyres, and ear-sticks. Of cane, baskets of many sizes and descriptions, fish traps of many kinds, bird traps, cages for fowls and pigs. There is an ingenious bamboo spittoon and strainer connected with the manufacture of toddy. The Nicobarese have found out the principle of Warren's Cooking Pot and use a wooden grating in an ordinary pot for steaming vegetables, pandanus and cycas paste.

Fire can be produced by an indigenous fire-stick arrangement, and must still be so for ceremonial purposes. For ordinary purposes, where matches are not forthcoming, bamboo fire-sticks are used as in Burma and the Far East, and produce a fire without much skill or practice.

The canoes are skilfully outrigged structures, light and easily hauled up and carried. They are made of one piece of wood hollowed out and burnt, and very carefully constructed: flat-bottomed, big-bellied, narrow towards the top, with a small raised taffrail,. battens for seats at regular intervals, and long and projecting bows. They are fast sailers, and, when properly managed, safe in surf and rough water. The racing canoes are specially built and costly, with ornamental masts and flag staffs in the bows. The indigenous sails are wide masts of clipped cocoanut of nipa leaves, and erected two to four at intervals, with which the canoes will sail fairly well. Cotton lateen and other sails of borrowed patterns are, however, nowadays more commonly used with skill.

The clothing is now nearly all imported and so are most of the ornaments worn. The Nicobarese man at home wears only an infinitesimal loin-cloth, or rather string, fastened behind with a waggling tag. This must have been his garment from all time, because of the persistent reports that these people were naked and tailed from the days of Ptolemy onwards to the middle of the 17th Century. The woman wears only a petticoat from waist to knee: nowadays of cotton cloth, but even still on occasion of the bark of the *ficus brevicuspis* and split cocoanut leaves. There is, however, from this point an infinite variety of clothing, the result of foreign trade and a fondness for European articles of dress. Anything he can get will be worn by the same man without regard to its appropriate use: "cylinder" hats, *sola topis*, blankets, shawls, coats, waist-coats, trousers, bits of uniform, Port Blair convict clothing of any kind. The split cocoanut-leaf petticoats are confined to Chowra and Teressa, are very neatly made and are three in number, worn one over the other. The inner one is six inches long and the others a foot each. The bark-cloth petticoat is confined to the Shom Pen and the Southern Group coast people.

As personal ornaments, ear-sticks with silver ends (usually four-anna pieces defaced), are generally worn and there is a sort of crown worn at Car Nicobar by young men returning from a journey to Chowra. As semi-religious ornaments (and also as a cure for sickness) a number of German-silver bracelets, armlets and anklets are worn by *menluanas* (priests) and *mafais* ("novices"), as well as necklaces of large silver beads. There are also ornaments of iron made on Chowra in imitation it is said of ancient weapons, which are costly and highly prized everywhere as curiosities and evidences of wealth. These are probably worth ethnographic enquiry.

External Trade.

The Nicobarese never cultivate cereals, not even rice, and very little cotton, though carefully taught in this by the Moravians; but they exercise some care and knowledge over the cocoanut and tobacco, and have had much success with the many foreign fruits and vegetables introduced by the Danish and other missionaries. They club together in making their gardens, which are industriously cultivated and always, if possible, out of sight. They domesticate dogs, fowls, and pigs (which they elaborately fatten to English prize condition), but not cattle and goats, as they require no milk. They tame parrots and monkeys for sale. The staple article of trade has always been the universal cocoanut, of which it is computed that 15 million are annually produced, 10 million taken by the people (in most places cocoanut milk is their actual drink), and 5 million exported, 2½ million coming from Car Nicobar and 2½ million from the remaining islands. The export consists of whole nuts and *kopra* (pulp prepared for expressing oil). There is some export, also, of edible birds'-nests, split cane, betel-nut, trepang (*beche-de-mer*), ambergris, and tortoise shell. The imports consists of a great variety of articles, including rice, cotton cloths, iron, cutlasses (*dahs*), knives, tobacco, crockery and pottery, glass-ware, silver and white-metal ornaments, sugar, camphor, wooden boxes and chests, biscuits, fishing nets, Epsom salts, turpentine, castor-oil, looking glasses, thread, string, matches, needles, Europeans' hats, old suits of clothes and cotton-clothing. Spirits and guns, though welcome, are contraband. As with all semi-civilised people articles of trade to be accepted must conform closely to fixed pattern. The foreign trade is in the hands of natives of India, Burmans, Malays, and Chinamen, who visit the islands in schooners, junks, and other small craft.

The system of trade is for the foreign trader to give the articles settled on for a certain quantity of cocoanuts to the local owner of trees in advance and then to work out their value from his trees himself. He must get the nuts down from the tree, make the *kopra* and take it away and the husks too, if he wants them, himself. All the Nicobarese does is to tally what he takes. It is a laborious system for the trader and requires systematic working. Lists of foreign trade articles now in use will be found in the Census Report, pp. 242-3, with their value in cocoanuts, and it is interesting to note that Busch in his Journal, 1845 (Danish Expedition), gives them as being then cloth, cutlasses (*i.e.*, *dahs*), hatchets, silver spoons, Spanish dollars and rupees, spirits, guns, knives, coloured cloths and European sundries, and Chinese and strong American tobacco. In 1857 the Austrian *Novara* Expedition stated the articles of barter as follows:—*dahs*, axes, muskets, calico and coloured cotton stuffs, salt meat, biscuit, onions, rice, American tobacco in stick, medicinal salts, spirits of camphor, peppermint, turpentine, eau-de-cologne, castor-oil, silver wire, beads, rum, old clothes, black felt hats.

Internal Trade.

There is an old established internal trade, chiefly between the other islands and Chowra for pots, which are only made there. Chowra is also a mart for the purchase of racing and other canoes, made elsewhere in the islands. The season for this trade is December to April. The Southern Group brings to the Central Group baskets, tortoise shell, split rattans for canoes, sestus bark and cloth for matting and formerly for general clothing, and a few canoes. These are passed on to Chowra with spears, and racing canoes of the Central Group make, in return for a certain class of iron pig-spears and pots, and are sold by the Chowra people to Car Nicobar for cloth, baskets of Car Nicobar make and a great variety of articles, valued at Car Nicobar in cocoanuts. There is a considerable trade between the Shom Pen and the coast people of Great Nicobar in canes, canoes, wooden spears, bark cloth, matting and honey for iron, *dahs* and cotton cloths.

Currency.

Without anywhere using coin, the Nicobarese have from all time been ready and quick-witted traders in their great staple, the cocoanut, using it also as their currency and obtaining for it even important articles of food which they do not produce, their clothing and many articles of daily use. In order to explain the cocoanut currency of the Nicobarese and its place in civilisation, it is necessary to go briefly into the general question. Barter is the simple exchange of possessions. Currency is the use of a definite article every one possesses and uses as the medium of exchange for all goods between two parties. Money is a conventional article or token, not otherwise of use, used as the medium of exchange. A gives his knife for B's adze, that is barter: A gives 10 pairs of cocoanuts for B's adze and subsequently B gives A 10 pairs of cocoanuts for A's knife, they are using a medium of exchange and cocoanuts are their currency. The cocoanuts here measure the relative value of different articles of use. A gives a coin, in itself of no other use, to B for his adze and B gives A another coin for his knife: they are using a token for their currency, *i.e.*, money. The essence of an article of currency is that it is used for general purposes and also to measure the value of other articles: the essence of an article of money is that it is useless except as a measure of the value of other articles. The Nicobarese have no money; cocoanuts are their currency. They also barter.

The following is an instance of barter:—In 1895 about 8½ acres of cocoanut-covered land from the villagers of Mus in Car Nicobar for the Agency compound had to be acquired for Government, and were bought at the people's own valuation as a pure matter of barter for 12 suits of black cloth, 1 piece of red cloth, 6 bags of rice, 20 packets of China tobacco and 12 bottles of Commissariat rum. Valued in cocoanuts the price would have been about 10,000 nuts. As a proof that cocoanuts really are Nicobarese currency: on the 5th April 1896 the people of Mus in Car Nicobar had occasion to buy a large racing canoe from the people of Chowra. It was first valued at 35,000 cocoanuts, but instead of being paid for in actual nuts it was exchanged for a large number of articles, each valued in cocoanuts and mostly actually purchased with cocoanuts from Burmese and other traders. The bargain was finally struck and the following articles were given for the canoe each valued as under:—

Red cloth . . .	5 pieces	at	1,200	each	6,000
Spoons, big . .	2 pairs	,,	1,000	,,	2,000
Baskets . . .	6 No.	,,	100	,,	600
Two-anna pieces . .	20 ,,	,,	15	,,	300
Silver wire . . .	3 sets	,,	1,000	,,	3,000
Silver rings . . .	10 No.	,,	100	,,	1,000
White cloth . . .	5 pieces	,,	800	,,	4,000
Knives . . .	6 No.	,,	50	,,	300
Spoons and forks . .	10 pairs	,,	500	,,	5,000
Pigs . . .	10 No.	,,	400	,,	4,000
Fowls . . .	3 ,,	,,	20	,,	60
Beads . . .	a quantity	,,	500	...	500
Chisels . . .	10 No.	,,	50	each	500
Dahs, large . . .	6 ,,	,,	200	,,	1,200
,, small . . .	6 ,,	,,	100	,,	600
Fish hooks . . .	12 ,,	,,	20	,,	240
Fishing line . . .	3 ,,	,,	50	,,	150
Rupees . . .	12 ,,	,,	50	,,	600
Axes . . .	6 ,,	,,	400	,,	2,400
Carpenters' axes . .	6 ,,	,,	200	,,	1,200
Iron spikes, large . .	6 ,,	,,	100	,,	600
,, ,, small . .	6 ,,	,,	50	,,	300
Sundry small articles . .		,,	450	,,	450
					35,000

Reckoning.

As reckoning is an important point of ethnography it is very carefully gone into in the Census Report, pp. 244-248, as regards the Nicobarese; especially as the enquiry goes far to show that the inhabitants of all the islands, including the Shom Pen, are really one people—a fact that is not very clearly apparent otherwise. It also infers a long history of foreign trade, and an old established civilisation of the present type, both of which facts can however be proved independently by direct historical evidence. The conclusions that may fairly be drawn by an examination of Nicobarese ordinary and trade reckoning and the terms used in them are:—The system is Far Eastern, it is the same throughout the islands even among the Shom Pen, the terms, the methods and the very peculiarities have become interchanged between the islands and the original sense of the terms themselves is now quite lost. These conclusions support the inference of a long growth, an old internal trade, and an ancient origin in the Far East. They further strongly support the inference of a unity of origin for the people. There is now no idea of the hand or multiplication in the terms for the smaller figures, but the term for "five" is a clear derivative of an obsolete root for "hand," and in one or other of the languages 8 and 4 are multiples of 2, so are 6 and 9 of 3, and 9 is also "one-less-ten." So the term for "and-a-half" applied to the score and score of scores contain clear lost roots meaning "lessened to half hand."

The Nicobarese keep no records of reckoning beyond tallies and have no proper method for any mathematical process beyond tallying. The basis of all Nicobarese reckoning is tally by the score and for trade purposes by the score of scores, and on this basis they have evolved a system of reckoning, which is naturally clumsy and complicated, but has become where trade is briskest simplified and made exact by an interesting series of rising standards up to very large figures. Tally is ordinarily kept by nicks with the thumb-nail on strips of cane or bamboo, and in Car Nicobar, where trade in cocoanuts is largest, by notches cut in sets on a stick.

For ordinary purposes Nicobarese reckoning stops at about 600, except on Car Nicobar where it stops at 2,000, but for cocoanuts it goes everywhere up to very large figures and even the Shom Pen, who have no trade, have no difficulty in reckoning up to 80,000. A set of commercial scales will be found at page 218 of the Census Report, 1901, and a detailed examination of the Nicobarese system of reckoning at p. 244.

The scales for reckoning cocoanuts stated in the European fashion are as follows, and show the extent of foreign trade per island: the greater the trade the greater the number of standards in the scale. It must be remembered however that the Nicobarese have no definite and only an instinctive scale. It will also be seen that the "wild' Shom Pen too have evolved a definite and useful scale for themselves, though without foreign trade:—

I.

For all islands.

10 *tafual* or *takoal* or *tahol* (pair) make 1 *inai* or *tom* score (20).

II.

Central and Southern Groups and Car Nicobar.

10 *tafual* or *tahol* . . . make 1 *inai* (20).
20 *inai* . . . . „ 1 *momchiama* or *michama* (400).

III.

Chowra Teressa, and Car Nicobar.

10 *tafual* or *takoal* or *tahol* (pair) make 1 *inai* or *tom* (score) (20).
10 *inai* or *tom* (score) . . „ 1 *la*, *nong*, or *'ong* (200).
10 *la*, *nong* or *'ong* . . . „ 1 *mamila* (*kaine*) (2,000).

IV.

Chowra.

10 *takoal* . . . . make 1 *tom* (20).
10 *tom* . . . . „ 1 *la* (200).
10 *la* . . . . . „ 1 *mamila* (2,000).
2 *mamila* . . . . „ 1 *metnetchya* (4,000).

V.

Car Nicobar.

10 *tahol* . . . . make 1 *inai* (20).
10 *inai* . . . . „ 1 *'ong* (200).
10 *'ong* . . . . „ 1 *kaine* (2,000).
10 *kaine* . . . . „ 1 *lak* (20,000).

VI.

Shom Pen

10 *ta-au* (pair) . . . make 1 *inai* (20).
20 *inai* (score) . . . „ 1 *teo* (400).

The ethnographic result of examining the methods of the Nicobarese for reckoning time is exactly that of examining their methods for reckoning currency (cocoanuts). It is one system throughout, even to its peculiarities, and the methods of applying it practically in different islands dovetail so into each other and into the whole general system of reckoning as to presume them to be the creation of a people having a unity of civilisation.

The Nicobarese keep rough calenders by notches on wood. They reckon time by the Monsoon, season or period of regular winds. Roughly the South-West Monsoon blows from May to October, the North-East from November to April, *i.e.*, for six months each. Two Monsoons thus make a solar year, though the Nicobarese have no notion of such reckoning. Within a Monsoon time is approximately divided by "moons" or lunar months. Each moon is divided clearly into days, or as the Nicobarese reckon them *nights*, up to 30 and more if necessary. As the Monsoons do not fall exactly to time but are "late" or "early," there is a rough and ready method of rectifying what would be otherwise obviously consequent errors in reckoning. The changing lunar months (September-October and March-April of our reckoning) have double names, according as the Monsoon is late or early, and are made to run on by intercalary days called *kanat* (*aiya-ap-chingeat* in Car Nicobar) or "moonless" in the former case. The first moon of the next Monsoon is cut short in the reckoning and thus the lunar months are made to fit into the year. Dark nights also when the new moon cannot be seen, are reckoned as *kanat* or intercalary days. By one or other method at their own appropriate time the Nicobarese manage to divide the solar year into two halves, of seven lunar months in Car Nicobar and six elsewhere, with sufficient approximation to keep the solar year straight, without having any idea of a solar year and using lunar months. The months are variously divided, but the principle is to recognise four phases of the moon in every month—waxing, waxed, waning, waned— of 10, 10, 5, and 5 days each in the South and of 10, 6, 10, and 4 days each in the North. In the first three phases the days are reckoned consecutively and in the last or uncertain period each day has its name. The detail of the Nicobarese method of reckoning the month will be found in the Census Report, pp. 249, 250. In talking with the Nicobarese it has always to be borne in mind that they never reckon by the year, but always by the Monsoon or half year.

Communications.

All distant communications are by water, but on Car Nicobar there are good clear paths from village to village, and this is true to some extent of Chowra, Teressa and Katchall. The sea distances have made the people experts in the feeling of direction, and as among other Far Eastern people the points of the compass are thoroughly understood and constantly in mind. A Nicobarese always knows intuitively the direction North, South, East, or West of any object, action, condition or movement at any time, and constantly so describes position in his speech.

Necessity has also made the Nicobarese study the stars and winds to a limited extent. The astronomical knowledge is strictly limited to actual requirements while sailing or paddling at night in calm weather and at neap tide from one island to another. Voyages are then made partly at night under star guidance as follows:—*Pole Star ahead.*—Central Group to Chowra; Southern Group to Nancowry; Chowra to Car Nicobar.—*Southern Cross ahead.*—Car Nicobar to Chowra; Central Group to Little Nicobar; Chowra to Central Group. Steering by the stars is, however, the old men's work, and the young men will have none of it, for fear of such uncanny knowledge shortening their lives or ageing them unduly. The Southing and Northing of the sun is perhaps, naturally attributed to its being blown out of its proper course by the North-East and South-West winds, which prevail roughly in the winter and summer, respectively.

The study and knowledge of the winds is also strictly practical and the terms used for the winds have no connection whatever with the points of the compass. Kapa is the North Wind and Lohnga the South Wind, but Ful merely means that the wind is Easterly, and Shohong that it is Westerly. The North-West, North-East, South-West and South-East are roughly, but indeed as exactly as in ordinary European colloquial speech, recognised by the combination of the appropriate terms, Kapa-Shohong, Lohnga-Ful, and so on. Two other terms are used in the Central Group to denote winds that will take a canoe direct to Teressa and Chowra, or direct to Little Nicobar; Kapa-Mahaichan, direct North, and Lohnga-Mahaichan, direct South, though in fact these are really North-North-West and South-South-East, respectively. The only clouds distinguished are rain-clouds, which again are merely called black clouds.

Internal Government.

Such government as the Nicobarese have is by the village. Each village has a chief, who is often hereditary, and recognised elders. In the chief is vested the land, but he cannot interfere with ownership of houses and products without the consent of the elders. Beyond a certain respect paid to him and a sort of right to unlimited toddy from his villagers, the chief has not much power or influence, except what may happen to be due to his personality. The maintenance of the chiefs or "captain" has been encouraged steadily for their own political convenience by all the foreign suzerains. Each chief has now a flag (Union Jack), a letter of appointment, and a book, in which shipmasters and other visitors can record their visits. This custom was started by the Portuguese in the 17th Century, and has been carried on by the Danes, Austrians, and English in succession. In the eyes of the people a man so appointed by the foreign suzerain, unless a chief or elder naturally, is looked upon merely as an interpreter for communication with the suzerain without any social standing or power. Other persons besides the chief and the elders who have acquired a certain political power are the witchfinders and sorcerers (*menluana*). Government is in fact simple democracy bound by custom. Property is everywhere safe.

In Car Nicobar where the villages are much the largest in the islands, the Government and the land seem to be vested in the chief (*matakkolo*) and three hereditary elders (*yomtundal*), who rule everything in it in council. All the village land is held by the people from the Council of Elders for cultivation, giving nothing for it beyond contributions at ceremonies. When Offandi, the Chief of Mus, sold land to the Government for the Mission and Agency without duly consulting the elders, he raised up much enmity towards himself, which it took a long time and many wordy quarrels to overcome. At the Census, however, only the appointed chief, his appointed deputy and each actual occupier of the land were recognised. At pp. 175-178 and 241 of the Census Report lists of these are given, which will be useful at the next Census for comparing facts and getting better at the real nature of the land tenure than was possible on this occasion.

There are great differences as to the meaning of the term "village" in the various islands, and here the Nicobarese show much difference in habits by "dialect."

Table of average number of huts in a village.

Island.	Huts.	Dialect.
Car Nicobar	58	Car Nicobar.
Chowra	21	Chowra.
Teressa	10	Teressa.
Bompoka	11	
Camorta	3	Central.
Nancowry	4	
Trinkat	6	
Katchall	2	
Great Nicobar	2	Southern.
Little Nicobar	2	
Kondul	2	
Pulo Milo	2	

From the above table it is clear that a village to the people of Car Nicobar, Chowra, and Teressa is a permanent collection of houses or huts, and that in the Central and Southern Groups it is the site of a couple or so of huts, presumably erected by individual owners as fancy or their needs direct. That they are really so erected on impermanent sites the following tables clearly show:—

Tables of villages and chiefs in 1883 and 1901.

Islands.		No. of Villages. 1901.	No. of Villages. 1883.	No. of Chiefs in 1901.	No. of sites inhabited in 1901 and not in 1883.	No. of sites inhabited in 1883 and not in 1901.
Car Nicobar		13	18	13	...	...
Chowra		6	5	6	1	...
Teressa	Teressa	11	8	10	3	...
Bompoka	Teressa	2	2	1	...	...
Camorta	Central	30	28	6	10	6
Nancowry	Central	13	15	2	3	4
Trinkat	Central	4	8	2	3	7
Katchall	Central	34	37	2	5	8
Great Nicobar	Southern	15	28	2	9	17
Kondul	Southern	3	3	1	...	...
Little Nicobar	Southern	13	17	1	3	7
Pulo Milo	Southern	2	2	1	...	...

Table of chiefs with more than one village.

Island.	Chief's name.	No. of Villages in 1901. Inhabited.	No. of Villages in 1901. Uninhabited.
Car Nicobar	......	...	...
Chowra	......	...	...
Teressa	Rupa	2	...
Bompoka	Shameak	2	...
Camorta	Din Muhammad	7	2
	Loham	7	...
	Kaepeho	5	...
	Jan	10	2
	Saran	2	...
	Chandu	6	3
Nancowry	Jemira	8	4
Trinkat	Frederick	5	...
	Do.	1	...
	England	3	7
	Yasin	20	2
Katchall	Maung Poen	14	6
Great Nicobar	Kontri	4	6
Kondul	Dang	11	10
	Do.	8	...
Little Nicobar	Shong Shire	18	7
Pulo Milo	Do.	2	...

On these last tables can be fairly based the following observations: In Car Nicobar is a thick trading population, dwelling in permanent villages, each with its own chief or headman and his second chief or successor. Such, also, are approximately the conditions on the still more thickly populated Chowra, which is a manufacturing as well as a trading island. In Teressa the population is much thinner, and the tendency to break up villages into hamlets is commencing; *e.g.*, the Chief Rupa is occupying fresh ground with a new "village" south of his own. The two hamlets or villages on Bompoka have always been under one chief. In the Central and Southern Groups, which are quite thinly populated, there are no fixed villages at all in the sense of those on Car Nicobar and Chowra. There men shift their huts and hamlets about to any convenient site, calling each site by a separate name, but acknowledging their own proper chief. There is thus a distinct difference in habits of life betweeen the north and south in the Nicobars. On pp. 153, 154 of the Census Report will be found a list of the villages and their chiefs and the accompanying island maps will show the different arrangements of the villages under their chiefs.

Relations with the British.

In 1882, during the occupation of the islands as a Penal Settlement, a system of control over all the islands was started by means of making formal appointments of all chiefs as from the British Government. The chiefs thus appointed are, as far as possible, selected by the people themselves, but the Government reserves to itself the power to depose any chief who misbehaves and to appoint another in his place. The whole of the islands have now quite acquiesced in this procedure, and by its means an effective continuous control is maintained. Each chief receives a formal certificate of appointment, an annual suit of clothes, a flag (Union Jack), and a blank leather-bound book. All these he is bound to produce at every official visit to his village and he undertakes to hoist the flag at the approach of every ship, to produce his book so that the commander may write in it any remarks he has to make, to report to official visitors all occurrences, especially smuggling, wrecks and violent offences that have taken place since the last visit, and to assist in keeping order. On the whole the chiefs perform their duties as well as people of their civilisation might be expected to perform them. In every other respect the people are left to themselves.

In addition there are two Government Agencies maintained, one at Camorta, and one at Car Nicobar. The duties of the Agents are to assist the chiefs in keeping order, to collect fees or licenses, to trade in the islands and to give port clearances, to report all occurrences, to prevent the smuggling of liquor and guns, and to settle petty disputes among the people themselves or between the people and the traders as amicably as may be. Excepting the ceremonial "devil" murders of Car Nicobar, there is scarcely any violent crime and very few violent disputes with the traders, and thus order and control are maintained perennially with hardly any hitches. The "devil" murders are dealt with directly from Port Blair.

CHAPTER IV.

THE PENAL SETTLEMENT.

Physical Geography.

The Penal Settlement of Port Blair consists officially of the South Andaman and the islets attached thereto, and covers 473 square miles. Of this area, at the present date, 327 square miles may be said to be in actual occupation. The unoccupied area consists of the densest imaginable jungle throughout every part of it. The occupied area is partly cleared for cultivation, grazing and habitation, and partly afforested. A great part of the unoccupied area is in the hands of the hostile Jarawas, but they are gradually retreating northwards under pressure of the yearly increasing forest operations extending step by step over the whole South Andaman, *i.e.*, over the whole official area of the Penal Settlement.

Coasts.

The South Andaman Island has a very deeply indented coastline comprising the harbours, on the east coast, of Port Meadows, Port Blair; on the south coast, of Macpherson's Strait; on the west coast, of Port Mouat, Port Campbell, Port Anson. In any one of these, vessels of any draught could anchor and trade with safety in any weather and in any season. If Baratang be added to the South Andaman as a natural appanage, Elphinstone Harbour must be added to the list. Smaller vessels would also find the following places safe for shelter and most convenient for work. On the east coast, Colebrooke Passage, Kotara Anchorage, Shoal Bay; on the west coast Elphinstone Passage in the Labyrinth Islands, and in some seasons Constance Bay; in Ritchie's Archipelago, Kwangtung Strait and Tadma Jaru, and in some seasons Outram Harbour.

Forests.

For forest trade, the staple trade of the islands, a more convenient natural arrangement is hardly imaginable. Port Mouat is only two miles distant from Port Blair over an easy rise, Shoal Bay is seven miles with an easy gradient from Port Blair and runs into Kotara Anchorage, and Port Meadows is but a mile from Kotara Anchorage. Creeks navigable for large steam launches run into

Port Blair from some distance inland. Five straits surround the island: two, Macpherson's Strait and Elphinstone Passage, navigable by ships; and the rest, Middle Strait, Colebrooke Passage and Homfray's Strait, navigable by large steam launches. Diligent Strait, fit for the largest ships and only four miles across at the narrowest point, separates Ritchie's Archipelago from the main islands, and the archipelago is itself intersected everywhere by straits and narrows mostly navigable.

Hills.

The whole of the Settlement area consists of hills separated by narrow valleys, rendering road-making and rapid land communication difficult. The main ranges are the Mount Harriett Range up to 1,500 feet, the Cholunga Range up to 1,000 feet, and the West Coast Range up to 700 feet. These run about parallel north and south down the centre of the island. To the north of the island the Cholunga Range breaks up into a number of north and south ridges more or less parallel. To the south of the island below Port Blair Harbour, the country is a jumble of hills rising to 850 feet and tending to form ridges running north and south.

Streams.

There is no stream in the island which could be called a river and on the east coast perennial streams are not common. On the west and north, however, there is much more surface water to be found, and perennial streams running chiefly south to north are fairly numerous. Fresh water is, however, everywhere obtained without much difficulty from wells, and there is everywhere any number of places where rain-water reservoirs (tanks) could be formed, to be kept perennially filled by the heavy rain of the islands falling in most months of the year. Navigable salt-water creeks are numerous and of much assistance in water carriage.

Administrative Geography.

The Penal Settlement centres round the harbour of Port Blair, the administrative head-quarters being on Ross Island, an islet of less than a quarter square mile across the entrance of the harbour. For administrative purposes it is divided into afforested and unafforested lands. As little change as possible is made in these, but the growing condition of the Settlement makes it sometimes imperative to effect small alterations in area. It is also divided into three districts and four sub-divisions. The sub-divisions remain constant, but their distribution between the districts has to vary according to circumstances from time to time. At present they are as follows:—Eastern District—(District head-quarters, Aberdeen)

Ross, Haddo; Western District—(District head-quarters, Viper Island) Viper, Wimberleyganj; Jail District—(District head-quarters, Cellular Jail) Cellular and Female Jail.

Stations and Villages.

Within the sub-divisions are "stations," *i.e.*, places where labouring convicts are kept, and "villages," where free or self-supporters, respectively, dwell. As these stations and villages perforce enter largely into the life and description of the place, a list is given here.

Eastern District.

Stations.	Villages.
Haddo Sub-division.	
Phœnix Bay.	Phœnix Bay.
Haddo.	Janglighat.
Navy Bay.	Niagaon.
Garacherama.	Birchganj.
Pahargaon.	Bumlitan.
Chatham.	Taylerabad.
	School Line.
	Garacherama.
	Prothoroepur.
	Austinabad.
	Pahargaon.
	Lamba Line.
	Dudh Line.
Ross Sub-division.	
Ross.	Aberdeen.
Aberdeen.	South Point.
Middle Point.	
North Bay.	
Hope Town.	
Madhuban.	
Rutland Island.	

WESTERN DISTRICT.

Viper Sub-division.

Stations.	Villages.
Viper Island.	Mitha Khari.
Dundas Point.	Namunaghar.
Port Mouat.	Ograbaraij.
Namunaghar.	Chouldari.
Elephant Point.	Port Mouat.
	Dhani Khari
	Homfrayganj.
	Manglutan.
	Baghel Singpura.
	Nawa Shahr.

Wimberleyganj Sub-divisions.

Stations.	Villages.
Shore Point.	Cadellganj.
Goplakabang.	Hobdaypur.
Wimberleyganj.	Tusonabad.
Middle Straits.	Manpur.
Kalatang.	Templeganj.
Bajajagda.	Bamboo Flat.
Bindraban.	Stewartganj.
	Wimberleyganj.
	Kadakachang.
	Mathra.
	Bindraban.
	Anikhet.
	Alipur.

JAIL DISTRICT.

Cellular Jail.
Female Jail.

History.

THE EIGHTEENTH CENTURY SETTLEMENT.

The old Settlement at the Andamans, established by the well-known Marine Surveyor Archibald Blair in 1789, was not a Penal Settlement at all. It was formed on the lines of several then in existence, *e.g.*, at Penang, Bencoolen, and so on, and was established under Lord Cornwallis, Governor-General, originally to put down piracy and the murder of shipwrecked crews. Convicts were sent incidentally from India to help in its development, precisely as they were sent to Bencoolen and afterwards to Penang, Malacca, Singapur, and Moulmein, and the Tenasserim Province. Everything that Blair did was performed with ability, and his arrangements for establishing the Settlement in what he named Port Cornwallis (now Port Blair) were excellent, as were his selection of the site and his surveys of parts of the coast, several of which are still in use. He established himself on Chatham Island where he built a wharf, had a clearing on Haddo, and cut a path through from Phœnix Bay to Navy Bay. In Phœnix Bay he built a small vessel, the *Union*, which he afterwards sold to the East India Company. Many of the names about the harbour of Port Blair date back to his time. The *Viper* was his own vessel, the *Atalanta*, *Ariel*, *Crown*, *Perseverance*, and so on, were His Majesty's ships of the day.

The Settlement flourished under Blair, but unfortunately on the advice of Commodore Cornwallis, brother of the Governor-General, the site was changed for strategical reasons to North-East Harbour, now Port Cornwallis, where it flourished at first but afterwards carried on an existence rendered miserable from sickness. Here it was under Colonel Alexander Kyd, an Engineer Officer, and a man of considerable powers and resource. On the abandonment of the Settlement in 1796, on account of sickness, it contained 270 convicts and 550 free Bengali settlers. The convicts were transferred to Penang and the settlers taken to Bengal. After that the islands remained unoccupied by the Indian Government till 1858 when the present Penal Settlement was formed.

HISTORY OF THE PRESENT SETTLEMENT.

Since its foundation, the history of the Penal Settlement up to the Census of 1901 is merely one of continuous official development. In January 1858 the Andaman Commission came to examine the islands for a possible site for a Penal Settlement. It was composed of Dr. F. J. Mouat, Dr. C. R. Playfair, and Lieutenant J. H. Heathcote, I.N., and produced an exhaustive and practical report. They fixed on Blair's original Settlement in 1790, and the harbour he worked in was named Port Blair in his honour. At the same time Captain (afterwards General) H. Man, as an experienced manager of convicts, was sent to re-annex the islands and found the Settlement commencing at Chatham Island. In March 1858 Dr. J. P. Walker, an experienced Jail Superintendent, arrived and with four European officials and 733 convicts cleared Chatham and Ross Islands, and started clearings at Haddo and Atalanta Points. He fixed the head-quarters on Ross Island where they have been ever since. He worked under enormous difficulties and with great energy, and his inadequate staff induced him to be very severe. In addition to the natural difficulties of his position he had to contend with constant escapes and attempts at escape and repeated attacks from the Andamanese. At this time was raised for the protection of the Penal Settlement the last Sebundy Corps ever formed in India. They were not a success, and were abolished in 1861. The Sebundies, once ubiquitous all over India, were the forerunners and the official lineal ancestors of the modern Military Police.

In October 1859 Captain (afterwards Colonel) J. C. Haughton, still remembered with affection as Jân Hâtan in the Settlement, of the Moulmein Commission, succeeded him, and at once introduced milder measures. He was much worried with attacks from the Andamanese, but managed to commence friendly relations with them. Colonel Haughton, in his isolation, had to face serious currency difficulties, and was obliged to issue first redeemable MS. card tokens as currency, and next, with the authority of the Government of India, copper rupee tokens redeemable at the Local Treasury. In these for some years under certain conditions the self-supporter convicts were paid for produce to prevent bribery and the influx of too much cash. The system failed to have effect because both silver money and the tokens were current together and in 1870 the copper tokens were withdrawn, when it was found that 17,788 of those issued in ten years had not been returned to the Treasury for redemption. They have entirely disappeared, and are now extremely rare. Up to Captain Haughton's time the Settlement was directly under the Government of India, but in 1861 it was ordered to be transferred to the Chief Commissionership of Burma, the transfer not actually taking place till April 1864. In May 1862 Colonel R. C. Tytler succeeded, continued Colonel Haughton's mild policy and effected a good deal of clearing, especially at Mount Harriett (named after Mrs. Tytler). At this period the cultivated land was only 149 acres: 76 by self-supporters and 73 by Government. A path ran from the Aberdeen (Atalanta Point) to Haddo clearings, and a road was commenced from Aberdeen to Jangli Ghat. There was a pier at Ross and a 10 horse-power saw mill at Chatham. In Colonel Tytler's time, with the help of Reverend H. Corbyn, a great deal was done in establishing friendly relations with the Andamanese, and the Andaman Home was started.

In October 1863 General Sir Robert Napier (afterwards Field-Marshal Lord Napier of Magdala) inspected the Settlement and wrote a Memorandum thereon, re-organising it; and much of what he instituted is still in force, especially in the arrangements for clothing, sanitation, buildings, and vegetable supplies. He also secured a grant for the Andamanese Home, still given, in recognition of Mr. Corbyn's services. Up to that time 8,000 convicts had been sent down altogether, and the Settlement consisted of Ross, Chatham, and Viper Islands, and small clearings at Aberdeen, Haddo, Mitha Khari, Hope Town, and Mount Harriett. At his suggestion Colonel Tytler drove a road with Mr. J. N. Homfray's assistance through to Port Mouat from Homfray's Ghat to Tytler's

Ghat, and formed a clearing at Mount Augusta. In May 1864 Colonel Tytler gave place to Colonel B. Ford, who wrote the first Annual Report on the Settlement, 1864-1865, much on the lines still adopted, and it is from his time that records are clear and almost continuous. He started with 149 acres under cultivation and 3,294 convicts, and by 1867, when he was transferred, these figures had increased to 724 acres cleared and 353 cultivated, and 6,965 convicts. He commenced the building of Viper Jail. He also placed Mr. J. N. Homfray in charge of the Andamanese, whose generous and judicious treatment of them laid the foundation of the existing system of dealing with them, and made them largely friendly. He was, on and off, ten years in charge of them, learnt their language colloquially, and travelled considerably about their country. He instituted the custom of using them to capture runaways and return them to the Settlement. Before his time their usual practice was to kill the runaways who escaped into the jungles. In 1867 Colonel Ford was so pressed for both silver and copper tokens that he had recourse to Colonel Haughton's plan, and issued redeemable card tokens while waiting for remittances. In the same year Colonel Nelson Davies, Secretary to the Chief Commissioner, Burma, made an inspection of the Settlement, and wrote a long and, unfortunately, biased Report against Colonel Ford's administration.

In 1868 Colonel (afterwards General) H. Man, who had ten years previously founded the Settlement, took up the Administration and formally introduced the discipline and system of the Straits Settlements. His was the first formal Code of Rules and formed the foundation for the existing law and Rules of the Settlement in almost every part of them, even to the system of the controlling returns. Colonel Man stayed on till March 1871, and afterwards in the late Sir W. W. Hunter's *Life of Lord Mayo* some cruel remarks were made on the state of the Settlement under him. As a matter of fact he did a great deal towards consolidating the system that has been so successfully pursued ever since. By the end of his time the more or less completely cleared area reached 2,814 acres, and the cultivated area to 876 acres, showing how much was accomplished in this direction in what may be called the preliminary stage of the development of the Settlement. The number of the convicts in the Settlement reach to 8,373. In 1869 the Settlement was removed from the control of the Chief Commissioner, Burma, and placed again under the direct orders of the Government of India, and in 1870 it was placed for judicial purposes under the High Court of Calcutta. In the same year the Nicobar Penal Settlement was founded which continued till 1888. In 1870 the Andaman Orphanage was started and continued until

1896 when it was merged in the Andamanese Home by force of circumstances. In 1871 Captain Darwood had charge of the Andamanese for a short while, and was the first to use the aborigines to collect jungle produce for the Settlement.

In 1871 General (afterwards Field-Marshall Sir Donald) Stewart became Superintendent to work up a scheme of reforms laid down by the Viceroy, Lord Mayo, who took a great personal interest in the Settlement. During that year Lord Mayo, drew up a Note which has had a distinct effect on the existing organisation of Port Blair. He directed that special attention be paid to cultivation, produce of the self-supporters, cattle-raising, timber, and produce from the Andamanese: also to the substitution of troops for police as a reserve force and their regular relief, to an increase in the convict strength, and to the codifying of Colonel Man's Rules into formal Regulations. Sir Donald Stewart's administration has markedly affected the Penal System ever since his time in very many aspects. In going through his correspondence one cannot help being struck with the influence of the principles and lines of action he laid down on the present working of Port Blair. In 1872 Lord Mayo visited the islands and, as is well known, was murdered by a convict on Hope Town Jetty at the foot of Mount Harriett on 8th February 1872. In 1872 Mr. Justice Scarlett Campbell visited the Settlement to report on all points in Lord Mayo's Note in conjunction with General Stewart. This resulted in creating the existing form of the superior establishment, in placing the Settlement under the Home Department of the Government of India, and in laying down the principle of considering penality firstly, and development of resources secondly, in the administration of the Settlement. In the same year the Chief Commissionership of the Andamans and Nicobars was created, and General Stewart became the first Chief Commissioner.

In 1874 General (afterwards Field-Marshal Sir Henry) Norman visited the Settlement and his report in conjunction with General Stewart had a most marked effect on the Settlement System. It confirmed and improved Mr. Scarlett Campbell's Rules, brought in term convicts, gave life convicts a promise of release after 20—25 years' servitude with approved conduct, provided for the personal security of officials, and created the existing system of guards and guard-ship. It resulted in the Andaman and Nicobar Regulation of 1874, and in placing the Settlement judicially under the Government of India direct, removing it from the jurisdiction of the Calcutta High Court. In 1874 Mr. F. E. Tuson (afterwards Deputy Superintendent) took charge of the Andamanese and introduced the free coming and going of the aborigines to the Home, and the existing system of providing an income for the Home from the work of the inmates in the jungles. In 1875 Mr. E. H. Man (afterwards for many years Deputy Superintendent), since so well known for his anthropological and other studies, took charge of the Andamanese and held it, off and on, for about ten years. It is due to his efforts that the accurate and extended knowledge of the Andamanese and their languages and the almost universal friendly relations with them now existing are chiefly due. His accuracy of observation and record is beyond praise, and though it has been at times impugned in details, he is still a safer guide than his critics even where attacked. In 1875 also General C. A. Barwell succeeded General Stewart, and in the following year a new and improved Andaman and Nicobar Regulation (III of 1876) superseded the previous one and is still in force, and was followed by various special Rules and Orders which, with the Superintendent's own Bye-Laws (Settlement Standing Orders), were consolidated into the Andaman and Nicobar Handbook drafted by Captain (now General M.) Protheroe, then Deputy Superintendent. It was at this time that epidemics began to destroy the Andamanese. In 1876 syphilis declared itself among them, said to have been traced to one Shera, the convict Jemadar in charge of the Home. This was followed by ophthalmia. In 1877 measles introduced itself disastrously and, with pneumonia and since then influenza, has, in combination with the general spread of syphilis, diminished the population to its present proportions. In 1879 Colonel T. Cadell, V.C., succeeded General Barwell and held the administration for thirteen years until 1892, and naturally greatly influenced the Settlement. His efforts were chiefly directed towards agricultural and forest development and improved communications, for all of which he laid a solid foundation. In 1882 the present regular Forest Department was established.

In 1885 Sir Alexander Mackenzie visited the Settlement and recorded the many improvements effected and suggested others of detail, and in 1890 Sir Charles Lyall and Sir Alfred Lethbridge arrived as a formal Commission to investigate the Penal System. Their Report resulted in a good many changes, chiefly in the direction of increased penality and discipline, in the construction of very large jails, in the reduction of the number of term convicts and in the separation of the "free" and "convict" district. Its immediate effect has been to convert the Settlement from an almost purely agricultural institution into one largely industrial, in order to construct the building required mainly from local resources. In 1886 the Andaman and Nicobar Handbook was redrafted as the Andaman and Nicobar Manual by Colonel W. B. Birch, Deputy Superintendent, and in that form the local law and administrative rules still exist.

In 1879 Mr. M. V. Portman was first placed temporarily in charge of the Andamanese, which he held at intervals until 1888 and then almost continuously till his retirement in 1900. He continued Mr. Man's researches into the languages and ethnography of the people, performed a great deal of anthropometry and scientific photography, and founded a knowledge of the Little Andaman. His work is, however, unfortunately marred by too much captious and not always accurate criticism of others engaged in the same line of research. In 1881 Mr. H. Godwin-Austen had charge of the Andamanese for a time and visited many distant places, confirming the friendly relations effected by Mr. Man. In 1883 Mr. Portman established some friendly relations with the Onges of the Little Andaman, and in 1886 Mr. T. Metcalfe, while in charge, discovered the value of the Andamanese as pilots in their own waters. From 1888, when Mr. Portman came into nearly continuous charge, he studied, so far as opportunity offered, the hostile Jarawa Tribe, but his accounts must be accepted with caution, especially his remarks on their timid character.

In 1892 Colonel N. M. Horsford succeeded Colonel Cadell, and early in 1894 was attacked and nearly murdered by a convict. He commenced the carrying out of the recommendations of the Lyall-Lethbridge Commission. In 1894 Colonel Sir Richard Temple, Bt., took over the Administration and was, up to the Census which was taken in his time, chiefly engaged in carrying through the orders of the Government of India resulting from the Lyall-Lethbridge Commission, *i.e.*, in developing the disciplinary and labour organisation, the industrial capacities of the convicts, forestry, communications, and, to some extent, agricultural products. Also in the construction of the large jails then ordered and in the employment of machinery. In 1895 Mr. J. P. Hewett visited and reported on the Settlement, confirming the details of the Lyall-Lethbridge Report. In 1900 Mr. P. Vaux took charge of the Andamanese, and with Mr. C. G. Rogers, who followed him, greatly increased the knowledge of the Jarawas and their country. He was unfortunately killed in an encounter with them on 24th February 1902.

Origin and History of the Penal System.

The Andaman Penal System is *sui generis*, has grown up on its own lines, and has been gradually adapted to the requirements of a Penal Settlement, covering officially an area of 473 square miles, of which 327 square miles are now occupied, containing grazing and arable lands, swamps, dense forests, large harbours and inlets, of the sea, hills up to 1,500 feet, and small villages for the ticket-of-leave (self-supporter) convicts, ex-convicts and free persons, convict stations, workshops, and jails. This system has also been independent of, and was never at any time based on, the Indian prison system and has been continuously under development for about a hundred years. The fundamental principles on which the system is founded are now substantially what they were originally, and have stood the criticism, the repeated examination, and the modifications in detail of a century without material alteration. The classification of the convicts, the titles of those who are selected to assist in controlling the general body, the distinguishing marks on their costume, the modes of occupying them, and their local privileges are virtually now as they were at the beginning.

It will be seen from the following brief history that the Andaman Penal System is at root the former system of the Straits Settlements. The first temporary Superintendent of the Andamans was Captain (afterwards General) Henry Man, who was generally instructed in January, 1858, by the Government of India as to the treatment of the convicts on the Straits Settlements lines and given his powers under the Mutineers Acts, XIV and XVII of 1857 (since repealed). General Man was trained in, and long Superintendent of, the Penal Settlements of the Straits. He was succeeded by Doctor J. P. Walker in March, 1858, who drew up rules sanctioned by the Government of India and based on his instructions, which were identical with those given to General Man. These were followed by the Port Blair and Andamans Act. XXVII of 1861 (since repealed), and by modifications of the rules by successive Superintendents and by (afterwards Field-Marshal) Lord Napier of Magdala, as the result of an official inspection of the Settlement in 1863. In 1868 General Man became permanent Superintendent and embodied in the Andaman system the Straits Settlements Penal Regulations, which he brought with him, and thus brought the system still more closely into line with that of the Straits Settlements. General Man's modifications still colour almost every part of it. Sir Clive Bayley took General Man's rules and drafted out of them a formal Regulation in 1871. This draft was given to (afterwards Field-Marshal) Sir Donald Stewart for comment by the Viceroy, Lord Mayo, who took a great personal interest in the Andamans, and was subjected to the scrutiny of Mr. (Justice) Scarlett Campbell in 1872 and of (now Field-Marshal) Sir Henry Norman in 1874, both formally deputed to inspect the Andamans, in consultation with Sir Donald Stewart, then Chief Commissioner and Superintendent. Their joint labours resulted in the Andaman and Nicobar Regulation, 1874, and in the Governor-General in Council's Rules and the Chief Commissioner's Rules of the same year. In 1876 a new Andaman and Nicobar Regulation was drawn up, but the rules under the Regulation of 1874 were continued. These rules together with the Superintendent's Bye-laws (Settlement Standing Orders) authorised thereby and modified from time to time by the Government of India orders and by the Commission of Sir C. J. Lyall and Sir A. Lethbridge in 1890, that form the still growing Andaman Penal System of the present day. The governing principles of the Andaman system are, therefore, those of the Straits Settlements system, *i.e.*, of the old Indian Penal Settlements system.

The methods employed were originally a new departure in the treatment of prisoners, its salient features being still those of the Andamans,—the employment of convicts, in any place desired, on any and every kind of labour necessary to a self-supporting community, their control by convicts selected from amongst themselves, permission to marry and settle down in the Penal Settlement after a given period ("self-supporter"). It arose thus: Indian convicts were first transported to Bencoolen in Sumatra in 1787 to develop that place, then under the Indian Government. At Bencoolen, the Lieutenant-Governor, Sir Stamford Raffles, drew up a despatch in 1818 to the Government, explaining the principles he had already successfully adopted for their management, and in 1823 he sent the Government a copy of his Regulations. In 1825 Bencoolen was ceded to the Dutch and the convicts there were transferred to Penang and Singapore. Penang was first occupied by the English in 1785 and convicts were sent there in 1796. When the Bencoolen convicts arrived, they took with them the Regulations of Sir Stamford Raffles, and in 1827 on this basis were drawn up the "Penang Rules." Malacca was occupied in 1824 and convicts were sent there at once from Penang and shortly afterwards they, too, were placed under the Penang Rules. Singapore was founded by Sir Stamford Raffles himself in 1819 and in 1825 convicts arrived from Bencoolen and India and in 1826 from Penang. At Singapore at first the "Bencoolen Rules" and then the "Penang Rules of 1827" were enforced, with modifications, for many years, until the first formal Rules and Regulations for the management of Indian convicts were drawn up in 1845 by Colonel Butterworth, the Governor of Singapore, and were known as the Butterworth Rules. These, with modifications by Major McNair, Superintendent of the convicts, made in 1858, were the Rules for the Singapore convicts. The Butterworth Rules were avowedly founded on the principles laid down by Sir Stamford Raffles in 1818 and on his Bencoolen Rules. The formal title of the Butterworth Rules was the "Straits Settlements Rules and Regulations for the management of Indian convicts," and in the making and working them General Man, to whom it fell to start the Andaman Penal Settlement in 1858, took a leading part. He carried them with him to Moulmein and the Tenasserim Provinces, to which places Indian convicts were also transported, and when in 1868 he was appointed permanent Superintendent of the Andaman Penal Settlement it was the "Regulations of the Straits Settlements as used in the Tenasserim Provinces for the management of convicts" that he brought over and embodied in the rules and orders he found already existing. The direct unbroken descent of the present Andaman Penal System from the original Indian Penal System is, therefore, quite clear. The intimate connection of the Andamans with the original Indian Penal System from the beginning is further illustrated by the fact that when in 1796 the Old Andaman Settlement at Port Cornwallis was broken up, the convicts there were transferred to Penang.

On the basis that the Penal Settlement is not a prison, but a place for the detention of a certain class of prisoners only, *viz.*, transported convicts, the present Andaman System is practically worked on rules contained in the Andaman and Nicobar Manual, consisting of two parts:—(1) Rules and orders issued under legal authority, and (2) Administrative and Executive orders. The system has always rested on the Indian Prisoners Act and the Andaman and Nicobar Regulation. The rules or orders having legal authority in the Andaman and Nicobar Manual, as they now stand, are— (1) Rules of the Governor-General in Council for the management of transported convicts, under Section 34 of Act V of 1871 (Prisoners), bearing date 29th July 1874, and since modified by many orders of the Government of India. (2) Subsidiary Rules of the Chief Commissioner with the sanction of the Governor-General in Council, under Section 18 of Andaman and Nicobar Regulation, 1874, dated 4th December 1874, and continued under Section 33, Andaman and Nicobar Regulation, III of 1876. (3) Governor-General in Council's Rules for licenses to reside, under Section 26 of the Andaman and Nicobar Regulation, dated 30th December 1882. (4) Bye-laws of the Superintendent [see Section 32 (*b*) Andaman and Nicobar Regulation, III of 1876, and Rule VI (7) of the Governor-General in Council's Rules for transported convicts, 1874]. These bye-laws are known as Settlement Standing Orders, and are included in the Manual and issued whenever necessary. The Prisoners Act, 1874, has been repealed by the Prisoners Act (III) of 1900, and, though no rule-making power is conferred by the new Act in this connection, the present Rules of the Governor-General in Council and the Bye-laws referred to therein are still in force under the General Clauses Act, X of 1897, Section 24.

The Convicts.

The gross number of the convicts sent to the Penal Settlement up to the date of the Census was 49,592, and the returns and statistics are so arranged that the full life history of every one of them while in the Settlement is immediately forthcoming. The persons transported to Port Blair are sent by the Government of India and are murderers, who for some reason have escaped the death penalty, and the perpetrators of the more heinous offences against the person and property. The sentences they have to undergo are chiefly for life, but a number, varying from a very few to a considerable amount, with long term sentences, are also sent from time to time. Except under special circumstances, convicts are not received under 18 years of age nor over 40 years; nor unless they are medically fit for hard labour previous to transportation. Youths between 18 and 20 are kept in the Boys' Gang under special conditions. Girls are occasionally received of 16 or thereabouts, but as all women locally unmarried are kept in the Female Jail, a large enclosure consisting of separate sleeping wards and worksheds, there are no special rules for them.

The ages of the convicts, while in the Settlement, consequently depend on their ages at conviction, and the length of sentences, none, except under special circumstances, being now received under 18, as above stated. The following general statement of them will be found to be of use in considering the value of economic and other statistics concerning them :—

Year.	1 to 16.	18 to 40.	40 to 60	Over 60.
1874	20	4,582	1,091	476
1881	...	8,730	2,180	512
1891	...	8,815	2,121	502
1901	...	7,261	3,945	625

Offences causing Transportation.

The following Table shows that murder and the heinous offences against the person, dacoity (gang robbery with murder or preparation for murder), and the other heinous offences against property make up nearly the whole total, all the other serious offences together accounting for but a few arrivals :—

Year.	Murder.	Against the person.	Dacoity.	Against property	Others.	Total.
1874	5,575	107	1,262	325	298	7,567
1881	7,445	158	2,444	1,012	381	11,440
1891	7,946	308	1,711	1,337	416	11,718
1901	7,795	817	2,262	904	196	11,974
1904-05 . . .	8,386	752	2,881	1,874	219	14,112
1905-06 . . .	8,559	812	3,050	2,038	237	14,696

These figures illustrate clearly the violent character of the convicts, and it is of value to examine their behaviour under continuous restraint. Between 1890 and 1900, the average proportion of convicts who committed or attempted murder was ·12 per cent., the figures rising to 1·54 in 1894. Neither the nature of the labour nor the discipline enforced appears to have any effect on the tendency to murder, and the motives traced are similar to those disclosed in similar cases among an ordinary population, while murderous assaults are usually committed quite suddenly on opportunity and cause arising.

Administration.

The Penal Settlement is administered by the Chief Commissioner, Andaman and Nicobars, as Superintendent, with a Deputy and a staff of Assistant Superintendents and Overseers, almost all Europeans, and Warders who are natives of India. All the petty supervising establishments are themselves convicts. There are, besides, special departments: Police, Medical, Commissariat, Forests, Tea, Marine, and so on, of the usual type in India, except that all Civil officers are invested with special powers over convicts. Civil and criminal justice is administered by a series of Courts under the Chief Commissioner and the Deputy Superintendent, as the principal Courts of original and appellate jurisdiction. The Chief Commissioner is also the chief revenue and financial authority.

Penal System.

The full penal system, as at present directed, is as follows:—The life convicts are received into the Cellular Jail for six months, where the discipline is of the severest, but the work is not hard. They are then transferred to the Associated Jail for 18 months, where the work is hard, but the discipline less irksome. For the next three years the life convict lives in barracks, locked up at night, and goes out to labour under supervision. For his labour he receives no reward, but his capabilities are studied. During the next five years he remains a labouring convict, but is eligible for the petty posts of supervision and the easier forms of labour; he also gets a very small allowance for little luxuries, or to save in the special Savings Bank. He has now completed ten years in transportation and can receive a ticket-of-leave (self-supporter). In this condition he earns his own living in a village: he can farm, keep cattle, and marry or send for his family. But he is not free, has no civil rights, and cannot leave the Settlement or be idle. After 20 to

25 years spent in the Settlement with approved conduct, he may be absolutely released. While a self-supporter, he is at first assisted with house, food, and tools, and pays no taxes or cesses, but after three to four years, according to certain conditions, he receives no assistance and is charged with every public payment, which would be demanded of him, were he a free man.

The women life convicts are similarly dealt with, but on altogether easier lines. The general principle with regard to them is to divide them into two main classes—those in and those out of the Female Jail. Every woman must remain in the Female Jail, unless in domestic employ by permission or married and living with her husband. Women are eligible for marriage or domestic employ after five years in the Settlement, and if married they may leave the Settlement after 15 years with their husbands, all married couples having to wait each for the other's full term under the rules, whichever, comes last, and they must leave together. If unmarried, women have to remain 20 years. In the Jail they rise from class to class and can become petty officers on terms similar to those for the men.

Term convicts are treated on the same general lines, except that they cannot become self-supporters and are released at once on the expiry of their sentences.

Convict marriages are carefully controlled so as to prevent degeneration into concubinage or irregular alliances, and the special local Savings Bank has proved of great value in inducing a faith on the part of the convicts in the honesty of the Government, irrespective of its value in inducing habits of thrift and diminishing the temptation to violence for the sake of money hoarded privately.

All the civil officers are Magistrates and Civil Judges with the ordinary powers of such as exercised by grades in India, and if a term convict misbehaves sufficiently seriously, his case can be tried magisterially and an additional punishment inflicted. In the case of a life convict any term of "*chaingang*" inflicted is added to the 20 (or 25) years that he must, in any case, remain. Under recent orders, however, confinement in the Cellular Jail has taken the place, in the case of shorter sentences, of punishment in the chaingang. Any offence under the Indian Penal Code or other law, except an offence involving a capital sentence, is punishable executively as a "convict offence," the exception to this rule being tried at Sessions in the ordinary manner. "Convict offences," though punishable executively, are all tried, however trivial, by a fixed *quasi*-judicial procedure, including record and appeal, so that the convict is made to feel that justice is, at all times, as secure to him, as to the free.

The whole aim of the treatment is that of a long education to useful citizenship, throughout which there runs continuous threads of practice in self-help and self-restraint and of inducement to profit by the practice. Effort to behave well and submission to control alone guide the convict's upward promotion in due course; every lapse retards it. And when he has his ticket-of-leave, it is only to himself that he has to look to provide that money out of his own earnings as a steady member of society, that is to provide him with a sufficient competence on release. The aim of the Penal Settlement is to educate the outcasts it receives into self-respecting citizens, habituated to provide for themselves in an orderly way. The incorrigible are kept till death, the slow to learn till they mend their ways, and only those that are proved to have good in them are returned to their homes. The root argument on which the system is based is that the acts of the convict spring from a constitutional want of self-control.

Classification of Convicts.

The convicts, while in the Settlement, are divided up in several ways. The great economic division for both sexes is into labouring convicts and self-supporters; the former perform all the labour of the place, skilled and unskilled, and the latter are chiefly engaged in agriculture and food supplies. The Commissiariat division is into rationed and not rationed: in the former class are nearly all the labouring convicts and in the latter all the self-supporters and some of the labouring convicts. The financial division is into classes indicating those with and those without allowances with numerous sub-divisions, all according to scale of allowances, thus:—

I.—Supervision.
- (*a*) Jemadar.
- (*b*) Tindal.
- (*c*) Peon.

II.—Monthly Allowances.
- (*a*) 1st Class—
  - (i) Rs. 2-0-0
  - (ii) R1-12-0
  - (iii) R1-8-0
  - (iv) R1-4-0
  - (v) R1-0-0
- (*b*) 2nd Class—
  - (i) A: R 1-0-0
  - (ii) B: R0-12-0
  - (iii) New: R0-12-0

V.—On Monthly Pay.
- (*a*) Self-supporter Hospital Compounders—
  - (i) R6-4-0
  - (ii) R8-4-0
  - (iii) R10-0-0
- (*b*) Self-supporter Government servants—
  - (i) R6-0-0
  - (ii) R7-0-0
  - (iii) R8-0-0
  - (iv) R9-0-0
  - (v) R10-0-0
  - (vi) R11-0-0
  - (vii) R12-0-0

III.—Invalids with allowances.

(*c*) 1st Class—

(i) R0-12-0

(ii) New: Rs. 0-8-0

(*d*) 2nd Class—

(i) A: R: 0-8-0

(ii) B: R0-4-0

(iii) New: R0-4-0

IV.—Without allowances.

(*a*) 3rd Class—

(*b*) Chaingang.

(*c*) Domestic servants.

(*d*) Self-supporters.

(viii) R14-0-0

VI.—Females.

(*a*) Supervision—

(i) Jemadarni.

(ii) Tindalani.

(iii) Daffadarni.

(*b*) Labouring—

(i) 1st Class A.

(ii) 1st Class B.

(iii) 2nd Class.

(iv) Refractory ward.

(v) Hospital ward servants.

(*c*) Self-supporters.

DISCIPLINE.

There are also disciplinary gangs all involving degradation either on account of bad character on arrival or while in the Settlement. These are known as Cellular Jail Prisoner, Viper Island Disciplinary, Chatham Island Disciplinary, Chaingang, Habitual Criminal Gang, Unnatural Crime Gang, "D" (for doubtful) ticket men. The *lingua franca* of the Settlement is Urdu (Hindustani), spoken in every possible variety of corruption and with every variety of accent. All the convicts learn it to an extent sufficient for their daily wants and the understanding of orders and directions. It is also the vernacular of the local born, whatever their descent. The small extent to which many absolute strangers to it, such as the Burmese, inhabitants of Madras, and so on, master it is one of the safeguards of the Settlement, as it makes it impossible for any general plot to be hatched. In barracks, in boats, and on works where men have to be congregated, every care is taken to split up nationalities, with the result that, except on matters of daily common concern, the convicts are unable to converse confidentially together. The "D" ticket comes about in this way. Prisoners in the 3rd class are obliged to wear wooden neck tickets, which tell the expert all about them. On the ticket is the convict's number, the section of the Indian Penal Code under which he was convicted, the date of his sentence, the date his release is due—if of "doubtful" character it has a D; if one of a gang of criminals in India it has a star, and the presence or absence of A shows the class of ration; if a life prisoner it has L. There is a class of "connected convicts." Prisoners convicted in the same case, marked by a star on the neck ticket, are all specially noted and never kept in the same station or working gang, under special arrangements sometimes involving considerable care and organisation, as when a large and dangerous gang of dacoits is broken up in India and arrives in Port Blair at times even 40 strong.

Free and Convict Districts.

There is a sharply marked division of the Settlement into what is known as the "free" and "convict" portions, by which the free settlers living in villages are separated from the ticket-of-leave (self-supporter) convicts also living in villages. Every effort is made to prevent unauthorised communication between these two divisions. No adult person can enter the Settlement without permission or reside there without an annual license, and certain other necessary restrictions are imposed on him as to his movements among and his dealings with the convicts, etc., on pain of being expelled the Settlement or punished under its laws. The "free" sub-divisions are Ross and Haddo. The "convict" sub-divisions are Viper and Wimberleyganj and the Jail Sub-division.

Convicts' Descendants.

A large proportion of the free settlers are "local born," *i.e.*, descendants of convicts born in the Settlement and permanently resident there. Like every other population the local born comprise every kind of personal character. Taken as a class they may, however, be described thus. As children they are bright, intelligent and unusually healthy. It is the rule, not the exception, for the whole of a local born family to be reared. On the score of intelligence they do not fail throughout life. As young people they do not exhibit any unusual degree of violence and inclination to theft, but their general morality is distinctly low. Among the girls, even when quite young, there is a painful amount of prostitution, open and veiled: the result partly of temptation in a population in which the males very greatly preponderate, but chiefly due to bad early associations—convict mothers not being a class likely to bring up their girls to a high morality. The boys, and sometimes the girls, exhibit much defiant pride of position, *i.e.*, in being "free" as opposed to being "convict," combined with a certain mental smartness, idleness, dislike of manual labour, and disrespect for age and authority that stand much in their way in life. Their defiant attitude is probably due to the indeterminate nature of their social status as has been observed of classes unhappily situated socially elsewhere. Heredity seems to show itself in both sexes rather in a tendency towards the meaner qualities than towards violence of temperament. The adult villagers are quarrelsome and as litigious as the Courts will permit them to be, borrow all the money they can, do not get as much out of the land as they might, and spend too much time in attempting to get the better of neighbours. At the same time, it would be an entire error to suppose that the better elements in human nature are not also exhibited and convicts' descendants have shown themselves to be upright, capable, hardworking, honest, and self-respecting. On the whole, considering their parentage, the local born population is of a much higher type than the inexperienced would expect to find them, though there is too great a tendency on the part of the whole population to lean on the Government, the result probably of the excessive "governing" necessary in such a place as a Penal Settlement.

Language.

The mother-tongues of the population are as numerous as the divisions and districts of India and Burma from which they are derived, but it is of value to ascertain them, as they are presumably a fair test of origin in the case of the convicts, and for that reason their places of origin are below tested by a comparative table of language with birthplace by provinces. For this purpose the languages of the convicts, as returned at the Census, are assigned to the various provinces and administrations, being necessarily grouped togethed. Thus:—

Indian Provinces.	Mother-tongues of residents in Port Blair.
Port Blair	Urdu.
Bengal with States and Assam	Bengali, Oriya, Assamese.
Bombay with States and Baroda	Gujarati, Mahrathi, Kachchhi, Kathiyawadi, Khatri, Konkani.
Burma	Arakanese, Burmese, Karen, Shan, Talaing, Siamese, Chinese.
Madras with States, Berar, Hyderabad, Mysore, Laccadives.	Tamil, Telugu, Canarese, Malayalum, Gadaba, Bellara.
Punjab with States, Frontier Provinces, Kashmir.	Panjabi, Dhanni, Dogri, Pahari, Peshawari, Pushto, Persian.
Sindh	Balochi, Brahui, Sindhi.
United Provinces with States and Central India and Central Provinces with States.	Hindi, Khweymi, Naipali, Khas, Gondi, Kharia.
Rajputana, with Ajmer-Merwara	Marwari.
Nicobars	Nicobari.
Straits Settlements	Malay.

On this basis province of origin by language and birth place can be stated thus:—

	Population by Language.	Population by Birthplace.
Bengal and Assam	1,766	2,596
Bombay	1,149	829
Burma	2,154	1,981
Madras	1,429	1,818
Punjab	1,761	2,119

	Population by Language.	Population by Birthplace.
Sindh	221	90
United Provinces and Central Provinces.	4,903	4,270
Rajputana	47	109
Nicobars	2	7
Straits Settlements	10	10
Portguese Settlements	16	14
Port Blair	2,419	2,039
Others	437	388
TOTAL .	16,256	16,256

The Urdu of Port Blair is thus not only exceedingly corrupt from natural causes, but it is filled with technicalities arising out of local conditions and the special requirements of convict life. Even the vernacular of the local born is loaded with them. These technicalities are partly derived from English and are partly specialised applications to new uses of pure or corrupted Urdu words. As opportunity has arisen some of these have been collected and printed from time to time in the *Indian Antiquary*. The most prominent grammatical characteristic of this dialect of Urdu appears in the numerals, which are everywhere Urdu, but are not spoken according to correct Urdu custom. Thus, the convicts and all dealing with them count up to 20 regularly, and then between the tens simply add the units, instead of using special terms, *e.g.*, a convict, whatever his nationality or mother-tongue, will give his numbers, say, 12,536, as *bara hazar panch sau tis chhe*, twelve thousand five hundred thirty-six. He would never say, even if born and bred in Hindustani proper, *bara hazar panch sau chhatis*. The convict must be addressed in the same manner, or he will most probably misapprehend what is said. Specimens of corrupted Urdu used in the Settlement will be found in the Census Report, pp. 362-364.

Many of the existing place names about Port Blair are English, and the corruptions thereof by the convicts and their native guards are interesting, showing that striving after a meaning which is so prolific of verbal corruptions all over the world. *E.g.*—Mount Harriett becomes Mohan Ret; Perseverance Point becomes Parasu Pet and Parson Pet; Shore Point becomes Suwar Pet; Navy Bay becomes Nabbi Beg; Phœnix Bay becomes Pinik Beg; and Barwell Ghat becomes Balu Ghat. Harriett was the name of the wife of Colonel Tytler, a former Superintendent. Perseverance and Phœnix were the names of Royal Ships in Blair's day. Shore Point is named after Sir John Shore (Lord Teignmouth), Governor-General. General Barwell was a former Chief Commissioner. There is also a large village called Anikhet (now often converted into Ranikhet), a conscious pun on the name of a daughter of a former Chief Commissioner, who was named Annie Kate. A steam launch in the harbour was named *The Belle* after a daughter of another former Chief Commissioner, which has proved an unfortunate name, for the vessel was invariably called by the Natives "*Belli Jahaz.*" The station of Elephant Point has been translated into *Hathi Tapu* and *Hathi Ghat.* The stations of Navy Bay, Dundas Point, South Point, and Phœnix Bay are all also frequently indiscriminately called *Chuna Bhatta*, because there is now, or has been at some former time, a lime-kiln at these spots. Convicts never forget a place at which there has been a lime-kiln: they hate the work so. So, also, there is a village called Chauldari (for *shuldari*) in the Southern District after a former convict camp at the spot; but the station of Middle Point, a long way off in the Northern District, is also commonly known to the convicts as Chauldari for the same reason. Sometimes the native names for places are merely corruptions of the English words, without any effort at a meaning; *e.g.*, *Ubten* for Hope Town where Lord Mayo was murdered, and *Hardo* for Haddo. Port Blair itself is always *Pot Biler* and Port Mouat always *Potmot.*

POPULATION.

The population of the Penal Settlement consists of convicts, their guards, the supervising, clerical, and departmental staff, with the families of the latter, and a limited number of ex-convict and trading settlers and their families. Detailed statistics have been maintained since 1874, and are shown as in the following table: but it must be remembered that in intervening years, the numbers of the convicts vary considerably. A point to notice in the figures is that the establishments had up to the Census increased since 1874 by 41 per cent., the free resident population by 257 per cent. and the convicts by 74 per cent., showing that the general increase in the population and convicts and the ever-increasing completeness in watch and ward and penal discipline has not been attended with a corresponding increase in establishments:—

Free Population.

YEAR.	ADMINISTRATIVE ESTABLISHMENT.					FREE RESIDENT POPULATION INCLUDING CHILDREN AND CONDITIONALLY RELEASED.		
	Civil.	Military.	Marine.	Police.	TOTAL.	Male.	Female.	TOTAL.
1874	50	426	19	330	825	466	372	838
1881	45	336	19	736	1,136	941	669	1,610
1891	85	460	39	541	1,125	1,357	1,340	2,697
1901	100	466	70	532	1,168	1,623	1,368	2,99[illegible]

Year.	Convict Population.			Total Population.				
				Adults.		Children.		Total.
	Male.	Female.	Total.	Male.	Female.	Male.	Female.	
1874	6,733	836	7,569	7,654	907	370	301	9,232
1881	10,325	1,127	11,452	11,766	1,329	636	467	14,198
1891	10,874	864	11,738	12,532	1,439	824	765	15,560
1901	11,217	730	11,947	13,235	1,477	773	621	16,106

Artificial Conditions.

The conditions under which the population of Port Blair lives are so artificial and so unlike those of an ordinary population that it is impossible to describe them on the usual lines. There are hardly any natural movements to observe and report. The following remarks aim therefore at a description of the social state of the convicts and the unofficial population in the regulated conditions of life imposed on them from outside.

General convict statistics for a series of years are given below:—

Particulars.		1874.	1881.	1891.	1901.	1904-05.	1905-06.
Number of convicts received	Male .	603	1,102	869	1,233	1,159	1,507
	Female .	97	100	53	80	43	56
Number of life convicts	Male . .	6,727	7,628	8,033	9,204	9,578	9,642
	Female . .	836	1,122	861	714	676	672
Number of term convicts	Male . .	6	2,657	2,840	2,037	3,816	4,239
	Female . .	...	5	4	19	44	42
Number of convicts released	Male .	355	64	665	215	161	300
	Female .	4	8	73	33	27	31
Admissions into hospital	Male . .	11,193	25,531	27,328	22,310*	24,630	25,991
	Female . .	842	827	1,094	1,240	1,046	1,246
Number died . .	Male . .	107	534	435	423	532	529
	Female . .	9	18	17	17		20
Number escaped and not re-captured.	Male .	24	15	14	5	21	12
	Female .	...	...	...	...	...	...
Number executed .	Male . .	6	13	12	6	6	5
	Female .	...	...	...	...	...	...

* Medical statistics are for 1900.

In the above Table the "escaped" are those who have not been heard of again. As a matter of fact such unfortunates, as a rule, die in the jungles or are drowned at sea. Very rarely does a convict escape to the mainland.

The social conditions in which the free residents live are as artificial as those that govern the lives of the convicts, and the restrictions under which they live have a distinct effect on the characters on those subjected to them from childhood to death, an effect which will become more and more apparent as generation after generation of convicts' descendants comes under their pressure. The free residents include Government establishments introduced from India, traders from India and Burma, domestic servants who have accompanied their masters, very few settlers from outside, and the descendants of convicts who have settled in the Penal Settlement after their release. The local born population is certain to become clearly differentiated in many respects from the corresponding population on the continent and is well worth watching in its every aspect. The statistics as to numbers are as follows:—

	Total.	Male.	Female.
1881	754	488	266
1891	1,499	1,288	211
1901	2,030	1,168	862

DISTRIBUTION.

The decennial census returns for Port Blair may be taken as quite accurate, as there are maintained, for local administrative reasons, a daily census of the convicts and an annual census (March 31) of the whole population. The daily Census of the convict population is effected by what is known as the "Morning Report," sent to the Superintendent daily from each district and checked by the "Strength Register" in his office, also made out from day to day. Besides these, there are the ration issues from the Commissariat Department made to the District officers on daily indents for supplies, which serve as an additional check on the labouring convicts, the class most likely to attempt escape. There is further an organised arrangement of patrols and surprise visits by police, overseers, and Settlement officers: a daily statement of the employment of all the labouring convicts, returns of the self-supporters, their residences, employments, and so on. The working of this system of report and check makes it impossible for the petty officers immediately responsible for the presence of labouring convicts and the village officials responsible for the presence of the self-supporter convicts to successfully attempt concealment of the absence of any one anywhere in the whole settled area of 327 square miles. Discovery would follow so quickly on such an attempt that none has been made in my considerable experience of the Settlement.

The District Morning Reports are designed to show the strength of those convicts who are rationed and who are not rationed and the total in each District daily, and are made in the following form. They form a daily Census of the convicts. The Morning Reports are first made out by writers (Munshis) station by station, collected in the District Offices, examined, checked and made out into the form above given and sent in separately to the Superintendent's Office, where they are checked by his "Strength Register." It will be observed that the details in the two sets of returns are entirely different, but that the totals for the whole Settlement must absolutely agree. By the system adopted a complete Census is daily secured and collusion between officials to conceal an absence made impossible. The Superintendent's Strength Register is designed to show per district the actual number present every day of every class and description of convict. It is primarily a financial return to check payments with numbers. It forms a complete check on the Morning Reports, and it shows daily the numbers present on the previous day and every convict withdrawn and added during the day for any reason in each class.

At the Census the population was shown as 16,256 including 150 persons, 114 male and 36 female, on board the mail steamer, which happened to be in the harbour. Details are shown in the following table:—

	Christians.		Hindus.		Mahomedans.		Buddhists.		Others.		TOTAL.	
	M.	F.	M.	F.	M.	F.	M.	F.	M.	F.	M.	F.
Civil .	42	...	40	...	18	...	...	...	...	...	100	...
Military .	163	..	166	..	183	...	...	...	...	...	511	...
Marine .	22	...	5	...	72	...	1	...	...	...	100	...
Police .	2	...	369	...	161	...	...	...	...	...	532	...
Free Residents .	21	60	514	535	195	148	...	1	1	...	731	734
Convicts .	40	2	6,582	539	2,766	191	1,817	8	10	...	11,217	730
Conditionally released convicts	...	...	41	13	2	1	...	...	...	...	44	13
Children of all ranks	40	27	576	444	196	140	2	...	...	...	773	621
TOTAL	328	90	8,242	1,510	3,596	480	1,820	9	11	...	14,006	2,098

The population was distributed over an occupied area of 327 square miles in 29 "stations," or places where labouring convicts are kept, and 34 "villages," or places where free residents or ticket-of-leave (self-supporters) convicts reside.

The principle of distributing the self-supporters is to keep them in fixed villages in the "convict sub-divisions," but as a good many are taken into Government and private service, these have to live at the stations nearest their work and some are accommodated in villages in the "free sub-divisions" and so the self-supporters are apparently distributed all over the Settlement as in the following Census Table, which is instructive in another way because it shows that to 1,768 men there were only 349 women and 404 children :—

—	Adults.		Children.	
	Male.	Female.	Male.	Female.
Total Self-supporters in villages	1,453	331	214	189
Total Self-supporters at stations	315	18	1	...
Gross Total of Self-supporters in the Settlement	1,768	349	215	189

Religion.

Every religion in India is represented among the convicts, but it was impossible to classify Hindus by sects at the Census, as convicts do not form a class who are at all sure about nice distinctions in religious matters. The Sikhs are represented chiefly in the Military Police Battalion, the Buddhists by the Burman convicts and the Christians by the British Infantry garrison and the officials. It is to be noticed that not one person is returned as a Jew among all the convicts. The details are as follows :—

—	Male.	Female.	Total.
All religions	14,122	2,134	16,256
Hindu	7,847	1,417	9,264
Sikh	326	44	370
Jain	49	12	61
Buddhist	1,848	12	1,860
Zoroastrian	2	...	2
Musulman	3,678	529	4,207
Christian	366	120	486
Others	6	...	6

Occupations.

The necessary work of the Settlement is all performed by convicts. Leaving out those employed as public servants, the occupations of the settlers recorded at the Census show how the ex-convict and free unofficial population supports itself, it being premised that disreputable occupations are not officially permitted in the Penal Settlement, though prostitutes and those about them exist *sub rosâ* in greater numbers than is at all desirable.

Livelihood of settlers (excluding convicts and Government servants).

———	Workers.	Dependants.	TOTAL.
Provision and care of animals	19	4	23
Agriculture	479	1,015	1,494
Personal, Household and Sanitary Service	90	116	206
Food, Drink, and Stimulants	58	61	119
Light, firing, and forage	7	4	11
Buildings	1	2	3
Supplementary Requirements	9	12	21
Textile fabrics and dress	22	5	27
Metals and precious stones	15	34	49
Glass, earthen and stone-ware	1	5	6
Wood, cane and leaves	14	11	25
Leather	6	10	16
Commerce	85	93	178
Transport and Storage	98	27	125
Learned and artistic professions	91	118	209
Earthwork and general labour	18	13	31
Indefinite occupations	64	34	98

At the Census 279 local born male adults were recorded to be earning their own living and maintaining their families in the Penal Settlement in the following manner :—

Occupation.	No. following it.	No. of adult dependants (elderly women, wives and sisters).	Total supported by it.
Government Service	84	76	160
Trade and shop	13	21	34
Agriculture	149	190	339
Private service	33	36	69
TOTAL	279	323	602

CASTE.

As the maintenance of caste among natives of India involves the maintenance of respectability, and as the aim of the Penal System is the resuscitation of respectability among the convicts, nothing is permitted that would tend to destroy the caste feeling among them. The tendency is always with them to "raise" their caste wherever that is possible, and occasionally some crafty scoundrel is convicted of illegitimate association with fellow Hindus in regard to caste. Two Mehtars have recently been detected in sucessfully managing this: one, a self-supporter, masqueraded for years in his village as a Rajput (Rajbansi), and another for years was cook to a respectable Hindu free family on the ground of being a Brahman. It is also not at all uncommon for low caste ex-convict settlers, with a view to raising their social status, to adopt a mode of dress and life, which would be quite inadmissible if they were to return to their native villages in India. In Port Blair, as elsewhere, the great resort of those desiring to raise their social status is the adoption of Muhammadanism. On the other hand, instances have occurred, in which men who were not so by caste, have volunteered to become Mehtars, debasing their social status in order to adopt what they have regarded as a less arduous mode of life than daily cooly labour.

In relation to the question of caste, all important to the natives of India, there is a considerable ethnographic interest attaching to the descendants of convicts, known in the Settlement as the "local born," as there is a marked difference maintained at present between the "free" introduced from India and the "free" with the taint of convict blood. In certain cases the barrier is broken down socially, but entry by marriage into a "local born" family has been observed to be looked upon as degrading to an immigrant from India. How long this will last and in what directions the barrier will be habitually broken through is worth watching. At present there is much greater sympathy on the part of the immigrants, temporary or permanent, with the actual convicts than with their descendants.

Although the self-supporter convict is entitled to send for his family from India, he very seldom does so, or at least their families very seldom consent to join the convicts, and the result is that the "local born" are nearly all the descendants of "convict marriages." A convict marriage comes about in this way. Any self-supporter may marry a convict woman from the Female Jail, under the conditions that they have the permission of the Settlement authorities and the marriage is in accordance with the social custom of the contracting parties. In the existing practice, an enquiry ensues on every application and covers the eligibility of the parties to marry under convict rules, the capacity of the man to support a family, the respective social conditions in India of both parties; *e.g.*, a Hindu would not be allowed to locally "marry" a Muhammadan woman, an undivorced Muhammadan woman with a husband living in India would not be allowed to marry at all, and so on.

When the preliminaries are settled to satisfaction, often after prolonged enquiry, permission is given and registered by the Superintendent, who then calls upon the parties to appear before him and certify on a given date that they have been actually married according to their particular rite. The marriage is then registered as such by the Superintendent and becomes legal. Owing to the enormous variety of marriage rites in India, the parties have to be left to their own statement as to having gone through the appropriate ceremonies, and as the desire for marriage is unquestionably genuine on the part of the contracting parties (of the woman at any rate) as much of the ceremonies as are binding in their eyes are no doubt gone through. At the very least they are legally married. In carrying out this practice there is no difficulty as regards Christians, Muhammadans, and Buddhists, endogamy within their group being easily ensured; but some difficulty has arisen as regards Hindus. The varieties of marriage customs among the Hindus are legion, differing indefinitely not only in every caste, but with every locality, and as the Hindu convicts come from every caste and every locality, in the strict narrow view of the question hardly any Hindu marriage contracted in Port Blair could be in accordance with customary endogamy, which, be it noted, is quite a different question from legality. In the Penal Settlement, however, the knot has been cut since 1881 by recognising only the four main divisions (*waran*, *varna*) of Hindus as separate "caste," within which there must be endogamy among the Hindu convicts, *viz.*, Brahmâns, Khatris (Kshatriya), Vaisyas, and Sudras. Before 1881, under pressure of the dominating conditions, the rule was merely Hindu to Hindu, Muhammadan to Muhammandan, Christian to Christian; Buddhists and others hardly then came into consideration. The fruit of such marriages, *i.e.*, "the Hindu local born" form therefore a most interesting ethnographical study.

The birth and growth of caste among convicts' descendants is then a question really of the growth and formation of new or special local Hindu castes—a question that can be studied obscurely perhaps in every part of India and clearly enough in all regions where Hindu propaganda are being carried among indigenous and animistic populations in the course of the natural spread of civilisation along new lines of communication. In Port Blair "caste" exists as strictly within its limits among the locally born Hindus as it does elsewhere among the natives of India, and the interest of the question lies in observing how the people have settled among themselves the exceedingly knotty point of the relative status among each other of the decendants of what in India would be looked on as the offspring of mixed castes—usually an unenviable position, but by force of circumstances not so in the Penal Settlement. Fond as they are of claiming and talking of their "caste," the locally born have naturally but hazy ideas on the subject, as it is understood in the localities from which their parents came. Firstly, they take the caste of the father, as they understand it, that of the mother being ignored. Secondly, they divide themselves into high and low caste generally, *e.g.*, the children of Brahman, Khatri, and Vaisya fathers hold themselves, so far as they can, to be of high caste and apart from the whole of the innumerable castes coming under the head of Sudra or low caste. Next a locally born man marries, so far as he can, into his own caste, *i.e.*, the daughter of a man of the same caste as his own father. But the time for this being possible generally is yet to come and the custom is to ignore the caste of the woman taken to wife, but to consider all the children to be of the caste of the father. Thus the full caste system of India is fairly on the way to being realised among the descendants of the convicts.

As regards the present custom as to marriages among the "local born," brought about by pressure of surrounding conditions be it remembered, the following questions were asked and answers received as under:—

(1) *Q*. When a local born boy marries a local born girl of lower caste than himself (*a*) who pays the expenses? and (*b*) does *his* father receive any present for allowing the marriage from *her* father?

A. The observance of caste in the case of "local born" Hindu marriages is not so rigid as in India. (*a*) When a local born boy marries a local born girl of a lower caste than himself the expenses are generally borne by the boy's parents. If they have not the means, the girl's parents undertake the expenses. The point looked to locally is whether the boy can keep the girl comfortably or not.

(*b*) No presents are given to the boy's father for allowing marriages like this.

(2) *Q*. Are local born girls married to local born boys of lower caste than themselves?

A. Yes.

(3) *Q*. When a local born boy marries a local born girl of his own caste, who pays the expenses?

A. The same rule as in the first question applies. The parents of the boy pay if they can; if not, the girl's parents pay.

(4) Based on actual returns of local born mixed-caste marriages the following question was asked, the second caste name representing that of the girls.

Q. Which is considered the highest caste locally of—

	Q.	A.
U	Bania or Lohar ?	Bania.
D	Kayath or Thakur ?	Thakur.
U	Kayath or Kaibarth ?	Kayath.
U	Kayath or Garasia ?	Kayath.
D	Khatri or Thakur ?	Thakur.
U	Khatri or Ahir ?	Khatri.
U	Dosadh or Namasudra (Madras) ?	Dosadh.
D	Dosadh or Baghdi ?	Baghdi.
U	Kurmi or Kachi ?	Kurmi.
D	Kurmi or Bania ?	Bania.
D	Bind or Thakur ?	Thakur.
U	Maratha or Kunbi ?	Maratha.
U	Sonar or Nonia ?	Sonar.
D	Pasi or Bania ?	Bania.

The letter U in the above Table shows where the girls married "up" and D where they married "down."

The question here is, of course, not which of these pairs of caste are held to be the higher in India, nor whether they would, in any circumstances, associate together in India, but which is locally the higher and why they will associate locally. In every one of these mixed-caste marriages the issue will be of the father's caste. In one case the opposite sexes in two families married each other: one family was Baghdi and the other was Dosadh. In some parts at least of India they would all have become of one "caste" and both families would have been "outcasted." In Port Blair the Dosadh girls in this instance have become Baghdi and the Baghdi girls have become Dosadh, and they and their children are so recognised socially.

The answers to the last and indeed to all questions show clearly that there is as yet no notion of hypergamy in the Penal Settlement and that under pressure of surrounding conditions caste has to be set aside in marriages and can only be maintained by ignoring the caste of the mothers. There is, however, a strong desire to marry into the same caste and wherever practicable it is no doubt done, and it is probable that caste maintenance in its strictness will commence in the Penal Settlement by isogamy which, in India, is so merged in hypergamy that it was left out of consideration in the last Census Reports. That in time caste will rule marriages and social relations in the Penal Settlement in all its accustomed force there appears to be little doubt.

The following table gives statistics of civil condition in 1901 :—

—	Males.	Females.	TOTAL.
Unmarried	3,762	625	4,387
Married	9,259	1,199	10,458
Widowed	1,101	310	1,411
TOTAL	14,122	2,134	16,256

The Census figures for unmarried females among the Hindus are of much interest.

Age.	Total females.	Married.	Unmarried.	Widows.
Under 5	182	2	180	...
5—10	126	11	115	...
10—15	123	38	82	3
15—20	101	79	15	7
	532	532		

After 20 and in a few cases under that age the only unmarried Hindu females are convicts. The very small number of Hindu female children married is primarily due to the rule, for strong administrative reasons, which does not recognise infant marriages under 16 in the case of the female children of convicts (self-supporters). But it would appear that this rule is affecting the custom of the whole Hindu population, so that even out of 101 girls of all sorts (children of the free and convicts) between 15 and 20 only 79 are married. The number of very young widows is also necessarily in quite small proportion.

Health.

Sickness and mortality are always matters of great consideration among a convict population, but the conditions are also always highly artificial, as there is one constant struggle between efficiency in discipline and labour and the maintenance of a low sick and death-rate by regulation and direct measures. The tendency on one side is to overstrain in the direction of penality and economy, on the other side to secure "satisfactory" health statistics at the cost of over-leniency and extravagance. Port Blair has had no exceptional experience of this struggle, which is perpetually maintained wherever prisoners are congregated in civilised countries. All convict sickness and mortality tables have to be viewed with this point in mind.

Effect of Rainfall.

It is usual in the East to compare on the same form or table, sick-rate, death-rate, and rainfall, but Tables and diagrams, covering 31 years of Port Blair in this manner, were found to show that annual rainfall does not there bear any real relation to either sickness or death-rate, and that the death-rate bears some, though far from a continuous, relation to the sick-rate annually. *Monthly* rainfall has a decided effect on the sick-rate, which greatly rises regularly every year during the rains (June-September).

Sickness and Mortality.

The following is a comparative table of sickness and mortality in the Settlement for the Census years, all the medical figures for the last Census being, however, for 1900 :—

Year.	Average daily strength.			Daily average sick.			Deaths in and out of Hospital.		
	Male.	Female.	Total.	Male.	Female.	Total.	Male.	Female.	Total.
1874 .	6,852	885	7,737	580	25	605	177	17	194
1881 .	9,966	,097	11,063	1,205	13	1,218	543	18	561
1891 .	10,739	837	11,576	664	24	688	461	24	485
1900 .	10,880	714	11,594	602	27	629	452	16	468

Year.	Ratio per mille of average strength.								
	Of admission.			Of daily number of sick.			Of deaths.		
	Male.	Female.	Total.	Male.	Female.	Total.	Male.	Female.	Total.
1874 .	2,102·16	1,291·53	2,009·44	84·65	28·25	78·20	25·83	19·21	25·07
1881 .	2,561·81	753·87	2,382·54	120·91	11·85	110·03	54·49	16·41	50·71
1891 .	1,607·13	1,342·89	1,588·03	61·83	28·67	59·43	42·98	28·67	41·90
1900 .	2,051·38	1,806·72	2,036·31	53·35	37·28	54·20	41·54	23·41	40·36

Statistics for isolated years such as these are, however, illusory, as, from some causes not yet reported, the sickness and mortality appear to rise and fall in the Penal Settlement in successions of years, as can be seen from the accompanying abstract.

Cycles of Health.

Serial No.	Period.	Years.	Death rate.	Average death rate per mille.
1	4 years . .	1871 to 1874 . .	Low . .	18·46
2	7 " . .	1875 to 1881 . .	High .	40·07
3	6 " . .	1882 to 1887 . .	Low . .	22·02
4	5 " . .	1888 to 1892 . .	High .	41·37
5	6 " . .	1893 to 1898 . .	Low . .	28·39
6	2 " . .	1899 to 1900 . .	High .	41·25

The worst year on record was 1878-79 (67·30). The first group is probably the end, and the last the beginning of a cycle. Sickness and death-rates for any given period or year are really due to a combination of causes, which are very difficult to examine, but an elaborate enquiry made in 1902, showed that the highest rates are among the latest arrivals. The general inference from the enquiry is that the health statistics for any given period depend largely on the number of new arrivals and convicts of short residence present, and it is possible, for example, that the high rates in 1878-79 are due to the weakness caused by the prevalence of famine in India.

The governing causes of the convict sick-rate are length of residence, personal character, mode of cooking food, nature of the labour demanded and place of residence. They all dovetail into each other and it is the combination of all these that produces any given sick-rate. This was the result of the enquiry in 1902 and it was also the result of the enquiry made by Dr. W. H. Rean in 1867. Elaborate statistics resulting from the elaborate enquiry in 1902 will be found in the Census Report, pp. 383-395. The Tables for the effect of length of residence on health show that there is a steady annual decline in the sick rate for the first six years, after which it remains pretty steadily at a low figure, and that it is the new arrivals who swell the general sick rate. But in reading such tables the following facts must be borne in mind. Third class convicts, chiefly those up to five years' residence, go to hospital as often as they think they will be admitted. The first and second class convicts have something to lose by going to hospital. No self-supporter ever goes to hospital if he can help it, as he loses thereby working time and hence income and also his means of looking after his property and land. As to the effect of personal character on health, it was observed that the highest sick rate of all is among the really bad—men with very bad or bad Indian character and very bad local character in the Settlement. Next in order come those with only local very bad character. No doubt long continued evil habits of life permanently affect health, and also in some of such cases successful malingering may be suspected. Personal cooking being the rule in India, for strong disciplinary reasons convicts are "promoted" from the "mess gang" to private cooking. In the result somewhat less than half are in "mess gangs." The Table of the effect of the method of cooking on health shows the sick rate to be five times greater among the mess gangs than among those who cook for themselves. These figures must, however, be read with caution, as in the "mess gangs" are included all the latest arrivals and the bad characters. They thus lose much of their relative importance. In reading the Tables showing the effect of convict labour on sick rate, it is to be remembered that all the labour in Port Blair is by way of being "hard," *i.e.*, a full task is to be exacted of whatever work a convict is put to, and all arrivals are presumed to be physically capable of a full task before despatch. But social antecedents, personal capacities, education, state of personal health from time to time, advancing years, and the nature of the work from time to time necessary for the welfare and progress of the Settlement, all tell in distributing tasks. The very varied tasks demanded are in this way divisible into indoor and outdoor, and then again into ordinary and hard. The indoor "hard labour" men are the bad and very bad characters in jails. The outdoor "hard labour" men include the chaingang, the habitual criminals, the unnatural-crime men, and so on. So character comes into play in gauging the "hard labour" sick returns. As to the effect of the place of residence in the Settlement on health, convicts have to be located as near as possible to the work that it is obligatory to impose on them and this is a point that has always to be remembered in fixing location. The sick rate, for all diseases, was found to be pretty equally distributed between the two districts of the Settlement, but to vary very largely for individual stations. It was however found to be doubtful whether locality within the Settlement limits had as such any preponderating influence on health.

In 1867, when the general conditions of the Settlement and the state of medical knowledge and terminology differed greatly from those now obtaining, Dr. W. H. Rean, Senior Medical Officer, wrote a very careful report on the health of the Settlement, and his general conclusions are much those above arrived at. At that time and previously the death-rate had always been very high, except in one year, 1865, when it was even then high according to present notions, 65·70 per mille; but then deaths from "ulcers degenerating into gangrene" were numerous, a state of things now happily passed away with antiseptic treatment. He noticed that the great causes of sickness and death were fevers and what he called "miasmatic diseases"—fever (malarial), dysentery, diarrhœa, and "others"; that the great mortality was in the first and succeeding years after arrival; that the nature of the labour affected health, out-door jungle and swamp work being the worst for health; that character did so too, the worst characters being the most sickly; and that few arrivals in a year combined with few arrivals in previous years sent down the sick and death-rates. He drew up one still instructive table which helps to illustrate the results above given:—

	Under 1 year.	Under 2 years.	Under 3 years.	Under 4 years.	Over 4 years.
Strength	1,803	2,698	748	558	1,743
Deaths	317	191	51	65	46
Percentage to strength	24·7	7·0	6·8	11·6	2·6

He also drew up two diagrams showing the prevalence of *fever* with reference to other diseases: one generally for the Settlement, where the enormous preponderance of fevers at that time becomes clear, and another for Viper Island showing the sick from the population of that island only, where there is a decided preponderance of other diseases over fevers. He attributed this to the early clearing of the island andthe absence of miasma, where now-a-days we should say it was due to the clean condition of a hilly island which prevented mosquitoes from breeding. These diagrams are still instructive, and are to be found at p. 367 of the Census Report.

Prevalent Diseases.

There appears to be no doubt that malaria, dysentery and phthisis are the main points requiring special attention and also that, if malaria alone can be successfully checked in growth, the health of the Penal Settlement will put on a new aspect. The following general figures may be taken as approximately exhibiting their relative importance:—

Disease.	Percentage of prevalence among the sick.
Malarial fever (47 per cent.) and dysentery consequent thereon (7 per cent.)	54
Ulcers and injuries	16
Phthisis	6
All other diseases including dysentery other than malarial (7 per cent.)	24
Total	100

Ulcers and injuries are classed together, as they are both ordinarily caused by outdoor work and are largely due to the carelessness of the convicts. The organisation of a mosquito brigade and other apparatus for reducing mosquitoes will perhaps largely reduce the importance of malaria. After fever, dysentery (caused by malaria and otherwise) is the chief disease, and is being combated by improved cooking, milk, and diet. Phthisis (with tuberculosis), as an infectious preventible disease likely to spread if unchecked, is being treated in a special hospital, and by other preventive measures.

Infirmities.

The infirm population of the Settlement is almost wholly made up of the insane and the lepers and thus of convicts who have become insane or have developed leprosy after arrival. The Census recorded insanity among the convicts to the extent of 11·20 per mille, a figure which may be expected among those convicted of serious crime, and it has been otherwise noticed that for social reasons lepers are liable to commit serious crime also. The proportion in Port Blair of lepers to convict male population is 2·80 per mille, which is presumably much higher than the proportion of lepers to population elsewhere. Blindness is sometimes self-caused by the convicts, who occasionally put lime and other deleterious substances into the eyes to avoid work. Of the whole afflicted population only 4 are children under 10: *viz.*, males— 1 insane, 1 deaf mute, 1 blind: female—1 insane. Details are given in the following table:—

	Total afflicted.	Insane.	Deaf mute.	Blind.	Leper.
Males . . .	194	145	6	9	34
Females . . .	2	2	...	...	...
TOTAL .	196	147	6	9	34

Enquiry into the offences committed by convicts however goes to show the general sanity of the convict class, as they are exactly such as might be expected of a violent and by nature an ill-disciplined description of mankind subjected to discipline—such as might be expected indeed in the same conditions of life of any body of human beings with the same characteristics, who have not been convicted of heinous crime and are regarded as sane. The actual amount of insanity among the convicts is shown in the accompanying statement, from which it will be seen that the overwhelming cause is mania:—

Type.	Total number.	Admitted in 1901.	Admitted in 1902 (10 months).
Mania . . .	122	10	11
Melancholia . . .	14	10	3
Dementia . . .	4	...	...
Epilepsy . . .	4	3	...
Effects of ganja (hemp) .	10	2	...
Effects of opium . .	1	...	1
Sequelæ of fever, etc. .	...	1	...
	155	26	15

Agriculture and Economics.

Only about 6 per cent. of the labouring convicts are employed as agriculturists, and those chiefly to supply special articles of food for the convicts and staff, such as vegetables, tea, coffee and cocoa. But agriculture is the main source of livelihood among the self-supporters, whose labours have contributed to the solid progress of the Settlement. Also rather more than half the adult local born population live by agriculture. The area of cleared land has increased from 10,421 acres in 1881 to 25,189 in 1905 and that of cultivation from 6,775 acres to 10,364 acres. Although the working of the Regulations has very largely reduced the number of self-supporters in the last decade, the result of steady agricultural labour for many years is shown by increased productive capacity in the land and a rise in the prosperity of the self-supporters. The value of supplies purchased from these rose from £1,913 in 1874 to £3,260 in 1881, £3,572 in 1891 and £7,116 in 1901.

Revenue System.

All the land in the Penal Settlement is vested in the Crown and all rights in it are subject to the orders of the Government of India. Practically the land is held at a fixed rent under license from the Chief Commissioner on conditions, which, *inter alia*, subject devolution and transfer to his consent and determine the occupation on compensation at a year's notice or on breach of the conditions. The working of the rules, framed primarily to meet the requirements of the self-supporter convicts, is in the hands of the District officers, through *amins* or native revenue officials. Village revenue papers like those maintained in India are kept up, and fixed survey fees are demanded.

House sites, except those of cultivators, which are free, are divided into four classes, and a tax is levied varying from Rs. 2 to Rs. 25, according to the net annual income of the holders.

Land for cultivation is divided into valley and hill land, the rent being fixed according to quality with a maximum of Rs. 4-8-0 per acre for the valley, and Rs. 2-4-0 for the hill land. Licenses are given for five years and may be surrendered on three months' notice. They are subject to special conditions for each holding and to general conditions among which are that the land is not surrendered or transferred without permission and that 5 per cent. of the amount paid by the transferree is paid to the Government as fine. Similar conditions are attached to licenses for house sites. Grazing-fees are levied by license for the use of the Government (common) lands for grazing or cutting grass for cattle, at the rate of Rs. 2 per annum per animal, and in the case of goats 8 annas per annum each: but cultivators may graze two bullocks free for each 5 to 15 *bighas* (1¾ to 5 acres) of land held by them.

Self-supporters, subject to good behaviour, can hold land on, *inter alia*, the following general terms: free rations and free use of village servants for six months; free grant of an axe, hoe and *dah;* rent, tax and cess free for 3 to 4 years with a limit of 5 *bighas*, if the land is uncleared jungle, or for 1 to 2 years with a limit of 10 *bighas* if the land is already cleared. Double holdings are permitted up to two years. Self-supporters must not sublet or alienate their holdings, must occupy them effectively, must assist in making village tanks, roads and fences, and must keep houses and villages clean and in good repair. Their houses may be sublet, with permission, to other self-supporters only, as free men and convicts may not live together in villages.

Cesses.

The following cesses and fees are levied: educational cess, collected with the revenue, on house sites and land, according to grade, from Rs. 3 to 6 annas per annum; village conservancy fees, from 2 to 4 annas per house per mensem, collected monthly; *chaukidari* (village officials) fees 4 annas for house or lodger per mensem, collected monthly; *salutri* (veterinary) fees, raised from possessors of cattle to provide for veterinary care and inspection of village cattle, at about half the educational cess.

The village officials, who receive fixed salaries, are the *chaudhri* (headman) and the *chaukidar* (watchman). The *chaudhri* is the head of the village, responsible for its peace and discipline and for assistance in the suppression of crime. He is the village tax collector, auctioneer and assistant land revenue official. The *chaukidar* is his assistant.

General Economic Conditions.

Generally speaking, a self-supporter has an income from Rs. 7 per mensem upwards, and an agricultural self-supporter can calculate on a net income of not less than Rs. 10 per mensem. As the peasantry of India go, the self-supporter is well off. The free resident population is probably not in so good circumstances, so far as it depends on the land.

Forests.

The forests are worked by officers of the general Indian Forest Department, as nearly as may be, on Indian lines, and there is a division of the Settlement for administrative purposes into afforested and unafforested lands. The reserved forest areas amount to about 156 sq. miles. As little change as possible is made in these, but the growing condition of the Settlement makes it sometimes imperative to effect small alterations in area. The labour of the Forest Department is divided up into the extraction of timber and firewood, the construction of tramways, and the conversion of timber at the steam saw-mills on Chatham Island. In 1904-05 it employed 1,102 men. Elephants are used to drag logs from the forests to tramways or the sea, and rafts are towed by steamers to Port Blair. This is a comparatively new department for utilising convict labour and is now the chief source of revenue in cash. The earnings under this head have increased from Rs. 1·6 lakhs in 1891 and Rs. 2·8 lakhs in 1901 to Rs. 6·2 lakhs in 1904-05. In the latest year the total charges amounted to Rs. 3·4 lakhs.

Trade and Manufactures.

Although the self-supporters and the free residents follow a number of occupations other than agriculture and Government service, yet the numbers so employed have but a comparatively small effect on the industries of the Settlement, and practically all the labour available in the community is found by the labouring convicts. The direction and supervision of the labour is a difficult task, for very few experts are employed and but little raw material is purchased from outside. In practice the officials have to learn each trade and then teach it to their unpromising pupils, the convicts, about 3 per cent. only of whom have any previous knowledge of the work they have to be put to in the Settlement. There is an unlimited variety of work, as can be seen from the following list of objects on which the daily labour is expended:—Forestry, reclamation, cultivation, fishing, cooking, making domestic utensils, breeding and tending animals and poultry, fuel, salt, porterage by land and sea, ship-building, house-building, furniture, joinery, metal work, carpentry, masonry, stone-work, quarrying, road-making, earth-work, pottery, lime, bricks, sawing, plumbing, glazing, painting, rope-making, basket-work, tanning, spinning, weaving clothing, driving machinery of many kinds and other superior work, signalling, tide-gauging, designing, carving, metal-hammering, electric-lighting, clerical work and accounting, compounding, statistics, book-binding, printing, domestic and messenger service, scavenging, cleaning, petty supervision. The machinery is large and important and some of the works are on a large scale.

The general heads of employments of labouring convicts can be seen from the following abstract of the average daily labour statement for the dry season of 1901 :—

Ineffective, excluding Departments, 1,589.	Departmental employ, 2,133.	Supervising Establishment (excluding Departments), 813.	Fixed Establishments, 2,489.
Sick and weakly . 1,065 Lunatics . 153 Lepers . 84 In Jails . 260 Others . 27	Commissariat . 220 Marine . 247 Medical . 269 Forest . 917 Tea . 333 Other Departments 147	Petty Officers . 813	Boats . 366 Private service 213 Government service . 169 Station service 735 Supplies . 392 Conservancy 115 Cartage . 327 Others . 172
Fixed works, 1,708.	**Artificers Corps, 908.**	**Miscellaneous Labour, 589.**	**Females, 366.**
Workshops . 429 Quarries . 117 Potteries . 22 Brickfields . 690 Jail buildings 450	Artificers . 548 Coolies . 360	At disposal of Officers for repairs . 589	Jail labour . 366

THE WORKSHOPS.

In the Phœnix Bay Workshops there is a great variety of work performed, divided under the heads of supervision, general, machinery, wood, iron, leather, silver, brass, copper, tin, and there are besides attached to the shops a Foundry, Tannery and Limekiln. This is a department that is always growing and has already grown considerably since the Census. The whole of the outturn is absorbed locally and no export trade is set up in the shops. The work done at Phœnix Bay has nearly all to be taught the convicts therein employed and is performed partly by hand and partly by machinery. By hand they are taught to make cane work of all sorts, plain and fancy, ropemaking, matting, fishing nets, and wire netting. They do painting and lettering of all descriptions. They repair boilers, pumps, machinery of all sorts, watches, and clocks. In iron, copper and tin they do fitting, tinning, and lampmaking; forging, hammering of all kinds. In brass and iron they do casting in large and small sizes, plain and ornamental, and fancy hammering. In wood they perform all sorts of carpentry, carriage-building and carving, and in leather they make boots, shoes, harness and belts. They tan leather and burn lime.

By machinery, in iron and brass, they perform punching, drilling, boring, shearing, planing, shaping, turning, welding and screw-cutting. In wood they perform sawing, planing, tonguing, grooving, moulding, shaping and turning, and in wheel-making they do the spoke-tenoning and mortising. Machinery is continually being added, in order to reduce establishment which can go to forestry and agriculture, the two descriptions of employment which are best calculated to make the Settlement finally completely self-supporting. Machinery will make it industrially and forestry *plus* agriculture financially independent: points that are never lost sight of and control the labour distribution.

Marine Department.

The work of the Marine Department about Phœnix Bay is chiefly connected with the building, finding, and working of the steam launches, barges, lighters, boats and buoys maintained.

Female Jail.

In the Female Jail the women are employed practically on the supply of the clothing of the Settlement, but they do also everything else necessary for themselves, and the only two men allowed to work inside the jail are the hospital assistant and the jail carpenter.

Exports and Imports.

The bulk of the exports consists of timber, either the property of the Government or of private persons, empties belonging to the Commissariat Department, canes and other articles of jungle produce, edible birds' nests and trepang. The imports consist chiefly of Government stores of various kinds for use in the different departments in the Settlement, private provisions, articles of clothing and luxuries.

Communications.

The modes of communication are by water about the harbour, by road, and by tram (animal and steam haulage). The means of communication are unusually good. By water there are eight large and two small steam launches and a considerable number of lighters, barges and boats of all sizes. Sailing boats except for the amusement of officers, are, for obvious reasons, not permitted. Ferries ply at fixed and frequent intervals at several points across the harbour. The roads, owing to convict labour probably, the best of any district in India, are practically everywhere metalled and are unusually numerous. Where convicts are situated it is a matter of importance to get to the spot quickly at very short notice. The road mileage is about 110 metalled and about 50 unmetalled. The animal-haulage tram-lines are chiefly forest, and their situation varies from time to time according to work. The steam tram-lines are: Settlement—Brickfields to South Quarries and Firewood area, 5 miles; North Bay to North Quarries, 2 miles; Forest—Wimberleyganj to Shoal Bay, 7 miles; Bajajag to Constance Bay and Port Mouat, 6 miles. There are besides short lines for work at a good many other places.

The harbour of Port Blair is well supplied with buoys and lights. The light-house on Ross Island is visible for 19 miles, and running-in lights have been fixed on suitable sites. There is also a complete telephone system connecting the different offices in the Settlement. Local posts are frequent, but the foreign mails are irregular. Wireless telegraphy between Port Blair and Diamond Island off the coast of Burma has been worked successfully since 1905, and various portions of the Settlement have been connected by telephone.

Post Office.

The external postal service is effected by the Port Blair post office, which is under the control of the Deputy Postmaster-General, Burma. The Chief Commissioner, however, regulates the relations of the post office with convicts. The following table gives statistics of the postal business:—

—	1890-91.	1900-01.	1904-05.
Number of post offices	1	1	1
Total number of postal articles delivered—			
Letters	69,082	65,119	92,498
Postcards	7,150	18,360	19,474
Packets	3,328	38,316*	18,018
Newspapers	36,686	10,620†	21,476
Parcels	3,276	2,568	3,952
Value of stamp sold to the public	Rs. 4,305	Rs. 3,810	Rs. 3,510
Value of money orders issued	‡	Rs. 1,40,820	Rs. 1,60,372

* Including unregistered newspapers.

† Registered as newspapers in the post office.

‡ The figures are included in those given for Bengal.

The Post Office Savings Bank is largely resorted to by the convicts who have allowances and by self-supporters, and the value of its work as part of the convict educational system pursued in the Settlement can be gauged by the fact that in 1904-05 the amount deposited by convicts therein reached Rs. 25,550.

PUBLIC WORKS.

The public works are constructed and maintained in all branches by the Artificer Corps, an institution going back historically, long beyond the foundation of Port Blair, in the Indian Penal Settlement System. Those men who were artisans before conviction and men found to be capable after arrival are formed into the Artificer Corps—craftsmen, learners, and coolies. This corps is an organisation apart, has special petty privileges and petty officers of its own under the title of "Foreman Petty Officer," who are artisans that have to labour with their own hands and also to supervise the work of small gangs and teach learners.

FINANCE.

The penal system is primarily one of discipline, financial consideration giving way to this all-important point. The labour of the convicts is firstly disciplinary; secondly, it provides for the wants of the Settlement so far as these can be supplied locally; thirdly, it is expended on objects directly remunerative. All necessary expenditure in cash is granted directly by the Government of India, and against this are set-off the earnings of the convicts in money. The following table gives the totals, for a series of years, in thousands of rupees, but a considerable variation occurs from year to year:—

—	1891.	1901.	1904-05.	1905-06.
Receipts, Total	4,74	5,71	9,80	9,10
Expenditure, Total	12,97	17,34	18,30	21,86
Net cost of Settlement	8,23	11,63	8,50	12,76
Net cost of the convict (Rs.)	69-10-11	99-4-9	60-6-4	88-4-3

The value of convict labour expended on local work and supplies is not included.

COST OF THE CONVICT.

The net cash "cost of the convict" at any given period depends, firstly on how far convict labour is employed on objects returning a cash profit, and secondly on the number of convicts permitted to hold tickets-of-leave and producing local supplies purchasable by Government at a far smaller cost than those procured from places outside the Settlement. Since 1891 very large jails and subsidiary buildings have been under construction by the orders of the Government of India and have absorbed labour that could otherwise have gone to forestry and other objects remunerative in cash, and the number of self-supporters has been greatly reduced by a change under the same orders in the regulations as to the grant of tickets-of-leave, resulting in a reduction of their agricultural holdings and the amount of jungle cleared annually. Both of these arrangements are disciplinary and go to show that the "cost of the convict" depends less on local administration than on general policy.

RECEIPTS AND EXPENDITURE.

The following table shows the progress of the principal sources of revenue and expenditure, in thousands of rupees :—

—	1890-91.	1900-01.	1904-05.	1905-06.
Land Revenue	35	36	30	31
Forests	1,58	2,78	6,21	5,83
Other Heads	2,81	2,57	3,29	2,96
Total Revenue	4,74	5,71	9,80	9,10
Salaries, establishment and contingencies	1,20	1,38	1,30	1,23
Tea cultivation	16	30	34	25
Education	5	5	5	6
Medical	37	40	44	44
Ecclesiastical	8	8	9	10
Commissariat establishment and supplies	4,14	6,10	3,00	7,18
Marine	12	22	24	25
Jail	10	24	26	28
Police	1,37	1,46	1,40	1,40
Subsistence money to convicts	92	71	83	84
Forest establishment and supplies	1,75	2,85	4,95	5,00
Clothing for convicts and police	33	38	44	58
Public Works	26	71	1,04	1,09
Purchase of stores	36	58	1,73	1,20
Passage money and freight on stores	1,63	1,73	2,04	1,75
Other charges	13	15	15	17
Total expenditure	12,97	17,34	18,30	21,86

MILITARY.

The total strength of the British and Native army stationed in the Islands in 1905 was 444, of whom 140 were British. The Andaman Islands are now under the Burma division. The military station at Port Blair is attached to Rangoon and is usually garrisoned by British and Native Infantry. Port Blair is also the head-quarters of the South Andaman Volunteer Rifles, whose strength is about 40.

POLICE.

The Police are organised as a military battalion 701 strong. Their duties are both military and civil, *i.e.*, in addition to their military duties they perform those of ordinary civil police. They are distributed all over the Settlement in stations and guards. They protect the Jails, the civil officials and convict parties working in the jungles, but they do not exercise any direct control over the convicts.

EDUCATION.

The local born population is better educated than is the rule in India, as elementary education is compulsory for all male children of self-supporter convicts up to 14 years of age. The sons of the local born and of the free settlers are also freely sent to the schools, but not the daughters—fear of contamination in the latter case being a ruling consideration, in addition to the usual conservatism in such matters. A fair proportion become sufficiently proficient in English for clerkships. Provision is also made for mechanical training to those desiring it, but it is not largely in request, except in tailoring, and there is a fixed system of physical training for the boys. Native employés of the Government use the local schools for the primary education of their children. All secondary education is carried on privately and so is the whole education of European children, who are usually withdrawn from the Settlement before ten years of age. Six schools are maintained, of which one includes an anglo-vernacular course, while the others are primary schools. In 1904-05 these contained 152 boys and 2 girls of free parents, and 55 boys and 40 girls of convict parents, and the total expenditure was Rs. 5,360. Owing to mistakes in enumeration the Census results for literacy are of no value.

MEDICAL.

There are four district and three jail hospitals in charge of the Medical Superintendent of the Cellular and Female Jails, who belongs to the Indian Medical Service, and four junior medical officers under the supervision of a senior officer of the Indian Medical Service. Medical aid is also given free to the whole population, and to Government officials under the usual Indian rules on the subject. The convicts unfit for hard labour are divided into sick and detained in hospital, convalescents, light labour, invalids, lepers and lunatics; for each of which classes there are special rules and methods of treatment under direct medical aid. Practically every child born in the Settlement is vaccinated.

APPENDIX A.

POINTS OF AGREEMENT AND DIFFERENCE BETWEEN THE ANDAMANESE AND THE SEMANGS.

The Semangs are found in Northern Perak, Kedah, Kelantan, Trengganu, and Northern Pahang in the Malay Peninsula. They have come considerably under outside influence and especially under that of the wavy-haired (Sakai) and the long-haired (Jakun, wild Malay) tribes of the Peninsula and even of the civilised Malays themselves.

Points of Agreement of Semang with Andamanese.

Hair: In colour and growth.
Height: Men 57 to 58 inches, women 53½ to 54½ inches.
Skin: In texture and colour.
Shape of head: Mesaticephalic and brachycephalic.
Eyes: In colour and shape.
Food: In its nature and elaborate preparation.
Huts: In leaf shelters; with the Onge-Jarawas, in communal huts, though not so good.
Funerals: In ceremonies and probable former disinterment of bones.
Belief: In the bridge to Paradise.
Bows: With the Onge-Jarawas only.

Points of Difference between Semangs and Andamanese.

Face: In the great variation of the Andamanese face.
Implements: In the blow-gun and *poisoned* arrows and spears.
Hunting: In trapping game.
Feeding: Men before women.
Quivers: In having reed quivers; Andamanese stick their arrows in the waist belt.
Ornamentation: In quality and artistic merit.
Ornaments: In personal ornaments, and in piercing the nose.
Huts: In rock-shelters, cave dwellings, tree huts, barricaded huts.
Clothing: Of hammered barks; loin-cloth for men, petticoat for women.
Magic: In its practice and in use of magical designs.
Music: In nose-pipe and bamboo castanets.
Songs: In their nature.
Marriage: Based on purchase and in ceremonies.
Beliefs: In Shamanism, metamorphism into tigers of living men, in ideas as to "God."

Language: In its mixture with Malay and Mon; basis can be proved *perhaps* to be (? Onge-Jarawa) Andamanese, though the specimens I have seen afford very little hope of this.

'Also a portion of the Semangs have fixed habitations and a rude agriculture, this latter capacity being entirely absent in the Andamanese.

APPENDIX B.

Tribal Distribution and Place Names, Andaman Islands.

1	2	3	4	5	6
No. on map.	Name of island, locality or encampment.	Andamanese name.	Tribal Territory.	Where situated.	REMARKS.
	East Island	Tàu-kàt	Chāriār	The following islands off the north and north-west coast of North Andaman, *viz.*:—East Island Landfall Island, West Island, Whitecliff Island, Thornhill Island, Reef Island, Paget Island, Point Island and Sugar-loaf Island.	The Coco islands are known to this tribe by the name Diki rai-chen.
	Landfall Island	Tébi chíroh	„		
	Cleugh Passage	Làu-chíroh	„		
	West Island	Tàu-rà-míku	„		
	Thornhill Island	Tar bólo	„		
	Whitecliff Island	Kareng-méo	„		
	Reef Island	Bà-pong	„		
	Paget Island	Tanmo-tát	„		
1	Paget Island (encampment on)	Kàra-bóronga	„		
	Point Island	Màra-bàlo	„		
	Sugar-loaf Island	Cha-ólo	„		
	Temple Sound	Tarà to lo-chíroh.	...		
	Cape Price	Pàro-júe	Kōrà	From bay opposite Craggy Island (East Coast of North Andaman) to Cape Price and thence along the North and West Coast to the North side of Casuarina Bay, together with all the islands off the Coast except Craggy Island and those constituting the territory of the Chāriār tribe.	
	Pocock Island	Kòi-cho	„		
	Cadell Bay	Kòto-par	„		
	Excelsior Island	Tàu-rà-míku	„		
	Port Cornwallis	Tólobu-tóng	„		
1	Do. (Ross Island at mouth of)	Po-chumbo (also Bo-pung)	„		
	Chatham Island (Port Cornwallis)	Tebi-chíro	„		
1	Trilby Island	Cho-à-póng	„		
1	Encampment on N. E. of N. Andaman near Reef Island	Tí-kò-dung	„		
1	Island encampment between Port Cornwallis and Temple Sound	Bòl-pòli	„	The interior is occupied by the Tābō tribe.	
	Craggy Island	Roth	...		
	Casuarina Bay	Kárate-tàt-chíro	Yére	E. Coast. From shore opposite Craggy Island in North Andaman Stream situated between Cooke Point and Kinserley Point in Middle Andaman, together with the islands of the Coast including Craggy Island.	
	Snark (? Shark) Island	Chíro-méo	„		
1	Casuarina Bay (encampment on N. side of)	Tórop-tot-chéto	„		
	South extremity of Lamia Bay	Rengo-to-tía	„		
	Point between Yulik and Lamia Bay	Ko-po	„		
	Do. North of Taralait	Yulik	„		

Tribal Distribution and Place Names, Andaman Islands—contd.

1	2	3	4	5	6
No. on map.	Name of island, locality or encampment.	Andamanese name.	Tribal Territory.	Where situated.	REMARKS.
	Eileen Bay . .	Pârô . .	Yere .	W. Coast. From North side of Casuarina Bay in North Andaman to Maramika-boliu in the same island, together with the island of the Coast.	
1	Cadell Point, North of	Tâ-burongo .	„		
1	Do. (Territory within a radius of few miles of) . .	Méo-pong .	„		
	Do. Point (Bay W. of)	Chaka-mit-kôito	„		
1	Camp Bay . .	Lau-tiche .	„ .	[This tribe has the Kôrâ tribal territory on its north side and the Kede on the south with the Tâbô in the interior.]	
1	Wreck Point . .	Chelop-râ .	„		
	Dot Island . .	Anâto . .	„		
	Kwangtung Island .	Karáne-teo .	„		
	Pembroke Bay . .	Tàu-kàt-chíro .	„		
1	Encampment at S. W. of Pembroke Bay .	Ina-ta-rà-jóle .	„		
1	Latouche Island .	Ar-kōl . .			
	N. Reef Island .	Tebi-chíro .	„		
1	Saddle Peak . .	Pàroto-míku .	„		
1	Do. (Adjacent hill on N. side of) .	Jíro-míku .	„		
	Stewart Island . .	Miriti-râ pong .	„		
	Sound Island . .	Tàul âr-míku .	„		
	Austin Strait . .	Pòròng-chíro .	„		
1	Do. (encampment at E. end of) . .	Tâu chàu .	„		
	Brown Point . .	Iltomata . .	„		
	Bacon Bay . .	Tára-chiro .	„		
1	Aves Island (also Berkeley group) .	Tàkla . .	„		
1	Casuarina Bay (encampment on S. side of)	Chàubalo râ-cheto . .	„		
1	Interview Island .	Tâu-tara-míku, also Ti-tara-míka, or in Bōa dialect, Tâu-l'ar-mūgu			
	Sea Serpent Island .	Tára-belo .	Kede . „	E. Coast. From southern border of the Yère territory (Middle Andaman) to Emej l'ar-tet (Middle Andaman).	
	Do. (Island adjacent to) . . .	Tâla-bucho .	„		
	Boudeville Island .	Jara-bōroin .	„		
	Bennett Island .	Chūrul-tong .	„ .	W. Coast. From Maramika-boliu (North Andaman) to stream opposite N. E. point of Flat Island (Middle Andaman) with all islands from Interview to Flat Island inclusive (as shown on map).	
	Anderson Island .	Tôro-tarà-chôu	„		
	South Reef Island .	Ti-pu-tâ .	„		
	Encampment on South Extremity of Interview Island opposite Reef Island . . .	Benge-l'un-tô .	„		
	Tuft Island . .	Burain . .	„		
	Hump Island . .	Lurwa . .	„		
	Flat Island . .	Tóba-chíra .	„		

Tribal Distribution and Place Names, Andaman Islands—contd.

1	2	3	4	5	6
No. on map.	Name of island, locality or encampment.	Andamanese name.	Tribal Territory.	Where situated.	REMARKS.
	Island between Middle Andaman and Long Island .	Pôr-lob .	Kôl .	*E. Coast.* From Emoj-l'ár-tet to Homfray Strait with intervening islands (as shown in chart).	
	Long Island . .	Mai-i-táng .	"		
1	Do. (Encampment on). . . .	Ïga-tóng-tà .	"		
1	Encampment in Yot jig . . .	Burka-chong .	"		
	Encampment in Boroïn-jig . .	Pili-orōnga .	"		
	Guitar Island .	Tōli-tàle .	"		
	Kwangtung Harbour (Encampment on N. side of) . . .	Môt-kunu .	Bojig-yáb	N. side of Homfray Strait with Báratáng and the islands bordering the East and West Coasts of that island. [Járawas have in recent years occupied the interior of Báratáng at intervals.]	
1	Encampment on N. side of Homfray Strait .	Tôli-chôrat .	"		
	Site of ancient kitchen-midden near N. E. point of Báratáng opposite North Passage Island . .	Wòt-a-emi .	"		
	Large island between Homfray Strait and Middle Strait .	Báratáng .	"		
	North Passage Island . . .	Toba-ōrema .	"		
	Colebrooke Island .	Pich-l'áka-chákan .	"		
1	Colebrooke (Encampment near N. W. point of) . .	Târa-chūlnga .	"		
1	Colebrooke (Encampment in S Bay of) .	Pàr-l'on-tà .	"		
	Colebrooke Passage (Encampment near S. end of) . .	Ōropa-chūlnga	"		
	Strait Island . .	Gereng kaicha	"		
	Diligent Strait .	Boroïn-jūru .	"		
	Homfray Strait .	Chàra-jūru .	"		
	Andaman (or Middle) Strait . . .	Godam-jūru .	"		
1	Barren Island . .	Taili-chapa .	...		
	Narcondam . .	Châto-l'ig-ba-ng	...		
	Duncan (or Entry) Island . . .	Kaichawa .	Bēa .	The whole of South Andaman and Rutland Island except where occupied by Járawas (*vide* map) also the Labyrinth Island, Spike Island and S. W. corner of Middle Andaman, as shown in map.	
1	Islet at mouth of Luru-jig inlet .	Chàr-tot-kaicha . .	"		
	Kwangtung Harbour	Karang-tóng-tà-chira .	"		
1	Do. (Encampment near W. mouth of) . .	Lekerà-l'on-tà .	"		
	Kyd Island . .	Dara-táng .	"		

Tribal Distribution and Place Names, Andaman Islands.—concld.

1	2	3	4	5	6
No. on map.	Name of island, locality or encampment.	Andamanese name.	Tribal Territory.	Where situated.	REMARKS.
	Port Campbell .	Kuro-pòng .	Bēa.		
	Do. Mouat . .	Gerengl'áka-chá-ti-jūru .	„		
	Rutland Island .	Tòko-pàt (Bēa) Ga-tin-a-Kwe-(Onge) .	„		
	North Button Island	Chāuga-l'on-jing . .	Balawa	The Archipelago and the three Button Islands.	
	Middle Button Island	Kaicha-wa .	„		
	South Button Island .	Āga-l'ot-baraij	„		
	Outram Island .	Tàr-mūgu .	„		
	Henry Lawrence Island . . .	Chārka-ērema .	„		
	John Lawrence Island	Parkit-ērema .	„		
	East (or Inglis) Island . . .	Jila-ērema .	„		
	Wilson Island . .	Bōroin-ērema .	„		
	Nicholson Island .	Kaichawa-ērema . .	„		
	Havelock Island .	Pūlunga-l'àr-mū-gu-ērema .	„		
	Sir W. Peel Island .	Tà-ērema .	„		
	Neill Island . .	Teb-jūru .	„		
	Sir Hugh Rose Island	Kòiohowra-bar	„		
	North Sentinel .	Pàtáng . .	Jarawa	North Sentinel and the interior of the northern half of South Andaman and Báratáng and Rutland Island, as shown in map.	
	Little Andaman .	Wilima-tára (Bēa) Gwábo-l'onge (Onge)	Onge .	Little Andaman and the islands between that island and Rutland, also South Sentinel.	
	Bumila Creek (north of Little Andaman) .	Kawáte-nyabo (Onge) .	...		
	South Brother . .	Gwaicha-nákwe (Onge) . .	...		
	North Brother . .	Té-ta-lé (Onge)	...		
	Sister Island (small)	Badgi-l'ar-rám (Bēa) Ta-jomad-a (Onge) .	...		
	Do. (large)	? àtla-cháng (Bēa) Ga ta-kwáte (Onge)	...		
	Passage Island .	Alaba-cháng (Bēa) Chōgo-da (Onge) .	...		
	Cinque Island (North)	Jēr tia (Bēa) Gwa-lu (Onge)	...		
	Do. (South)	Jēr-tia (Bēa) Ga-ta-kwe (Onge) . .	...		
	South Sentinel .	Yádi-l'ig bang (Bēa) Ináng-go-gwe (Onge)	...		

APPENDIX C.

List of Villages and their Chiefs in the Nicobar Islands with the total population of each Village as taken in the Census of 1901.

No. on map.	Name of Village.	Name of Chief.	Total population.
	I. CAR NICOBAR.		
12	Arong	Tom Dixon	341
5	Chukchuachia	Sam	151
10	Kakana	Sanelnga	100
11	Kemios	Silima	203
6	Kenyuaka	Corney Grain	142
2	Kinmai	Young Gwyn	205
3	Lapati	Edwin	755
9	Malacca	Saibu	148
1	Mus	Offandi	536
8	Perka	Kanaiñe	199
7	Tamalu	Hikka	240
4	Tapueming	Lawi	114
13	Sawi	Sampson	317
		TOTAL	3,451
	II. CHOWRA.		
4	Kotasuk	Malohla	31
2	Olheon	Liawa	51
3	Ol-teak	Filik	12
5	Pol	Anaka	69
6	Raichafe (also called Hiwah)	Teka	55
1	Sanenya	Tamkoi	304
		TOTAL	522
	III. TERESSA.		
10	Aöang	Ahúa	61
1	Bengala	Gibson	119
11	Chanumla	Hinaila	8
2	Enya	Kafin	32
9	Hinam	Komponi	62
5	Kanom Hinot	Kintoich	7
6	Kerawa	Rupa	60
7	Kolarue	...	2
8	Laksi	Wanechia	151
4	Pahiala	Kintoich	27
3	Trae	Nialu	95
		TOTAL	624
	IV. BOMPAKA.		
1	Poahat	Shameak	69
2	Yat-kirãna	Do.	9
		TOTAL	78

No. on map.	Name of Village.	Name of Chief.	Total population.
	V. CAMORTA.		
14	Chang-hõa	Din Mahomed	35
35	Chaug-manyap	Kaepshe	26
16	Chanol	Loham	9
4	Dak-an-feama	Kaepshe	30
11	Domyau	Din Mahomed	34
28	Domyuk	Jan	6
15	Fop-dak	Din Mahomed	15
8	Hentoin	Suran	6
19	Hentoin	Loham	3
17	Hoau	Loham	42
13	Hoe-chafâ	Din Mahomed	...
5	Hóe-mattai	Chandu	84
7	Inaka	Surau	31
20	Karau	Loham	9
36	Kehol	Kaepshe	21
37	Koi-hoa	Do.	13
24	Koilakama-shang	Jan	10
3	Ia	Chandu	...
4	Lanunga	Do.	10
23	Maru	Jan	9
10	Monak	Din Mahomed	9
31	Mon-chong-hoang	Jan	...
6	Moshoit	Chandu	30
30	Mush-lam-huye	Jan	2
12	Oal ek-heak	Din Mahomed	4
21	Okchoaka	Loham	3
22	Ok-dak	Do.	12
33	Ok-dok-tat	Kaepshe	50
9	Olenchi	Din Mahomed	...
27	Ol-loe	Jan	13
18	Oploapa	Loham	4
25	Ota-mush	Jan	8
26	Panoha	Do.	10
1	Takaro-ait	Chandu	...
29	Takayua	Jan	...
32	Talarom	Do.	5
2	Ta-weng-toaka	Chandu	...
		TOTAL	488
	VI. NANCOWRY.		
3	Alipa	Jemira	...
7	Chong-pi	Do.	15
5	Henkoi	Do.	...
1	Hendaha	......	...
2	Hoi-mange	......	...
6	Inuanga	Jemira	21
4	Itoe	Do.	22
13	Kabila	Frederick	12
12	Lanoanga	Do.	2

List of Villages and their Chiefs in the Nicobar Islands with the total population of each Village as taken in the Census of 1901—continued.

No. on map.	Name of Village.	Name of Chief.	Total population.
	VI. NANCOWRY—*contd.*		
9	Malacca	Jemira	58
15	Matai-ta-thoe	Frederick	5
8	Oal-dana	Jemira	13
11	Oal-ta-he·k	Frederick	23
10	Ong-yuang	Jemira	9
14	Tapong	Frederick	44
		TOTAL	224
	VII. TRINKAT.		
1	Höetamin	England	...
11	Lahom	Frederick	4
3	Okchuâka	England	84
8	Ol-neal	Do.	...
5	Ong-yang-la	Do.	9
7	Pia	Do.	...
2	Taka-shim	Do.	...
6	Tapiyang	Do.	5
1	Tapoa-an	Do.	...
4	Tarakṇk	Do.	...
9	Ta-wing-oank	Do.	...
		TOTAL	102
	VIII. KATCHALL.		
28	Chang-kmoe	Yusin	11
36	Chang-taneak	Do.	4
3	Chanohat	Moung-Poen	...
34	Chong-ipoh	Yusin	4
38	Chong-yuela	Do.	6
11	Hakoan-hala	Moung-Poen	2
10	Hoktak	Do.	...
27	Hanoka-dak	Yusin	5
32	Hoe-mattai	Do.	11
17	Hoin-henpoan	Moung-Poen	2
14	Hoin-ipoh	Do.	4
9	Kaiyi-domoanga	Do.	...
1	Kapanga	Do.	12
13	Kayila-heng	Do.	...
4	Kire-henpoan	Do.	4
20	Koila-tapain	Do.	14
23	Koi-mekeah	Yusin	7
42	Komlanga	Do.	5
26	Mattai-kaling	Do.	3
2	Misha	Moung-Poen	2
15	Moih-payala	Do.	7
39	Mosh-yuela	Yusin	8
25	Oal-dana	Do.	2
21	Oal-hake	Do.	...
35	Oal-hetaih	Do.	20
40	Oal-kandeal	Do.	5
30	Oal-kolo-kwak	Do.	18
29	Oal-menkoan	Do.	10
8	Oal-ta-ful	Moung-Poen	...
24	Oal-taming	Yusin	13
	VIII. KATCHALL—*contd.*		
7	Oal-ta-neak	Moung-Poen	21
41	Oal-tewila	Yusin	...
31	Ok-mange	Do.	8
19	Olenchi	Moung-Peen	24
18	Oyau-tapah	Do.	20
22	Shake	Yusin	4
6	Shanang-koal	Moung-Poen	7
33	Shanoya	Yusin	9
16	Tapain	Moung-Poen	2
12	Tawing-kaling	Do.	...
5	Tawing-kenhoha	Do.	5
37	Tawing-menyan	Yusin	2
		TOTAL	281
	IX. GREAT NICOBAR.		
17	Aka-noat	Dang	...
7	Bananga	Kontri	...
12	Chang-ngeh	Dang	7
21	Chanoha	Do.	4
6	Chisen	Kontri	...
32	Dak-lam	Dang	...
27	Dak-oank (or Pulo Kunyi)	Do.	4
28	Dak-omkeih (or Pulo Pet)	Do.	...
29	Dak-shiton	Do.	...
8	Ehonga-dak	Kontri	...
15	E.:henya-lôe	Dang	2
11	Enlowa	Do.	...
14	Henhcaha	Do.	3
18	Henkota (or Pulo Kota)	Do.	13
20	Henpoin	Do.	6
22	Kanalla (or Pulo Babi)	Do.	12
25	Kashindon	Do.	3
23	Koai	Do.	8
4	Koal-tapain	Kontri	...
26	Kopenheat	Dang	4
1	Laful	Kontri	13
2	Layom	Do.	...
13	Loka-fum	Dang	...
10	Mataita-anla	Kontri	2
19	Mush-pannya	Dang	...
5	Panok	Kontri	...
16	Shanonya	Dang	...
24	Tá-sanga	Do.	...
31	Ta-wing-fong	Do.	...
9	Tefap	Kontri	...
3	Tenlaa	Do.	...
30	Yashindo	Dang	...
		TOTAL	87

List of Villages and their Chiefs in the Nicobar Islands with the total population of each village as taken in the Census of 1901—concluded.

No. on map.	Name of Village.	Name of Chief.	Total population.	No. on map.	Name of Village.	Name of Chief.	Total population.
	X. LITTLE NICOBAR.				X. LITTLE NICOBAR —*continued.*		
19	Anula . .	Shong Shire	...	4	Sharonta-endenya .	Shong Shire .	7
14	Dit-dak . .	Do. . .	...	5	Ta-foap . .	Do. . .	5
10	Ekoya . .	Do. . .	15	2	Taaha-haya .	Do. . .	...
8	Endoana . .	Do. . .	2	12	Temain . .	Do. . .	2
16	Enfok . .	Do. . .	10	13	Tiden . .	Do. . .	...
18	Enhokta . .	Do. . .	...				
1	Ileya . .	Do. . .	4			TOTAL .	67
8	Kanduaka .	Do. . .	2				
17	Koila-oal .	Do. . .	7				
20	Maka-chian .	Do. . .	...				
21	Oal-heshoi (and Pihainsp) .	Do. . .	1		XI. KONDUL.		
6	Olenchi . .	Do. . .	2				
11	Oruanka .	Do. . .	...	2	Moyai-ya .	Dang . .	7
9	Pahonk . .	Do. . .	4	1	Oal-dowa .	Do. . .	17
15	Pahua . .	Do. . .	1	3	Oalnga-nat .	Do. . .	14
7	Patua . .	Do. . .	2				
22	Pituh . .	Do. . .	3			TOTAL .	38

BIBLIOGRAPHY.*

THE ANDAMANS.

BOOKS.

1669. Voyage de Gaul Schouten aux Indes Orientales.

1800. Symes, Embassy to Ava.

1825. Alexander, Travels from India to England: London.

1836. Malcom, Travels in Southern Asia: London.

1859. Selections from the Records of the Government of India, Home Department, Calcutta. No. XXV.

1863. Mouat, Adventures and Researches among the Andaman Islanders: London.

1871. Yule, Marco Polo: London.

1877. Man and Temple, Lord's Prayer in the Bojigngijida (South Andaman) Language: Calcutta.

1880. V. Ball, Jungle Life in India: London.

1883. Man, Aboriginal Inhabitants of the Andaman Islands: London (many references to older writers).

1887. Portman, Andamanese Manual.

* A great deal has been written about the Islands since 1875, chiefly in scarce Government Reports, in books usually rare and published in small editions, and in pamphlets and journals not easy of access.

1893-98. Portman, Record of the Andamanese: XI volumes MS. in India Office, London, and Home Department, Calcutta.
1898. Portman, Notes on the Languages of the South Andaman Group of Tribes: Calcutta (Government): (many references to older writers).
1899. Portman, History of our Relations with the Andamanese: Calcutta (Government): (many references to older writers).
1902. Kloss, In the Andamans and Nicobars: London.
1902. Alcock, Naturalists in the Indian Seas: London.
1906. Schmidt, Mon-Khmer Völker: Vienna.
1906. Skeat and Blagden, Pagan Races of the Malay Peninsula: London.

JOURNALS.

Anthropological Institute. Man (many); Lane-Fox (Pitt-Rivers); Thompson; Portman; Skeat.
Asiatic Researches. Colebrooke (1794); Fontana (1800); Buchanan; Leyden.
Asiatic Society of Bengal. Blyth; Tickell; Fytche; de Roepstorff; Nevill (many); de Niceville (many); Prain (many); V. Ball (many); Hoskyn.
Bombay Natural History Society. Butler; Cory.
Calcutta Review. Temple; Birch.
Encyclopædia Britannica. Yule (Andamans); Temple (in Supplement, Andamans).
Ethnological Society. Belcher; St. John.
Geographical Journal. V. Ball (1894).
Indian Antiquary. Man; Temple (many, including all the information in the India Office concerning Blair, Kyd, Ritchie and others in the Eighteenth Century); Portman.
Journal des Savants (Paris). De Quatrefages, November 1884; February 1885.
Microscopical Society of Calcutta, Holland.
Philological Society. A. J. Ellis (1882).
Royal Asiatic Society. Temple; Man; Portman; Gerini.
Royal Geographical Society. Mouat (1862); Yule; Portman; Temple; Man.
Royal Institution. Flower (Pygmy Races of Men: February 13, 1888).
Royal Irish Academy. V. Ball.
Society of Arts. Temple (1899).

Straits Branch, Royal Asiatic Society. De Quatrefages (1884).
Zoological Society, Godwin-Austen (1895).

MAGAZINES.

Botanical Magazine. Hooker, 1893.
Calcutta Monthly Register. November 1790.
Geological Magazine. V. Ball, February 1889; 1893.
Our Monthly, Rangoon, 1883.
Scottish Geographical Magazine, February 1889.

PAMPHLETS.

1879. De Folin. Mollusques des Isles Andaman: Bordeaux.
1885. De Quatrefages. L'Homme Tertiare: Paris.
1896. Campbell. Anchylostomiasis in the Andamans: Port Blair.
1899. Temple. Theory of Universal Grammar as applied to the South Andaman Language: London.
1899. Temple. Commercial Value of Wireless Telegraphic Communication with the Andaman and Nicobar Islands: Calcutta.
1901. Temple. Brief Account of the Andaman and Nicobar Islands: Port Blair.
1902. Miller. Mammals of the Andaman and Nicobar Islands (Smithsonian Institute, No. 1269): Washington, U. S. A.

REPORTS.

1858. Report of the Andaman Commission.
1864 and onwards. Annual Administration Reports.
1867. Report on the Andamans: Colonel Nelson Davies.
1869. Annexation of the Nicobars: Colonel Man.
1872. Report on the Andamans: J. Scarlett Campbell.
1874. Report on the Andamans: Sir H. Norman.
1884. Report on the Geology of the Andamans: Oldham.
1885-86. Reports on the Topographical Survey of the Andamans: Hobday.
1886. Andaman Forests: Ferrars.
1886 and onwards. Forest Administration Reports: Andamans.
1890. Report of the Commission of Sir Charles Lyall and Sir Alfred Lethbridge.
1890. Vegetation of the Andamans: Kurz.
1893. Cyclone Memoirs, No. V: Eliot.

1894. Prospects of the Andaman Forests : Temple.
1895. Forests of Stewart Sound : Buchanan.
1897. Report on the Nicobar Forests : Prevost.

SAILING DIRECTORIES.

1780. Dunn.
1809 and onwards. Horsburgh.
1874 and onwards. Taylor.
1892 and onwards. Bay of Bengal Pilot.

BARREN ISLAND AND NARCONDAM.

Barren Island and Narcondam, uninhabited, are included in the Andaman and Nicobar Administration and have an extensive bibliography of their own in scientific Journals and Magazines.

Mallet. Memoirs of the Geological Survey of India, XXI, 1885: Records of Geological Survey of India, Volume XXVIII, 1895 (with a valuable bibliography).

Dana. American Journal of Science, Volume XXXI, 1886.

Carpenter. Records of the Geological Survey of India, Volume XX, 1887.

V. Ball. Volcanoes of the Bay of Bengal, 1879 (from Geological Magazine, January 1879).

THE NICOBAR ISLANDS.

The Bibliography of the Nicobars is largely mixed up with that of the Andamans, but the following notes form a separate bibliography.

BOOKS.

1697. Dampier, New Voyage Round the World : London.
1733. Renaudot, Mohammedan Travellers (Arab Relations) : London.
1785. Hunter, Kingdom of Pegu : Calcutta.
1810. Lettres Edifiantes : Volume XI : Toulouse.
1867. Maurer, Die Nikobaren : Berlin (valuable bibliography : English, Danish, German, 1799-1863).
1870. Selections from the Records of the Government of India, No. LXXVII, Nicobar Islands : Government, Calcutta (valuable bibliography).
1871. Yule, Marco Polo : London.

1875. De Roepstorff, Nicobar Vocabulary: Calcutta, Government (valuable references, French, Danish, German).

1884. De Roepstorff, Dictionary of the Nancowry Dialect: Calcutta (valuable references to Danish works).

1888. Man, Nicobar Vocabulary: London.

1889. Man, Dictionary of Central Nicobar Language: London.

1894. Chavannes, I Tsing's Travels: Paris.

1896. Takakasu, I Tsing's Travels: Oxford.

JOURNALS.

Anthropological Institute. Man (many); Flower; Distant; Lane-Fox (Pitt-Rivers); Solomon; Skeat.

Asiatic Researches. Colebrooke (1794): Fontana, Volume III (1802); Hamilton, Volume II (1801).

Asiatic Society of Bengal. De Roepstorff (1870).

Indian Antiquary. Man (many); Temple (several).

Internationales Archiv fur Ethnographie (Leiden). Svoboda (die Bewohner des Nikobaren-Archipels, 1893): (coloured plates and a Continental bibliography).

Journal of the Indian Archipelago. Chopard (Volume III, 1844).

Philological Society. A. J. Ellis (1882).

Straits Branch, Royal Asiatic Society. Blagden.

PAMPHLETS.

1812. Latrobe. Letters from the Nicobars.

1845. Busch. Journal of the Schooner L'Espiegle.

1846. Barbe. Notice of the Nicobars.

1886. Flower. Nicobarese Skull: London.

1893. Man. Nicobar Pottery: London.

1894. Man. Narcotics in the Nicobars: London.

REPORTS.

1870 and onwards. Administration Reports (especially for 1888-89).

1886-87. Topographical Survey of the Nicobar Islands. Strachan.

1897. Tour through the Nicobars (Forests). Provost and Heinig.

SAILING DIRECTORIES.

1780. Dunn.
1809 and onwards. Horsburgh (especially 1836).
1874 and onwards. Taylor.
1892 and onwards. Bay of Bengal Pilot.